Praise for *The Accidental Zillionaire*

"Why is this the first book to be written about Paul Allen, the enigmatic tech wunderkind who has spent much of his adult life high atop the World's Richest Men list? Rich digs deep into Allen's past to offer us a quick-paced, entertaining, and illuminating glimpse into the life of a man who plainly has so much to prove despite his untold riches."

Gary Rivlin, author, *The Plot to Get Bill Gates*

"A disquieting look into high-tech's enigma, Paul Allen. Once Laura Rich's tale begins to unfold, we are treated to a roller-coaster inventory of odd and interesting facts from Allen's love affair with Monica Seles to his make-over by David Geffen. Her depictions at first bring to mind the Great Gatsby but quickly and disturbingly evolves into a dark portrait of a lost soul. A must-read."

John C. Dvorak, columnist, *PC Magazine*

"Paul Allen is the Loch Ness monster of the Internet age. Thankfully, Laura Rich got the definitive snapshot, down to the last eccentric detail: his passion for technology, his Jimi Hendrix obsession, his remarkable propensity for failure. In this fast-paced, gripping book, Rich for the first time captures Allen's awkward efforts to make high-tech, Hollywood, and Wall Street fit together."

James Ledbetter, business editor of *TIME Europe*, and author of *Starving to Death on $200 Million a Year: The Short, Absurd Life of The Industry Standard*

"*The Accidental Zillionaire* combines smart analysis of Paul Allen's multifaceted and complex business dealings along with eye-popping details about his billionaire lifestyle and personality."

Alan Deutschman, author, *The Second Coming of Steve Jobs*

"Paul Allen is the sort of billionaire you almost feel sorry for. A geek by nature, he seems ill-suited for many of his pursuits in business and often lives in the shadow of Bill Gates, his childhood friend. An excellent chronicle of a strange and fascinating character who at the heart of it all just wants to be cool."

Melanie Warner, senior writer, *Fortune*

"After reading this book, I will never look at Paul Allen the same way again. He's an odd duck."

John Motavalli, author, *Bamboozled at the Revolution*

# THE
# ACCIDENTAL
# ZILLIONAIRE

# THE
# ACCIDENTAL
# ZILLIONAIRE

## DEMYSTIFYING PAUL ALLEN

## LAURA RICH

 JOHN WILEY & SONS, INC.

Copyright © 2003 by Laura Rich. All rights reserved.

Published by John Wiley & Sons, Inc., Hoboken, New Jersey.
Published simultaneously in Canada.

For general information on our other products and services please contact our
Customer Care Department within the United States at (800) 762-2974, outside
the U.S. at (317) 572-3993, or fax (317) 572-4002.

Wiley also publishes its books in a variety of electronic formats. Some content that
appears in print may not be available in electronic books. For more information
about Wiley products, visit our web site at www.wiley.com.

*Library of Congress Cataloging-in-Publication Data:*

Rich, Laura, 1970–
   The accidental zillionaire : demystifying Paul Allen  /  Laura Rich.
      p.   cm.
Includes bibliographical references and index.
   ISBN 0-471-23491-5 ((CLOTH) : alk. paper)
   1. Allen, Paul, 1953–   2. Businesspeople—United States—Biography.
I.  Title.
   HC102.5.A49 R53 2003
   338.7'610053'092—dc21

                                                              2002012694


10   9   8   7   6   5   4   3   2   1

For my parents

# ACKNOWLEDGMENTS

I was often asked during the writing of this book whether I'd spent much time on Paul Allen's jets, at his parties, or in any of his many homes around the world. For a moment, I would imagine with them a sort of fabulous lifestyle I'd been leading since taking on this book. Then, I'd tell them that Allen didn't work with me on this project and my thoughts would turn to the many people who went out of their way and risked their relationships with one of the world's richest and most powerful men to help me tell this story. Some of them offered up exhaustive amounts of their time—quite literally. At the end of one marathon interview, one former executive of an Allen company begged off, claiming he was "tired now." But, he said, he'd had fun. That's good. If there's one thing Allen is concerned about, it's trying to enjoy life as often as possible. I thank those sources for their stories and their enthusiasm.

Paul Allen's story would remain untold were it not for the vision of Matthew Holt, my editor at John Wiley & Sons, who conceived of a book on Allen. Matt's eagerness fueled this project through every stage. I cannot thank him enough for that, and for his down-to-earth good nature. It was a comfort whenever new questions or concerns arose as the book was coming together.

My agent, Susan Barry at the Swayne Agency, must be thanked for bringing this exciting and rewarding project to my attention in the first place. As the project unfolded, she remained a trusty source of help. I am indebted to her.

There were many people who gave hours of their time in various ways. I would like to give special thanks to those who put in hours reading over pages of the manuscript in various stages, acting as sounding boards and offering words of wisdom from their own, similar experiences: Melanie Warner, who is a very dear and longtime friend, as well as a respected journalist; and Gary Rivlin and James Ledbetter, two esteemed journalists and authors whom I have the honor and pleasure to call former colleagues from our days at *The Industry Standard*. Melanie, Gary, and Jim kept me thinking about the bigger picture among the stories unfolding on these pages.

I would also like to thank Laurieanne Gilner, Laura Roe Stevens, Hane Lee, Bill Brazell, Mark Gimein, Maryann Thompson, Hugh Garvey, and Holly Rich for taking time out of their busy schedules to give me their thoughts about the book in progress, and to hear me out as I agonized through sections along the way. Friends and family deserve this special note for the support and encouragement they've given over the years. My parents and sister have always been faithful sounding boards, never more so than when I was consumed by doubts and concerns about this book. Much love and gratitude to them for everything.

L. R.

# CONTENTS

# INTRODUCTION

Paul Allen stood gazing over the guests aboard his 300-foot yacht, the Tatoosh, docked in New Orleans along the Mississippi River. The yacht had arrived in January of 2002 for that year's Super Bowl, and had remained there for months. Now, it was May and a cable-industry conference was underway. A few years back, Allen, whose $20.4 billion fortune made him the third richest person in America, had decided to dabble in cable. Well, maybe more than dabble. He had already spent $18 billion to make cable the lynchpin of his plan to change the way people communicate. Since 1974, he'd been dreaming of a world where everyone was connected through machines, whether it was through a computer, a television, a handheld gizmo, or some other unforeseen means. Inside this "wired world," as he's been calling it since the start of the 1990s, all kinds of things would take place. New kinds of entertainment, shopping, and socializing would be born. Cable was one way of connecting people. Now, in 2002, he'd invited dozens of business executives and politicians to a party to introduce them to Digeo, the company he was backing that he believed would, finally, deliver his wired world.

Around the yacht, little stations were set up to give guests a closer look at Digeo, which was also the name of a device equipped with fancy interactive-television features. Waiters offered local and exotic delicacies on silver trays and a live band pumped up the energy of the whole affair. It was just like those decadent dot-com parties that were quickly becoming a faded memory. But Allen was pulling out all the stops now because he was anxious to stir up excitement around Digeo, which, to his mind, was going to turn the cable box into something truly interactive.

Most people seemed to be there to bask in Allen's presence, not to play with his latest favorite toy. Amid the side presentations and hors d'oeuvres trays, guests angled for a word with the man with the means and the moxie to back their own projects. In this setting, Allen couldn't get a moment to himself.

Yet, two days later, Allen was dining alone. Here he was at a cable show as one of the most powerful people in cable, thanks to his ownership of the country's fourth-largest cable company, Charter Communications. Even so, Allen couldn't seem to get a lunch date. He sat hunched over a table in the convention hall cafeteria, two bodyguards at separate tables some distance from Allen. This was the other Allen—just a regular guy enjoying his pizza.

There's a view you hear a lot when the topic is Paul Allen. Often the view is offered with smugness or perhaps some snideness: It is that the best thing that ever happened to Paul Allen was meeting Bill Gates. So much has been written about Microsoft's other founder that somehow Allen's contribution seems diminished, if not beside the point. Gates has had a posse of public relations people carefully cultivating his image in the press, which have eagerly covered his nearly every move. He has become so clearly defined in the media, he's almost become a cliché: Gates as the uber-geek, the ultimate revenge of the nerds. He has been called a "genius"; he's a recognized business leader and a world figure. Gates is so huge that some reporters have forgotten that two people started Microsoft, referring to Gates, alone, as "founder."

Allen, on the other hand, has a reputation for being misunderstood. He's not a big public speaker and his public relations people don't spend much time on his image. He's such a mystery that even those who've spent some time with him find it easier to describe Allen in relation to Gates, as "more easygoing than Bill," "more laid-back than Bill."

If anything, many people think of Allen as a computer geek, like Gates, in part because of the billions he's spent on technology investments. But Allen's other activities—the sports teams he owns, the phantasmagoric rock museum he's built in downtown Seattle, the Hollywood studio he's funded—contort that initial presumption. If Allen is so enamored of sports, music, and movies, the thinking goes, he can't be all geek.

Maybe Allen's just a rich guy enjoying life. He's poured money into new homes for himself around the world, bulked up a stable of yachts and planes, and thrown lavish parties for the famous friends he's met because he's rich. A guitar junkie since he was a kid, he seems best of all to like meeting rock stars and often has one in tow on various jaunts he takes around the world to run errands or attend parties where other celebrities will be.

But Allen's wealth is held against him, while it isn't with Gates. They both started Microsoft, but Gates is still putting in the long hours there. Allen left the company in 1983 and has simply collected his dividend checks—and what dividends they are. It makes some people uncomfortable: One should *earn* money or good fortune, and since Allen hasn't worked at Microsoft in two decades, he seems, to many people, just "lucky."

Over the years, journalists have struggled to define Allen. The local newspapers in Seattle, where he lives, have provided windows into his life, as have writers at *Fortune*, who have talked with him about his businesses and his relationship with Gates. But Allen has generally remained unspecific and undefined. In 1994, *Wired* famously reviewed his life in business and fell in with the skeptics, giving Allen the one title that has stuck: "accidental zillionaire."

I received some initial indications from Paul Allen's office that I might get some support on this project. This made sense. Though he's been called "press shy" for his low-key public image, he has also occasionally been quoted as saying he was frustrated by how misunderstood he felt. What's more, no one had ever written a book about Allen. Maybe he was tired of living in the shadows of the many books that have profiled Gates. Besides, I was talking about a business profile. Allen guards his personal life to the extent that employees at his wholly owned operations must sign agreements that they will never talk publicly about the Allen family (Allen, his mother, and sister Jody). But a business profile would not delve into his personal affairs, except where those matters help to inform who he is as a leading businessman in America.

It wasn't too long before Allen's reps backed off, though they dangled a vague indication of collaboration in the future. They seemed to want to stay on generally good terms and told me that their reasons for backing off were "no reflection on" my publisher or me. They just said that, at the moment, they were all busy with other things and, unfortunately, would have to tell people who called—sources I contacted for the book who checked in with Allen about it—that they didn't want anyone to cooperate with me.

Several months passed. I carried on with my work, interviewing friends, family, and business associates who had known Allen throughout the years (those I knew personally or who, despite his views of the project, wanted to help tell Allen's story, anyway). And then, the final "no, thanks" arrived in my in-box from Jason Hunke at Vulcan:

> Laura—Mr. Allen and Vulcan remain very concerned, and quite frankly, disappointed in your ongoing disregard for his privacy, and the continued invasion of his personal and professional

relationships. We evidently had unrealistic expectations about how you would try to balance your "contract" to write a book and any respect for Mr. Allen's privacy—it is now clear that you have no regard for Mr. Allen or his wishes. We do not support this project, and will continue to communicate our position to all relevant parties. I question your ability to produce a manuscript that is remotely factual and balanced, given the variety of people who have refused to talk to you, and again encourage you and the publisher to evaluate the validity of the project.

All I can do is respectfully request that you stop harassing Mr. Allen, his associates, friends, family and business relationships—your tactics will in no way change our position and only reinforce the negative perceptions that have already been created about the project, your approach, and the motives of the author and publisher.

Disregard for privacy . . . harassing . . . strong language, but not all that surprising to me. From what I had learned of Allen's professional style, this was par for the course: "Mr. Allen" was a very powerful person, and those who wanted to do business with him fell in line. In 1993, he had tried to force America Online's board to give him control of the company; when they wouldn't grant it, he walked away from the company entirely. So even if Allen's staff were aware that I was not personally "harassing" anyone, knowing what I did about Allen's need for privacy and control, it wasn't that strange that such an e-mail found its way to me.

This wasn't the first profile that was to be written without Allen's initial consent. *Wired* undertook that charge in 1994 with a profile of Allen as an investor. According to the article's author, Paulina Borsook, Allen's group behaved similarly: They said "No, thanks," when first approached, and asked people not to participate in the piece. But Borsook and her editors took this response to mean there was a story worth digging into. Borsook plowed ahead. The Allen camp pursued ways to halt the article, but in the eleventh hour, when they realized the piece was going to come out, anyway, they conceded to granting interviews with Allen and several senior executives within his organizations. The piece in its final form was, as they seemed to have feared, unflattering. A rumor spread through the *Wired* offices that Allen would buy up every newsstand copy to prevent its being read. (He didn't.)

By the time the e-mail arrived from Allen's spokesperson, it was really too late to turn back, anyway. I had become hooked. So had my publisher. To us, Allen had been mistakenly overlooked. Allen had earned his place as an influential businessperson in large part because of his enormous wealth—but there was more. While Gates was off obsessing over a single company (a tactic that obviously made him one of the most important business leaders of all time), Allen had taken a more creative approach to business and investing that had its own legitimacy. He held on to what had started Microsoft in the first place: a keen interest in the possibilities of technology and a fervent belief in pursuing dreams, no matter how far-fetched they seemed.

Allen's concerns about privacy were understandable, but unrealistic. He had become a public figure who had a very significant effect on business and communications. To let Allen and his varied business interests go uncovered would be almost irresponsible.

When I was a reporter at *The Industry Standard*, a magazine that covered the Internet boom from the beginning to bitter end, we kept our eyes on the ever-active, provocative Paul Allen. We called him "prescient" when he invested in cable in 2001, but also noted that he wasn't extremely successful in other areas. I covered his 1999 investment in a Hollywood start-up called Pop.com, an idea from the principals of DreamWorks SKG that burned through cash and never launched. It was easy to see that one coming, since online entertainment had struggled even before Allen put in for Pop.com. But I called it wrong in 2001 when I covered his cable company's dispute with ESPN, which wanted to stream for free some of its broadcasts over the Internet, in addition to cable. Allen's Charter thought that ESPN's plan would devalue the content carried on their networks. They were probably right, but at the time, it looked like a step backward in the technological innovations that were taking place on the Internet.

This is the problem with Allen: His inconsistencies make him difficult to perceive in any generic terms. Is he smart? Sure. Though he didn't attend an Ivy League school like his Microsoft counterpart, he beat Gates's score on the SAT college entrance exams. Is he lucky? Of course he is. But, then, so is Bill Gates.

Allen and Gates became friends in high school and developed a dynamic that served them each well. They bonded over the new machine in their school, a Teletype that could dial into a real computer and allow them to start learning about software. Allen, Gates, and a couple of other boys quickly began offering these new skills for hire and even set up a little business called the Lakeside Programmers Group. The partnership between Allen and Gates really came together after high school, however, when they started thinking about a technology business they could start together. The partnership solidified into a business in 1975, after Allen famously spotted a magazine cover that gave him the idea for a product that became the basis for the formation of Microsoft.

Between the two of them, Allen was always driven by the inner workings of technology, while Gates was mainly motivated by money. Allen just wanted to be right about an idea, as he was with a new version of BASIC, the product that formed the basis of Microsoft. Gates, by contrast, was interested in the idea, but immediately sought to turn it into a commercial endeavor. Together, the two made Microsoft into a company that caught the attention of IBM in 1980, when it was piecing together plans for its own personal computer. IBM chose Microsoft to provide the operating system, transforming Allen and Gates's company into a global player.

What happened after IBM designated Microsoft as a major software company really isn't Allen's story, since he left the company in 1983, after being treated for Hodgkin's disease, a form of lymphoma. Yet, he's been tethered to the company ever since through the valuable stock options he earned as a cofounder, options that have provided almost the entire basis for his profound wealth. As Microsoft has done well, so has Allen. From a low-level spot on *Forbes*'s list of richest people in 1987, Allen ascended to No. 2, in 1999. He fell back in 2001 to No. 3 after the tech bubble burst and the value of his Microsoft stock and other tech investments shrank slightly.

Allen is often called a "tech mogul," which is fair, but that doesn't quite get to the heart of who he is. He isn't like Gates, who has made one company a single-minded focus for himself. That would never satisfy Allen. "Even as a kid, every year I was interested in something different," he told *Fortune* in 1994. Once he left Microsoft, Allen seemed out to prove it. He stayed in the technology field and started his own company, Asymetrix, in 1984, but as soon as he had the means—once Microsoft went public in 1986—he began to diversify his investments, from the personal to the professional, and seemingly less for monetary gain than to enjoy the trappings of wealth. In 1988, he bought himself a basketball team, the Portland Trail Blazers. By then, Allen had also acquired a personal jet and an estate on Seattle's posh Mercer Island. In 1990, when his personal fortune grew to $1 billion for the first time (again, almost entirely from Microsoft stock), he began to pick up the pace of those investments, launching a fund aimed at technology and becoming more active in personal and social pursuits, like plans to build a museum in Seattle in honor of his rock idol, Jimi Hendrix.

If Allen is known for anything, it's his "wired world" theory, inspired by a 1991 investment in the interactive TV company SkyPix. SkyPix's plan to deliver interactive experiences by satellite into people's homes got Allen thinking again about an idea he had first had in 1974. Now, it came together as the wired world strategy and became the aim of his investment arm, Vulcan Ventures, whose activities have often been seen as random, no doubt because the wired world is a broadly defined theory and has yet to be either proven or financially viable. As such, the wired world strategy seems to be to blame for Allen's failed attempt to pull America Online into his mix of companies. It has also been behind some seemingly wise investments, such as Charter and DreamWorks, and some clearly bad ones, like the failed dot-coms Value America and Mercata.

The wired world has not delivered any major hits for Allen—none on the scale of Microsoft, leading some critics to believe he can't do it without Gates by his side. Worst of all, Allen makes his bets in million-dollar increments, while other investors play in smaller change—thousand-dollar or hundred-thousand-dollar spreads. It makes Allen's moves all the more obvious, his blunders more apparent.

Allen doesn't seem to care. Yet, he does. In the interviews he's given over the years, he's regularly defended his mixed investment record with statements like, "When you're involved in as many things as I am, you're going to have some things turn out great, some things that are okay, and some that don't turn out like you expect them to," as he told the *Seattle Times* in 1994. Clearly, he doesn't like to be misunderstood—none of us do—but then he virtually guarantees that he will be. He brandishes nondisclosure agreements on a frequent basis, and has once fired a personal assistant just because he thought someone might be able to get information about his schedule out of her without her knowledge. When approached about this book, Allen and his immediate family chose not to participate. He's not like Gates or most other business leaders. He almost never makes himself accessible, and never courts the press.

Fortunately, Allen has spoken publicly about his life and work on occasion, and there is almost no end to the number of people who have known him, to varying degrees. For a man as rich as he is, Allen really gets out where the regular folks are. He tours convention hall floors and shops at his local video store. Because of his vast investment history, he has come in contact with people in many sectors, but mainly in technology and entertainment, where my own career has centered.

Even those who have known Allen for years still have trouble defining him, because he is always looking into new areas and finding new things that appeal to him. No single effort could cover the enormous breadth of Allen's holdings and interests. This is just a first attempt to offer a glimpse into some of the experiences he's had.

At this point, the world can only wait to see what Allen does next with the billions he's wagered on the wired world. Charter Communications is currently the best equipped cable system to deliver the broadband entertainment future Allen has been envisioning for decades. Few people are holding their breaths, knowing that even with the best tools on hand, Allen's made missteps in the past. But one thing's for certain: No stingy billionaire, Allen can be expected to keep on spending.

# GET EXPERIENCED

aul Allen's story begins most inauspiciously. Unlike his future business partner Bill Gates, Paul Allen wasn't born into wealth or status. No Roman numeral weighted down the end of his name, nor did he have well-bred roots that guaranteed a potential for success in life. Allen came from humble beginnings. His parents just managed to stretch their meager salaries far enough to give their son a good education and passed on their own love of books and theater to further expand his world.

Born into Oklahoma's Dust-Bowl poverty, Allen's parents each grew up in one-room houses and moved around a lot. Sometimes they didn't have any running water. Their families weren't alone; everyone in Anadarko, 70 miles south of Oklahoma City, was having a hard time of it. The Depression had struck and they were all just scraping by. Allen's parents, Kenneth Allen and Edna Faye Gardner, didn't let it slow them down.

Allen's father was the son of a struggling farmer. Mrs. Allen didn't work, but spent her days raising her three boys—Kenneth, Louis, and Bob. The Gardners were just as poor. Everyone in Anadarko—a town of 5,000—worked whenever and wherever they could to put food on the table. Times were hard. "It was very rough back then," says Kenneth's brother, Louis.

While they struggled at home, Kenneth and Edna Faye excelled at school. They were among the most popular kids in their classes at Anadarko High School. Kenneth was voted "All-Around Boy" and Edna Faye was voted "All-Around Girl." Every year, students awarded the title to the girl and boy who were most popular and most involved in school activities. Certainly, these two had a full schedule. Kenneth was president of the student council and a star athlete who lettered in four sports.

Kenneth was a star in the drama department, too, and his future wife was just as drawn to the stage, a fondness they'd pass on to their daughter, while their son preferred the stage on screen. In the William H. Smith play, *The Drunkard*, Kenneth played the villain, Squire Cribbs, while Edna Faye played the role of the cunning spinster, Miss Spindle. Edna Faye was also a singer. She was a member of the Girls' Glee Club and vice president of the Girls' Quartet. It was a busy schedule, but that wasn't all of it. She joined the student council as the representative of trade and industry and was asked to join the exclusive Pet Club, a type of sorority. It was little surprise Kenneth and Edna Faye were too busy to date during their high-school days.

"Not many folks dated back then," recalls Mayme Philips, one of Edna Faye's classmates. "Most people couldn't afford to."

Kenneth and Edna Faye were also immersed in their schoolwork. Eldon O'Donnelly, one of Kenneth's former classmates, remembers that Kenneth was a "good football player and a good student." And Philips says that all of the students thought Edna Faye was "really smart." Kenneth and Edna Faye were expected to go far.

They did—to California, 1,300 miles west of Anadarko. As drought conditions continued, towns emptied of people in search of work. Some folks went to southern California for the steel factories cranking up production of planes for the war. Eventually Kenneth and Edna Faye followed this path, but for a different reason. Edna Faye worked at the local library, where she met Kenneth after they had graduated from high school. They began dating and were married. Meanwhile, Edna Faye enrolled in the University of California at Los Angeles and was joined in Los Angeles by Kenneth after the war. Edna Faye earned a degree in sociology in 1948. Soon after, Kenneth and Edna Faye moved on again, this time to Seattle, their final destination.

Though tucked away into the farthest corner of the country, thousands of miles from the nearest major city and hemmed in by the Cascade Mountains and unrelenting overcast skies, Seattle has rarely been a sleepy town. Over the years, this out-of-the-way place has hosted political protests, riots, and become the No. 1 destination for teenage runaways.

At the end of World War II, Seattle was just as unsure about its future as other cities. Faced the new Cold War, Seattle had its share of Red scares with government groups on the prowl for Communist sympathizers. But Seattle boomed, too. Poor farming conditions in the Midwest had brought families to the Northwest during the war years in search of new work and new lives. New communities sprang up. To accommodate the influx of newcomers, no fewer than 15 new suburbs were formed across Lake Washington on Seattle's Eastside, including, in 1954, Bellevue, where the Allens' son would ultimately set up a base for his myriad holdings. But for now, Bellevue, Redmond, and other Eastside communities were just beginning. In 1950, when the Allens settled in the area, they stuck to central Seattle and chose a burgeoning middle-class neighborhood called Wedgwood, just north of the University of Washington.

By this point, Seattle was still a very new city, not even a hundred years old. Settled in 1861 by the Midwestern Denny family, it had been named for the friendly local Indian chief Seattle. Fire and earthquakes had rocked the city, which twice had been totally rebuilt. Then, around the turn of the last century, some local miners struck Klondike gold. Fifty years after California's gold rush, Seattle experienced a gold rush of its own.

When the Allens arrived, Seattle was more of a science and technology town, with airplane maker Boeing at its center. During the war, Boeing had pumped out planes. Before the decade was out, Boeing sent out the first commercial flight, firmly affixing the "Jet City" moniker to Seattle's identity.

From dusty, dry, and depressing Anadarko, the Allens had come far—2,100 miles from home. This quiet, hardworking couple was hopeful that Seattle would be the place for new beginnings. Kenneth looked for work and eventually found a job as the assistant director in the library at the University of Washington; his wife earned a certificate to teach elementary school. On January 21, 1953, they gave birth to their first child, Paul Gardner Allen.

Paul Allen would never have to struggle the way his parents had. By the time he came along, the Allens had pretty much achieved the American dream for their growing family: a two-story home in a middle-class community and enough income to live comfortably. Compared to his parents, Allen was spoiled.

For his first few years, Paul was an only child who had his parents' full attention. Faye, as she now was called, doted on her son. As a mother, she wanted to pass on the love of education and activities she'd enjoyed as a teenager. When Paul was just three months old, Faye began reading to him, anxious to get him started on books. He grew into a quiet, thoughtful child, like his parents. He read a lot and didn't really play sports—mainly because allergies to grass kept him off the fields. That was actually okay with his father, the all-around boy athlete. In high school, Kenneth had been injured a few times and now lived with a knee injury from one Anadarko football game. Instead of playing sports together, Kenneth and Paul bonded over their love of the game as spectators. They read sports pages, watched games, and talked shop about players and teams. Kenneth took Paul to Seattle Sonics basketball games. The two had no idea then that Paul would someday own his own National Basketball Association team.

Kenneth spent a lot of time talking with Paul and gave him some advice he never forgot. "He told me that you should love whatever work you do. You should try to find something you truly enjoy," Allen later wrote on his Web site.

If anything really captured Paul's attention, it was figuring out how things worked. He spent hours taking things apart and examining them. With patience and discipline, he built model airplanes and performed science experiments from hobby sets. He sometimes plowed through dry manuals so he could learn more about how things worked and, when he was old enough, he tagged along with his father to the university library to pick out books on electronics and rocket science. He was a product of the science-and-math Sputnik generation, but Paul was already somewhat of a geek in his own right.

The Allens as a whole were a fairly quiet, contemplative bunch. Even Paul's sister Jody, who became a drama star in school (like her parents), was thoughtful and reserved. The two siblings were as close as a brother and a sister separated by four years in school might be, but Jody had less interest in her brother's science projects, so they found other things to enjoy together. They saw movies at the newly opened Cinerama downtown. In 1968, they took in *Planet of the Apes* and in 1973, they saw *The Exorcist* there. They were friendly siblings who enjoyed each other's company.

The elder Allens permitted the movies, but this pair of academics preferred to fill their children's heads with more intellectual pursuits. They gave them reading schedules and taught them about music. On a couple of academics' salaries, they managed to buy an old piano for the kids. Jody learned to play classical piano, but Paul wasn't much interested. He did like the family's summer outings, though. Almost every year, the four Allens piled into Kenneth's 1963 Buick Electra—the first new car he ever bought—and drove eight hours south to the southern border of Oregon to attend the annual Oregon Shakespeare Festival. Paul grew to love Shakespeare.

In 1966, Paul learned to love something else, and it wasn't part of Kenneth and Faye's intellectual-stimulation program, although it was partly their doing. That year, they decided to take a vacation, leaving Jody and Paul with a neighbor whose 14-year-old daughter was a friend of Jody's. This girl had an impressive record collection and it was here that Jody and Paul learned about the latest bands. Each time they visited, Jody's friend pulled out a record. The first one was by The Monkees. After hearing the band, Paul went out and bought his own copy. Thanks to this neighbor's interest in music, he started his own collection of records.

The next year, Jody's friend pulled out a record by an artist named Jimi Hendrix. The album was called "Are You Experienced?" She removed the record from its case and placed it on the turntable. All of a sudden, strange noises began pouring from the speakers. A low, deep bass built first into a scraping rhythm and climaxed with a chromatic climb. The notes whinnied and growled. It was one of the most incredible sounds Paul had ever heard. "I felt immediately touched," Allen later recalled to *Rolling Stone.* "It was like hearing music from another planet."

Paul had liked the contemporary music of the day, but nothing like this. He became zealous over Hendrix's music. He bought Hendrix's album "Electric Ladyland" and played it endlessly, much to his parents' chagrin. "Our parents didn't like it," Paul confessed later to the *Seattle Times.* He eventually wore out the album, but replaced it with another.

Paul sought a solution to indulge his new passion without disturbing the other family members. "My mother said it sounded like noise," Paul said years later. He resorted to headphones when playing his Hendrix records.

Eventually, Faye found some good in all this noise. Paul hadn't picked up the piano, but he'd been drawn to this music, which may have seemed to her better than no music at all. She even encouraged him to learn to play the guitar and found an old used guitar for him at a rummage sale. He immediately learned to play it and figured a way to hook it up to the stereo so he could play along to his records—with headphones, of course. "And not bother the rest of the family," he recalled to the *Times*.

His love of Hendrix music even changed Paul's appearance. He started wearing a black leather jacket and a wide-brimmed hat. "He looked like Buffalo Springfield," says former classmate Dan Asia. He grew Fu Manchu sideburns. He wanted to be Hendrix-cool.

Like Paul, Jimi Hendrix was from Seattle, but by the time Paul heard his "Are You Experienced?" in 1967, Hendrix was 24, living in London, and playing on the global stage.

Hendrix was a sensation because he was changing rock-'n-roll. He drew out of the electric guitar not new notes and melodies, but new ways of using the instrument to create explosions, screeches, and a blending of sounds. He reinvented guitar playing, finding new ways to play the same old songs, like his infamous rendition of "The Star-Spangled Banner" that bangs and screeches its way melodically to the end.

Hendrix's sound was loud and he combined it with the use of amplifiers turned all the way up. Sometimes this created feedback, but this was where Hendrix's artistic mastery came in. He learned to tame that high-pitched sound and weave it into the melodies and guitar riffs in his music. Young Paul connected with this experimentation in music.

Paul had much in common with his new idol. Like Paul, Hendrix as a child was shy, soft-spoken, and, like Paul, inclined toward mechanical things (Hendrix learned to play songs on a one-stringed ukulele). Paul and Jimi even shared a name: James Marshall Hendrix was the name given to Jimi Hendrix by his father when he was three years old, but he was born Johnny Allen Hendrix in 1942.

Paul was growing into a very average teenager. He loved rock-'n-roll like all the other kids. He liked movies and sports. And, like lots of kids his age, he didn't care so much about his schoolwork. The Allens would fix that.

Faye grew alarmed when she discovered that her son sat in the back of the classroom and read books to pass the time. The public school was just the right price—it was free—but it wasn't doing much for Paul. Faye and Kenneth realized there was another alternative, but they didn't know if they could do it. The prestigious Lakeside School could offer their son a higher level of education, but it was expensive—$5,000 per year, even more than Harvard's then-tuition of $1,760. But the Allens already knew something about scraping by. They could manage it again for their child's sake. They told him their plan.

Paul didn't want to go. He was happy in the back of the classroom with his books. He had friends in the public school and didn't want to leave. Begrudgingly, he agreed to take the test for Lakeside, but privately, he determined to flunk it. "Except, when I started taking it, I thought it was pretty interesting," he later told *Rolling Stone*. Allen passed with flying colors and entered Lakeside in 1968 as a sophomore.

Lakeside School opened in 1919. Until the year Allen attended, its all-male student body was required to wear suits and ties, say prayer before meals, and call their teachers "masters." The freewheeling 1960s finally caught up with the place, though, and Allen arrived in his trademark leather jacket and hat. Lakeside was progressive, now. Open-minded teachers held students to a loose regular academic agenda and encouraged them to find the areas that interested them most. Allen's former classmate Asia, now a music professor at the University of Arizona, found out at Lakeside that he liked to compose music, so he spent more time in the music department than anywhere else. Another student, Harvey

Motulsky, found his own interests lay in science and math. He became a math-hall regular.

Allen didn't really have a niche at Lakeside in his first year. He attended his classes and made passing grades, but he was discovering cars and girls, and he still loved to play his guitar. But when Allen entered school in the fall of 1968, he noticed something new in the science and math building that would take him away from his classes, away from his books, and sometimes, even, away from Hendrix: a clunky old machine that looked a lot like a typewriter—except, it wasn't.

Lakeside School was the best thing that ever happened to Paul Allen. It was here that he met Bill Gates, with whom he would create Microsoft, one of the most successful startups in American business history.

For now, all there was between them was this machine. In what was being called the "computer" room in the math hall, the machine banged, clacked, and gurgled. It shook violently every time it was geared up to pump out data, but the rest of the time it just sat there. The odd contraption intrigued Allen, Gates, and some of the other kids. They were told it was a computer—well, sort of a computer—and they wanted to know what it could do.

The machine wasn't a computer. It was a Teletype ASR-33. It had a keyboard like a typewriter, as well as a hole-punch that translated typewritten commands into a pattern of holes on a roll of tape. On its own, this machine didn't do much more than punch holes in the tape, but when it was hooked up to a modem (a phone hooked up to the machine with its receiver placed in two cups), it could communicate with a computer in downtown Seattle. Basically, the Teletype was just the way to get into the real computer, a room-sized PDP-10 from Digital Equipment

Corporation (DEC). The computer was owned by General Electric, which had begun a time-sharing program of leasing access to the computer to businesses around Seattle.

Allen, Gates, and other students eyed the machine, and then they got to work. From their math teacher, Fred Wright, who'd been put in charge of the "computer," they learned the language used by the PDP-10, BASIC (Basic All-purpose Symbolic Instruction Code). With simple commands, they began to create programs. Gates devised a game of Tic-Tac-Toe. Harvey Motulsky taught the machine how to play Monopoly.

Soon enough, the computer room became the nexus of technology lovers at Lakeside. Gearheads and math geeks spent hours there, eating pizza and just sitting around. They almost had to. A simple program like Tic-Tac-Toe could take up to five minutes to relay a single move to the remote PDP-10 and receive back confirmation. But each time the machine sprung into action, the boys' eyes lit up with the wonder of what this thing would do.

What they really wanted was access to the PDP-10 itself. The Teletype was fine, but it was too far removed from the seat of the action. It was also expensive. General Electric was sending the school bills for the boys' time on the Teletype, and before long, the price was too high for the perceived benefit. The Lakeside Mothers' Club stepped in and raised $3,000 for computer time. But after a few months, what they thought would last a year had run out. The boys in the computer room were disappointed. They thought their brief little experiment was over. They had no idea that soon, in one easy transaction, they'd get free computer time *and* access to the PDP-10 and a chance to change computer technology.

Computer Center Corporation changed the lives of at least a few boys from Lakeside. Computer Center was a new

company set up by four former University of Washington profes-
sors who had an idea for a multiuser software program for Digital's PDP-10. They were nearing completion of their project, but
needed some help testing the system and working out the kinks.
What did this mean for the now quite-bored Lakesiders? One of
the cofounders happened to be the mother of a student at Lakeside. Through her son, she'd learned about the school's predicament and come up with an idea: If the boys could help them look
for bugs in the system (basically, find ways to crash it), they could
get free computer time in exchange.

"It was manna from heaven," Gates told the authors Stephen
Manes and Paul Andrews in *Gates.*

Indeed, it must have been like winning the golden ticket to
Willy Wonka's chocolate factory. Computer Center opened the
door and said, "Come on in and take a look. Play around." These
kids weren't just offered access to the PDP-10, as they'd hoped—
they were asked to poke around in the bowels of the machine,
looking for glitches here and there.

Some of the boys were more competitive than others. Allen
and Gates were among them. They welcomed the challenge of
trying to beat the machine. Gates went after security crashes,
while Allen looked at every aspect of the system, program, and
machine. Allen "got into it more than the rest of us," recalls
Motulsky. "He got into the details." He wanted to know everything. He'd ask the programmers at Computer Center about how
parts of the machine worked—only to be handed a manual. He'd
return with the manual and ask another question. Again, he got a
manual for an answer. But he was learning.

One time, Allen "got his hands on the source code and improved it. He got into the guts and made it easier to use," says
Motulsky. Source code eventually became a very big issue with
Gates and Allen when they were at Microsoft. They fought (and
beat) the entire computer industry against the practice of distributing it. But back in high school in Seattle, they didn't know the

difference, and naturally delighted in seeing the lines of code that went into designing computer programs.

Days and nights of free time at Computer Center came to an end once the project was completed. The boys glumly went back to the old Teletype at Lakeside. But now, they were a little smarter. They'd learned a thing or two about the PDP-10 from all the time they spent picking it apart. They used that knowledge and started digging around inside of the machine from their outpost at Lakeside, five miles north of Computer Center's offices. They found a chess game they weren't supposed to. They found accounting files—and they changed them so that the individual accounts for the boys were much lower than they were supposed to be.

They weren't that good, though. They got caught. According to an account in the book *Gates*, an intimidating visit from one of the Computer Center principals to one of the teachers at Lakeside scared them into curbing their bad behavior.

By now, some of the boys had earned themselves the beginnings of a reputation within the nascent computer industry. Word of their work on Computer Center's system found its way back to Digital Equipment Corporation, and now that company had an assignment for the boys: crack its latest security software. It took less than two hours. It was a catch-22 for Digital and Computer Center: The boys were talented, but it made them a security risk—they'd already proved their ability at mischief making. Allen and Gates, the primary culprits, were banned from the system in the summer of 1969. (Allen got himself computer time, however, on the PDP-10 and PDP-11 that were used at the University of Washington, where his father worked.)

The computer had just been a hobby—though a passionate hobby—for the handful of boys, including Allen, Gates, Motulsky, and two boys named Ric Weiland and Marc McDonald, who would become the first and third employees at Microsoft. There were other boys who were part of the computer crowd, too, but one very essential member of this group was Kent Evans. For Evans, it was important that the boys consider making their computer skills a business. He led the formation of the Lakeside Programmers Group.

Evans was the most business-minded kid anyone had ever seen around Lakeside. He carried a briefcase filled with the latest copies of *Fortune, Business Month*, and the *Wall Street Journal*. He schemed constantly ways to create businesses and make money.

Evans was Gates's best friend. Gates had always dreamed up ideas of things he could do to make a lot of money, but Evans may have been even more of a diehard than he. "The notion from day one was to make money, barrels of money," recalls his father, Reverend Marvin Evans. "This was the eighth grade!"

Evans says his son and Gates spent hours on the phone talking about businesses they'd start. Evans says one idea they had was to "put a computer on every desk in America." That's what Gates later claimed was always the goal behind Microsoft.

Gates was also friendly with Allen in high school, but it wasn't a fast friendship. Gates was two years younger than Allen and not very personable. He was short, scrawny, and his voice squeaked when he spoke, which was often, loudly, and arrogantly. Usually, he was insisting his was a smarter, faster, or more correct point than anyone else's. The other kids found him obnoxious and aggressive. "He went out of his way to ridicule and belittle me," says one former classmate. In their law class, Gates turned on this boy and, raising his voice, explained to the class why his last answer was wrong. "He was always trying to prove something," says the former student.

In contrast to Gates, Allen was tall for his age and chunky. He liked to go around looking like the rock stars he idolized. Allen wasn't shy, but he was quiet and didn't say much. He took his time to think things through and when he spoke, "you listened," recalls Harvey Motulsky, who was a year ahead of Allen.

The future cofounders of Microsoft were very different. While Allen was solidly middle class, Gates was among the privileged students who attended Lakeside. His mother came from a prominent Seattle banking family, and his father was a successful attorney. Bill Gates was known as "Trey" then, his full name was William Gates III. Even the name reeked of upper crust.

Despite their differences, Gates's arrogance actually appealed to Allen. He was amused by this younger kid and thought it would be fun to catch him at his own game. "If you're so smart," Allen was taunting Gates, "see if you can figure this out." Then he'd produce a programming challenge for Gates. Most times, Gates would figure it out and they'd talk over the program together.

They soon began getting together outside of school. Gates went to Allen's house one time and was blown away by his collection of science fiction books and technical manuals. "He had read four times as much as I had," Gates told the authors of *Hard Drive*. "And he had all these other books that explained things. So I would ask him, 'How do guns work? How do nuclear reactors work?' Paul was good at explaining stuff. Later, we did some math stuff and physics stuff together. That's how we got to be friends."

Allen and Gates bonded primarily through the Lakeside Programmers Group, made up of four boys: Allen and Ric Weiland, who were seniors, and Evans and Gates, then sophomores. Eventually, the group whittled down to just Allen and Gates.

Evans's plans for the Lakeside Programmers Group were coming along swimmingly. The group did very well for a bunch of teenage boys. They never made much money, since most of the deals were brokered in exchange for computer time, but if they had been paid in cash, the boys would have logged tens of thousands of dollars in fees.

It had begun with Computer Center. Allen and Gates figured that if they could offer work to Computer Center, they could get back on the PDP-10 and score free computer time. Allen landed an assignment on a BASIC compiler (language that converts software commands to hardware commands to make it run). The company gave Gates SYSTAT, which helped the system keep track of which programs were in use on the system. At the end of that school year, Computer Center ran out of money and had to shut down. For Allen and Gates, the bankruptcy was a lesson in how fragile companies could be.

Evans was anxious to keep the group going, so he thought about where they could offer their services—but the phone rang first. It was a company in Portland, Oregon, called Information Sciences, Inc., that had heard about the boys and needed their help. The referral came through Computer Center, actually, where one of ISI's executives used to work. The assignment? Help ISI develop a payroll program to market to clients. In return, they'd get free computer time. At first, the job went to Allen and Weiland, but they became disinterested in the arcane project that involved understanding state tax requirements, payroll deductions, and the like. Allen wasn't in it for the money, and this gig was mainly about money. It wasn't giving him any new insights into computer technology. He bailed.

Evans and Gates took over and, being the more business-minded among the four, insisted the Lakeside Programmers Group earn a share of the licensing fees ISI charged its clients. Evans was making an impression on Gates: Royalties became Microsoft's own preferred way of earning income.

As the Lakeside Programmers Group carried on, Allen kept up with Hendrix and playing the guitar. He attended two Hendrix concerts during high school, and continued to collect his albums. He was finding those things he really loved, like his father suggested, and none of them seemed to be school. He was a regular no-show in his classes at Lakeside, and even though he earned a higher score than Gates did on his SATs, Allen didn't follow the path of most Lakeside boys to an Ivy League college. Instead, he stuck close to home and attended Washington State University, which was three hours east—close enough to stay in the loop with the Lakeside Programmers Group and, importantly, Gates.

Meanwhile, Gates and Evans never got to carry on their friendship because Evans, who was not a very athletic boy, had decided to go on a fatal mountaineering trip in the last semester of his senior year of high school. His parents thought he was a bit rundown at the time and not up for the trip, but he insisted. Evans slipped and fell to his death. Gates was crushed. But the loss of Evans made way for a new sidekick in Gates's life: Allen. Allen needed Gates. Gates's interest in making money and Allen's fiddling with technology would turn out to be a good match. But for now, Allen was off to school and Gates was carrying on at Lakeside.

2

# MAKING MICROSOFT

When Paul Allen's parents pulled him out of the public school system and enrolled him in the private Lakeside School, it seemed they just might turn their son into an academic scholar. That was hardly the case. Allen didn't care about the lessons he was getting in the classroom, whether it was at the public school or at Lakeside. He had heeded his father's advice to find the things he liked and go with them—first to his parents' dismay and then nearly to his own detriment. In the public school, his biggest crime had been reading in the back of the class instead of paying attention. But at Lakeside, he skipped so many classes to hang out in the computer room that he nearly didn't graduate. Educating Allen the traditional way had become a losing battle.

Not that he wasn't smart—Paul Allen was very smart. Bill Gates is sometimes regarded as a genius, but Allen beat Gates's score on the college SAT exam. Their academic interests were different. Gates loved the challenges in the classroom; he liked sparring over ideas, and he loved to win. Allen had always been more introverted. He preferred to explore things on his own, as he had when he was learning about the PDP-10 machine from the programmers at Computer Center Corporation. He read everything he could get his hands on. He became fascinated by the inner workings of machines.

Allen became preoccupied by what was happening in the world of computers. He read all the magazines that covered computers. He'd been bitten by the bug at Computer Center and wanted to just go with it. Things were moving fast and he was anxious to stay involved out of fear that, otherwise, he would be left behind.

In the fall of 1971, when Allen was a freshman at Washington State University in Pullman, Washington, he picked up a copy of the November 15 issue of *Electronic News*. Buried deep in the magazine was an ad for a new product called the Intel 4004. It was touted as the world's first microprocessor. "Whoa," thought Allen. This could change everything. A microprocessor was a faster, better, and cheaper way of running computer technology and Intel's was an affordable, efficient little model. This combination could make all kinds of things more efficient, and ultimately reduce the size of the mammoth computers of the day. He quickly telephoned Gates back in Seattle and explained what a big deal this was. "This microprocessor's only going to get better and better," he said. Gates listened to him, but what he heard was that the 4004 wasn't actually all that impressive. It could only handle a small amount of characters. Since it was originally designed for the booming calculator market of the day, though, that kind of power was plenty. But Allen and some others in the computer industry saw that over time and with improvements, the chip would easily be able to do more than just serve calculators.

Allen and Gates talked over the implications of better microprocessors. Years later, Gates recalled to *Fortune:* "From the very beginning, we wondered, 'What would it mean for DEC [Digital Equipment Corporation] once microcomputers were powerful and cheap enough? What would it mean for IBM?' To us, it seemed that they were screwed. We thought maybe they'd even be screwed tomorrow. We were saying, 'God, how come these guys aren't stunned? How come they're not just amazed and scared?'" Seeds of a partnership were planted, but for now, Allen and Gates were on separate paths. It wasn't until tragedy struck that the two boys, as different in appearance and temperament as Mutt and Jeff, came together again.

Paul Allen was off to college and for a while, it looked like he was the one leaving the other behind.

At Washington State University, Allen made a new friend in his roommate Bert Kolde. Kolde was from Seattle, but he'd attended Roosevelt High School (Jimi Hendrix's alma mater) in the public system. Kolde was no gear-head like Allen, but he was keen on business. Over late-night orders of pizza, the two bonded as they discussed business ideas and played games of chess (a favorite with Gates, too). After a while, they became brothers in the fraternity Phi Kappa Theta. Allen wasn't the all-around geek that Gates had been considered in high school; he was still listening to Hendrix and still had the long-hair look, now styled more like a ZZ Top member with a full, bushy beard. He was having experiences beyond business and computers.

Phi Kappa Theta's national alumni included John F. Kennedy, Gene Kelly, Bob Hope, and basketball Hall of Famer Ed McCauley, but on fraternity row at Washington State, it was only distinguished by its steep front lawn. This lawn could only be mowed with the help of two people, one to push the mower across and the other to stand at the top of the hill and hold one end of a string that was attached to the mower to keep it from tipping over. The house itself was obscure—literally. It sat so far back on the lot it was easy to miss. Phi Kappa Theta wasn't a typical frat; its members were a mix of hippies, intellectuals, and Army ROTC members. Allen sometimes joined Phi Kappa Theta's intramural flag football team in center position. Though no one knew it then, Phi Kappa Theta was coming to the end of its 20-year run at Washington State University, which lost the chapter in 1976. Two decades later, in 1996, Allen returned to breathe new life into the chapter by building a new house with all the latest high-tech gadgets and connections. By then, Allen and Kolde had been reunited for 11 years and worked side by side in Allen's businesses.

As a student at Washington State, Allen was no more of a scholar than he had been before, but at least now, he had more control over the classes he took. He packed his schedule with computer classes and spent hours in the Johnson Hall computer center. He was getting to know better how computers worked, but he wasn't working on any projects in the real world any more. He kept in touch with Gates by phone to find out what was going on.

Bill Gates had entered his junior year of high school looking for a new project for himself alone or the remaining members of the Lakeside Programmers Group (basically, himself and Kent Evans). Before long, he got going on a project analyzing traffic patterns. It was a slow, tedious process and he recruited other Lakeside students to help him get the job done.

For the rest of the school year, the traffic job was Gates's main gig. But in the spring, a new, more prestigious project landed on the doorstep of the Lakeside Programmers Group. Lakeside was merging with the girls' school St. Nicholas and faced a potential class-scheduling nightmare. Administrators asked some of the computer-savvy teachers to come up with a computer program to handle scheduling. But when the teacher in charge died suddenly in a plane crash, the school looked elsewhere for help. Gates and Evans stepped right up. It wasn't a project they shared for long. A week after they got the project, Evans was killed on his ill-fated mountaineering trip. Gates was devastated by his best friend's death. After a period of grieving, Gates resumed the project and turned for help to Allen, now back home in Seattle for the summer after his freshman year at college. Their bond was rekindled, this time, nearly for good.

Allen came back to Seattle, worked with Gates on the grueling scheduling project and then reluctantly returned to college in the fall. By now, the two had grown closer than ever. For Gates, Allen may have filled two friendships: the one they already had, and the one he lost in Evans. Over the scheduling project, their minds raced through other things they could do together. Allen wanted to get started right away, but his parents insisted he go back to school. From college, Allen began to rack up huge phone bills making long-distance calls to Gates in Seattle.

Gates told Allen about his project analyzing traffic data. He complained about how cumbersome it was and how there must be a better way to do it. Allen talked Gates's ear off about what was happening in computer technology. That Intel 4004 chip he'd talked about last year was ancient history now. It wasn't even worth the cheap silicon it was made of. The new thing was the Intel 8008, which could handle the entire alphabet, and more. Allen insisted they build a computer before someone else built one first.

Gates agreed to build a computer, but only because Allen came up with a compromise: They'd make one that would handle the traffic-analyzing business. Gates had had to be convinced because he didn't think the 8008 chip alone was enough reason to build a computer. Even though it was better than the 4004, he still didn't think it was good enough. But he liked Allen's idea for a computer to transform his traffic-analyzing business: They could design this computer especially to handle a software program they'd write to analyze the data. Presto, they would have an automatic traffic analyzer. They'd sell it to municipalities. This made perfect sense to the business-minded Gates.

They scraped together the $360 necessary for the Intel 8008 chip, got some computer manuals, and recruited a local computer hardware guy they knew named Paul Gilbert. While Gilbert built the box and guts—the hardware—of the computer, Allen, back at school, was trying to create a bridge between the hardware and software so that Gates could write a program in the BASIC language he'd learned from the DEC machines. They christened their new business Traf-O-Data.

Traf-O-Data was many things, but a portent of things to come it was not. Allen's work became the single surviving legacy of the Traf-O-Data business. Time and again, he'd simulate the environment of one machine on another so that software could be written even before the intended machine was ready. But the business as a whole suffered almost from the start because they hadn't really thought it through. Allen and Gates went on to create one of the most successful companies in the world, but as their first business try showed, success was never guaranteed.

Traf-O-Data moved quickly at first. Allen, Gates, and Gilbert worked around the clock through the fall of 1972. During Christmas break, Gates joined Allen in freezing-cold Pullman, Washington, and together they pulled all-nighters on the college's computers. Allen's progress on the simulator was coming slowly. After a week, they headed home to spend the holidays with their families.

About that time, they landed a little reprieve from their start-up work. A job referral had come in for a new project at the tech firm TRW. TRW was about to create a power-management system for the Bonneville Power Administration to control the flow of water and electricity to its customers. The company was short of hands and was tapping all the sources it had, including a couple of kids named Allen and Gates. Without hesitation, the pair agreed to do it. Allen dropped out of school for that semester; Gates arranged to have the work classified as a "senior project" at Lakeside. For the next semester, it was Allen and Gates's job to keep TRW's PDP-10 system from crashing while the project was installed.

While they worked, they continued to discuss where technology was going and what they could do about it. Allen kept tabs on the computer industry through the magazines he read. The potential of these things boggled his mind. One day, over lunch at Shakey's Pizza, he wondered aloud to Gates, "Eventually, everyone is going to be online and have access to newspapers and stuff and wouldn't people be willing to pay for information on a computer terminal?" Allen had no idea at the time just how much he was personally going to be a big force in trying to make that happen. He held on to the notion for years and eventually dubbed it his "Wired World" theory, into which he'd pour billions of dollars. For now, he was putting a few precious bucks into his lunch.

With all these ideas and all this experience he was gaining, Allen was ready to work, but not without Gates. He begrudgingly went back for a full year of college. Gates, meanwhile, found he was happy at Harvard, so he suggested Allen join him at the end of the school year. He even arranged a job for him at Honeywell, near Boston. In the summer of 1974, Allen got in his car and headed across the country, leaving behind a college education for good. He had no idea how good.

Traf-O-Data never happened the way Allen and Gates hoped it would. When they started out, they really thought they were on to something big. After all, they knew there was a market for traffic-analysis. Many companies provided traffic-analysis services to municipalities, but they often did it by hand. This was both slow and expensive. Gates and Allen saw a big opportunity in offering a machine that would speed up that process for a tiny fraction of the cost. What they didn't realize was that most cities were tied in with their data contractors in a way that was not easy to disrupt. In addition, the Traf-O-Data machines were "buggy." In one presentation Gates gave to a representative of the King County Engineering Department, the machine wouldn't even turn on. Dispirited, Gates and Allen moved on, but they retained legal ownership, leaving the company in the hands of Paul Gilbert for the next 10 years until it finally disappeared. For the future Microsoft duo, it became a lesson in how things could go wrong.

In Boston, Allen dutifully fulfilled his job at Honeywell, where he worked on small- and medium-sized computers. But he wasn't having much fun. His work at Honeywell was nothing like his other jobs, where he worked on technology's cutting edge. Here, there were no envelopes being pushed; it was simply a grind.

When he wasn't working, Allen was often in Gates's dorm room at the Currier House, home of Harvard's math and science crowd, or dining with him in the dorm cafeteria. Gates was developing new relationships at school, playing a lot of poker, and occasionally attending classes. He found many people to goad, just like in high school. At Harvard, however, these people argued back, especially when he was talking about his silly ideas of how computers were going to become ubiquitous and connected. Allen and Gates argued, too. Over the years, their arguments became legendary. Allen was a good match for Gates, who often wore people down. Sometimes these two raised their voices together in pitch; other times, Allen drove Gates crazy with his stubborn perseverance.

They continued to talk about Traf-O-Data and considered themselves full-time principals of the company. Allen was still anxious to broaden the technological scope of their partnership, but Gates needed a business reason, first. One thing they had absolutely ruled out was building computers from the ground up. The Traf-O-Data experience had been one sorry lesson that building computers was not their strong point. They were better at the things that made the computers run and made them useful. Those were the kinds of projects they worked on at C-Cubed, ISI, and TRW. Allen and Gates were programmers.

Allen continued to report to Gates what he read in his magazines. He was still expecting a computer built around the Intel chip to hit the market any day. "Paul saw that the technology was there. He kept saying, 'It's gonna be too late. We'll miss it,'" Gates later recalled. When that day came, it sent Allen into a near panic.

What transpired next has become an often-repeated tale shrouded in folklore. On one December day as he crossed Harvard Square in Boston, Allen stopped casually by a newsstand on his way to Gates's dorm room. He picked up a copy of the January 1975 *Popular Electronics* and was about to page through it when the cover headlines jumped out at him: "World's First Minicomputer Kit to Rival Commercial Models; Altair 8800 SAVE OVER $1,000." The words rang out in Allen's ears. Ever since he'd first read about Intel's 4004 chip, he had an inkling this would happen. "I bought a copy, read it, and raced back to Bill's dorm to talk to him," Allen told the *Seattle Post-Intelligencer*.

This time when he showed Gates a story from a magazine that got him excited, Allen had less trouble convincing him they had to act fast. Now, they both believed they were getting left behind. But what could they do? The article explained that the Altair was small enough to sit on a desktop and was built around the Intel 8080, a new chip generations better than the 8008 that could handle loads more memory and new ways to manipulate data. The article also said that the makers of the Altair, Micro Instrumentation and Telemetry Systems (MITS) in Albuquerque, were looking for a computer language for the Altair.

"Well, here's our opportunity to do something with BASIC," said Allen to Gates. They'd cut their teeth on BASIC and believed it was the best, most efficient language for a simple computer. Those Intel chips still weren't anywhere near as powerful as what was driving the mainframes of the day, so to Allen and Gates, BASIC seemed to be about the right size. It made sense to them to work on rigging it for this new machine. The article had even suggested BASIC would be the right one.

Gates was just as excited as Allen, but it took them a few days before they did anything about it. Then, they decided to go ahead and tell MITS they had a BASIC that was ready to go. It was Gates's idea that they might as well get themselves some business before they got going.

They sent a letter to MITS in Albuquerque. MITS' president, Ed Roberts, got the letter, but it was on Traf-O-Data letterhead, which still listed Paul Gilbert's parents' home as the return address and phone number. Roberts was ready to do a deal, but when he tried the number and didn't find anyone who knew anything about Traf-O-Data, he gave up on them.

Fortunately, Allen and Gates placed a follow-up call. By then, 50 people had called up to say they had a version of BASIC for his Altair. "I told them, 'The first one that showed up with a working BASIC would get the deal,'" says Roberts. But there was also a delay at MITS. The company was still working out kinks in the computer's memory. If Allen and Gates wanted to come out, they should come, he told them, but they would have to wait a month until the Altair was ready for their BASIC. With that promise in hand, Allen and Gates got down to business.

What was so exciting about the Altair wasn't that it was the first minicomputer. Digital Equipment Corporation had been selling minicomputers. A small computer called the Mark 8 was also on the market. And Xerox's esteemed research lab, Palo Alto Research Center, had developed its own minicomputer called the Alto. But the Altair was affordable and available. It brought the idea of owning a computer closer to the mainstream. Once it was there, however, it didn't do much. The Altair's front was a mess of switches and lights that could be made to do little more than blink. Most people wouldn't know what to do with the machine, but hobbyists took to it instantly. One hobbyist figured out that the Altair emitted radio signals. He put a radio next to it, set it on an empty frequency and, after flicking a series of switches, made the Altair send a song through the radio. From hobbyists like him, MITS was taking up to 50 orders for Altairs each day. "We were increasing the world's supply of computers by 1 percent every month," says Roberts. Allen and Gates had picked the right company to do business with—MITS seemed to be soaring.

MITS didn't start out with computer ambitions. When Roberts, a hefty World War II vet with a booming voice, retired from the air force in the 1950s, he started the company to sell toy rockets. In the 1960s, the company moved into the trendy calculator market, but that failed to make Roberts rich. In 1973, the banks had come calling for the money they'd continued to loan him. That's when Roberts sold them on the idea of a minicomputer for hobbyists to stave them off.

The Altair was designed by Roberts and his air force buddy William Yates. What customers ended up getting was a kit that included the nuts and bolts of a computer—literally. For things like extra memory, or even one of those Intel chips, customers had to go elsewhere. Still, it made the beginnings of a personal computer widely available. Roberts saw the possibilities for his new machine—he was as much of a technology dreamer as Allen. In the future, he believed, computers would let people buy movie tickets, book travel, and buy goods and services.

For all of Roberts' dreams, the Altair in its present state wasn't likely to be the machine that did all that. For now, it needed something to make it do more than blink—something like BASIC. This language could be the basis for writing software programs around Roberts's plans for the machine. But no one at MITS had software expertise. They needed Allen and Gates, badly.

Once they got started on building BASIC for the Altair, Allen and Gates were very secretive. They told few people of their plans, and when, over a meal in Gates's dorm cafeteria, they asked another Harvard student, Monte Davidoff, to help them out, Allen and Gates told him little until they could meet in private. Their instincts told them that they were onto something big and didn't have much time to do it. They'd been surprised by the appearance of the Altair, but they were desperate not to be beaten by someone else with a version of BASIC for the Altair. It seemed more likely that other people—like the hordes of hobbyists in Silicon Valley—would be the ones to deliver BASIC. These two didn't think that way. Gates skipped classes and Allen cut his hours at Honeywell to work on their project. They were determined to be the first to produce BASIC for the Altair.

Davidoff went back to Gates's dorm room and they filled him in on their plans: They were going to create the language that turned Altair from a silly blinking box into a real computer. Allen didn't say much, at first. "He was a really quiet guy. But when he did talk—he was excited about things and talked louder, faster, and more emotionally. He was a lot more emotional than Bill. Not in a bad way," says Davidoff.

Though these three were frantically pulling together BASIC, it wasn't as if the entire world had turned its attention to the Altair. "Of my friends and the people I was involved with, hardly anyone noticed the *Popular Electronics* cover," says Davidoff. "It took Paul's insight to recognize what he was seeing."

Despite the view from Albuquerque that personal computer kits were all the rage, only about 50 people in the world were trying their hand at a version of Altair BASIC. Allen and Gates were two of them and their panic over the project was part of a paranoia they were developing for being first with an idea.

Making BASIC for the Altair wasn't a snap, but it turned out to be a better experience than making Traf-O-Data. Perhaps their biggest hurdle was creating it without the machine it was to run on. They didn't have an Altair. They didn't even bother to get one. Allen's process of simulating one machine on another had worked before; they tried it again. Using some manuals and specification sheets for the computer, Allen rigged up an Altair-like environment on a PDP-10, just as he'd done when the Traf-O-Data machine was being built. It was a process that would serve the future Microsoft again and again as it moved forward into new territories before those territories were ready.

"Paul's part was really crucial because a lot of the other people writing software weren't using a simulator or emulator," says Davidoff. Like these three, they, too, weren't using an Altair. MITS had received hundreds of orders, but they hadn't shipped a single kit. The techies back in Albuquerque were still having problems getting enough memory into the machine. Once they had that, they'd ship it out. Until then, those hundreds of hobbyists' purchases would sit on back-order.

Gates gets a lot of the credit for BASIC. He did write the bulk of BASIC, with Allen and Davidoff contributing the rest. Allen was always more interested in how people would use the machine. From then on, he would make a lifelong career of focusing on what came to be known as the "user interface"—how the computer presented itself to the people who wanted to use it. Gates was more esoteric. He liked being among an elite club of people who marveled at the genius of the code behind the scene.

As they worked, Allen and Gates talked a lot about Seattle. They rehashed their Lakeside days on the Teletype, hacking into computers remotely, or working on the latest, greatest machines from Digital at Computer Center Corporation and TRW. "It was clear that it was a big part of their lives," says Davidoff, who enjoyed the work on BASIC. "I got caught up in it from Bill and Paul," says Davidoff. "My studies suffered during that time," he admits.

They stayed in touch with MITS occasionally, especially when they had questions about the Altair. One issue had left them particularly perplexed: How did the Altair get data in and out? They asked Roberts that question. "No one had asked him that before," says Davidoff. "That's when he knew they were for real." He told them to pack their bags and prepare to come to Albuquerque.

Working through the nights, Gates, Allen, and Davidoff finished their version of BASIC just in time. Gates and Allen had decided Allen would make the presentation in Albuquerque because he looked older than Gates, who was still as scrawny and puny as he'd been in high school and still had his same high-pitched voice. Plus, Allen was easier to deal with, though no one really brought that up.

Sometime in March 1975, the night before Allen was to leave for Albuquerque, Gates put in his last all-nighter on their BASIC, making sure all the code looked just right. Allen slept. The next day, Gates saw him off for the airport, anxious about the outcome. The final product looked right to Gates, but who knew whether it would work—Allen had created a nice, simulated environment in which it worked just fine, but maybe he'd set it up wrong. They were both eager to find out if their experiment had worked.

It almost didn't. Their BASIC program would not have worked if Allen hadn't realized on the plane to Albuquerque that they'd overlooked one crucial step in the program: telling the Altair where to load BASIC onto the machine so Allen could access it. In the several hours it took to get to Albuquerque, Allen wrote up a series of code that he would have to input by hand when he got there. The anticipation was building.

When Allen arrived in Albuquerque, he didn't get the chance to show off BASIC. Not at first, anyway.

The entire trip so far had been full of disappointments in Allen's view. In the months since they saw the *Popular Electronics* cover, Allen and Gates had spent hours talking about MITS and what it was like. They believed it was a huge company taking over the computer world. But MITS wasn't very impressive to Allen. When he first landed at the airport, he was met by Roberts, a big, lumbering fellow who didn't seem at all like the president of a fast-moving high-tech firm. (To be fair, Roberts was underwhelmed equally by Allen, who was a kid just out of school, when he thought he was meeting an executive from a serious software company.) When they arrived at MITS' offices, Allen was disappointed even more. MITS wasn't some elegant enterprise in cool, sleek office space. MITS was in cramped quarters in a storefront office next to a massage parlor in a decrepit strip mall. Hardly the sort of place for the center of computer breakthroughs, Allen thought.

Still, he was there to catch a ride on this wave of Altairs that was sweeping at least some parts of the country. As soon as they stepped inside, Roberts showed Allen the Altair. But it wasn't ready to go. Workers were still testing the new memory boards to make sure the machine was capable of trying out something like BASIC. Allen would have to wait until the next morning to try BASIC.

The next morning came, no doubt following a fitful night of sleep at a hotel Allen couldn't even pay for. ("He didn't have enough room on his credit card," recalls Roberts, who picked up the tab. "He still owes me money.") During a nerve-racking five minutes, Allen flicked the switches over and over again using the loader code he'd written on the plane. Roberts and other MITS colleagues stood around, chuckling. This amateur style, they thought, could only mean they had a dud on their hands, like many of the other BASIC demonstrations they'd had. But this time, BASIC worked.

Allen was as shocked as the rest of them when the machine sprang into action. It sent out the okay prompt; Allen responded by telling it to PRINT 2 + 2, then began a game of Lunar Lander with the machine. Everyone was impressed; Roberts gave Allen a deal on the spot. "Come work for us," he said. Allen accepted and phoned Gates right away. "It worked!" he cried. They celebrated when Allen returned to Boston.

Allen appeared to like working at MITS. The people were nice, but more importantly, MITS was just about the center of the universe in computers at the time. As director of software, Allen was in charge of his own new division at MITS. He was finally working on the cutting edge.

Allen stayed in Albuquerque. Even while he continued to work on his company with Gates, he was becoming part of the MITS team. He really hit it off with his rough-edged boss and was liked by the rest of the staff.

Roberts was a burly, gruff fellow. He was as tough as Gates, but less whiny and anxious. He liked to talk, but he didn't like to be disobeyed or contradicted. He demanded his employees tow the line. At one company meeting, he was particularly irked by the fact that some people had shown up late. "Next time we have this meeting," one former employee recalls he said, "We're going to reduce the staff by the number of people who are late!"

But Allen liked Roberts and it was mutual. The two were men with wide-ranging interests. They talked for hours on a range of subjects. Gates, on the other hand, knocked heads with Roberts more than a few times. Because former employees thought that

Gates could win, they'd send him in to do battle. It didn't endear him to Roberts at all.

"Paul was, as far as I was concerned, our software guy. Gates was just a programmer—he'd probably take umbrage at that," says Roberts. "Paul was much more important to MITS, because Gates was hard to deal with. He assumed everyone was stupid, but Paul would listen to what was being said. He realized you needed hardware to run software and vice versa. Paul was a major factor at MITS. He was one of our major assets. He was probably involved to some extent in almost everything we did, because you had to integrate software and hardware."

Allen wasn't always punctual himself, but he was hard working. He also was somewhat of a hardware junkie, as Roberts said. At MITS, he created a circuit board that plugged in to the Altair so that an attached monitor could display lower-case type as well as upper case. Also for MITS, he set up a software applications center in Atlanta, which would distribute any programs developed by MITS or MITS customers who needed distribution. Allen also worked alongside other hardware teams on monitors, assemblers, and program editors. "He was one of the guys," says David Bunnell, the company's technical writer who went on to launch tech magazine *PC Week*.

Not that Allen was shirking his responsibilities to his business partner. By day a software director, Allen spent his nights working on his company with Gates. In 1975, Gates came out to Albuquerque during the summer and occasionally took semesters off from Harvard. Micro-Soft—as it was called then—had basically set up shop inside the Sundowner Motel, a dumpy motel across from MITS' offices. Later, it was moved to Allen and Gates's two-bedroom apartment and their small company worked from there. After a couple of years, the company expanded to about a dozen people and moved to office space in downtown Albuquerque.

Even though Allen had visited MITS first in March, the deal for BASIC was signed on July 23, 1975. It gave MITS exclusive, worldwide rights to BASIC for 10 years. Allen and Gates were guaranteed royalties on the sale of BASIC to Altair users. Part of the agreement later resulted in a contentious lawsuit after Gates complained that MITS failed to make an effort to sell the product to other computer makers. Roberts never made this a priority (Gates believed he even blocked some such deals), and it became the basis of a nasty court battle in which MITS lost BASIC.

Allen and Gates had one other stipulation in their contract with MITS: They insisted that MITS require BASIC users to sign a secrecy agreement before they were shipped a copy of BASIC. But MITS found the process a bureaucratic headache and dropped it before long.

MITS and the legal partnership of Allen and Gates—soon to become Micro-Soft and then Microsoft—were never a happy couple, mainly because Gates and Roberts butted heads from the start. The two companies needed each other, but their revenue interests didn't line up. MITS didn't need BASIC to make money; the $395 Altair kit did that.

Microsoft, on the other hand, had only BASIC as its source of income. It was hard, under the terms of the deal, for Microsoft to make money through MITS. MITS sold BASIC for just $75 to customers who also bought an Altair, but they charged them a whopping $500 for a standalone copy. Most people who already had the Altair skipped the $500 fee and hunted around for boot-legged copies of BASIC, instead. It threw Gates and Allen into a tizzy, while MITS didn't really care. "BASIC added nothing to the bottom line. Most of it went to pay the royalty to Microsoft," says Roberts. "But certainly it helped make Altair a viable product," he concedes.

"Viable" was an understatement. The same hobbyists who'd been content to experiment with a row of switches and blinking lights were thrilled to discover BASIC. So thrilled, in fact, they'd get it any way they could, which often meant, to Allen and Gates's dismay, bootlegging copies.

After more than two years of tumult, the relationship between MITS and Microsoft came to an end. It was a nasty split; Microsoft sued MITS. With the help of Gates's father's law firm, Microsoft claimed MITS hadn't done enough to market BASIC to anyone else. By this point, MITS had sold itself to a company called Pertec, which kept up the fight for BASIC, a big part of why Pertec had bought MITS. Microsoft carried on its legal tussle for almost a year and won. At the end of 1977, Microsoft got back its reason for being, BASIC.

While Microsoft was fighting with MITS, Gates fought with Allen. They couldn't always agree on what Microsoft should do next. They would each get excited about different new languages and try to push the other to his side. Allen liked FORTRAN; Gates liked APL. They screamed and shouted. "There were times Paul would walk out to cool down," recalls Monte Davidoff, who worked two summers for Microsoft in Albuquerque between academic years at Harvard. Davidoff says Allen was always the employee's employer. "He was much more easygoing," he recalls. Allen was the one who would invite people over to his apartment to watch sports or movies on his big-screen television. He was also fairly busy with his duties at MITS.

Maybe that's why Gates believed it was fitting that he should get the lion's share of the company. At some point in the first two years in Albuquerque, Gates and Allen huddled over the future of their partnership, which looked to be growing into a company with employees and clients. That's when they came up with a new name to replace Traf-O-Data and all its connotations. They came up with Micro-Soft—an abbreviation of microcomputer software—

and split up the company between them. Only, Gates got most of it. At first, they split the company 60–40, but after some time, Gates felt that with Allen at MITS while he was full-time at Microsoft (when he wasn't at Harvard), he should get more. They made it a partnership of 65–35. Over time, this proved to be a huge gap, but back in 1976 or 1977, when he was arguing for more of the company, it was measured in thousands of dollars, not tens of billions. But it was a sign of things to come. Over the years, Gates would foil and backstab Allen again and again.

All this time, Microsoft had grown. Once Microsoft was its own company, Gates ran around signing deals for the fledgling company. For staff, Gates recruited first the people he knew from Lakeside, Harvard, and MITS. Ric Weiland from the Lakeside Programmers Group joined Microsoft for a summer between years at Stanford University. Chris Larson and Marc McDonald, old buddies from the computer room, became full-time employees. The company grew to about a dozen and stayed that size for a while.

Allen and Gates were establishing themselves in the industry, but the company they'd started, Microsoft, was hardly the household brand it became. In 1977, it had revenues of just $381,715 and it really only had one product on the market. More eyes were on up-and-comers like Apple Computers' Steve Jobs, who were making entire computers, not just a little language. It would take several years and one key deal for Microsoft to hit everyone's radar screen. Until then, Allen would continue to push the company in new directions, his mind still aswirl with computers' possibilities.

In a January 1977 issue of *Personal Computing*, the magazine David Bunnell started after leaving MITS and for which Allen and Gates wrote a regular column, Allen wrote about the next step in the individualized computer dream: laptops, which he expected would become very commonplace and regularly toted around. He viewed it as "a companion that takes notes, does accounting, gives reminders, handles a thousand personal tasks." In his mind, the possibilities were endless. "Leaving everything to the computer opens the possibility of accidentally paying 20 years of insurance premiums in advance and things like that, but other kinds of accidents happen already and we learn to deal with them," he wrote. "New questions are raised. In addition to playing games, calculating income taxes, and all that, what are the uses of the home computer? What will inexpensive computers do? These are chiefly software questions."

Even with all the potential still far out on the horizon, it was probably in Albuquerque that Allen first lost enough interest in Microsoft to be able to leave the company he started after he was diagnosed with cancer in 1983. In Albuquerque, the company had become all Gates: It was about being small and fast, getting clients, and making a lot of money. "It was not an intellectual challenge," says Davidoff.

Once the lawsuit concluded and Allen left MITS for Microsoft, he started to talk to Gates about how he was getting sick of the desert. He wanted to go home. Let's move Microsoft to Seattle, he suggested. Gates thought Silicon Valley would be the better move. It was where Jobs and others were pushing a high-tech revolution. They argued over the company's move. Allen won, and Microsoft moved to Seattle in 1978.

3

# YIN AND YANG

Paul Allen and Bill Gates were not cut from the same mold. From the very beginning, they were different in every way. Gates was rich; Allen wasn't. Allen was large and mature looking and mainly pleasant. Gates was puny, squeaky-voiced, and rude, but they shared a fascination for computers and what they could do. They spent hours in deep discussion over the intricacies of programming code. Sometimes they grew passionate enough about it to launch into shouting matches that left one or the other of them drained from the experience.

It was a good partnership. It was yin-and-yang. Gates loved to argue; he'd argue with anyone over anything and for the longest time, until he won. He just liked to win his arguments. Allen needed Gates for his own intellectual stimulation. He loved to be challenged by ideas and it was easy to engage Gates that way. But when it came to business, the real yin-and-yang became evident: The difference between Gates and Allen was that Gates wanted more than anything to make money; Allen wanted more than anything to be the first to spot a technological idea, like the Altair's need for BASIC. In many ways, it was a partnership made in heaven—it worked.

When Allen and Gates brought Microsoft back to Seattle in 1978, it was, legally, still a partnership, even though the company was now 11 people strong and had $1.4 million in sales that year.

In the office, both young men were considered the leaders of the company, but Gates was often off signing up new computer company customers who wanted BASIC in their new machines. When he was around, he acted like he ran the place, which was fine with Allen, who enjoyed the intellectual challenges of pushing Microsoft to the next new frontier. They did argue though—heatedly—over company strategy. One time, it was Allen who kept Gates in line when Gates had become hung up on a trendy new computer language called APL. Gates insisted Microsoft put out its own version of APL. Allen argued that APL was a passing fad. Gates won that one, but it was an empty victory. Microsoft made APL, but no copies were ever sold.

As time went on, Gates may have felt he really was the one doing more for the company. He was constantly on the road getting customers–signing income-generating deals. He dropped out of school several times to get back to Albuquerque and keep the company going. In Albuquerque, while he was still at MITS, Allen had given his evenings and weekends to Microsoft, so in one way, their contributions were fairly equal: They were both absentee bosses. Most of the hard labor in the beginning was done by the employees that they recruited from Seattle and Harvard to come out and work for several-month stretches in the desert. Eventually, Gates and Allen were involved full-time, but, ultimately, Gates seemed greedier. When it came time to split the company, he persuaded Allen of his greater involvement in the company and secured himself a 65 percent ownership stake in Microsoft.

When they got to Seattle, Allen and Gates were still friends, like always. But their business relationship looked much less friendly. Gates had taken the president title for himself, as well as the premium office space, a palatial, corner office in the bland former Old National Bank building in Bellevue, Washington, where they'd leased space. Allen spent more time with the programmers, where he could focus on pushing the technology.

They weren't completely unaware of their differences. Gates later told the authors of *Gates* that he had always been the one who was "crazily competitive," while Allen was "the ideas guy who keeps us out in front in research and development."

That appeared to be true. It was Allen who came up with several breakthroughs at Microsoft, including the company's biggest since BASIC: an operating system that it would sell to IBM and become the most important company to come out of the PC revolution. But only after Gates, to the exasperation of some of his top executives, told IBM that it had an operating system. Allen was good at pushing actual technology, but Gates kept the company out in front by creating an image that was bigger than itself. It became a trademark strategy that worked. Over the years, Microsoft developed a reputation for coming up with "vaporware"—products that didn't exist. Eventually, the long-promised product would come out. It would often flop on its first try, but the company learned from its mistakes. It would either copy successes it saw in other companies, or work harder on version two. Gates had his head up looking around the field and Allen had his head down, buried in the possibilities of the machine.

Allen was happy to be back in Seattle. He worked the long, crazy hours that were becoming Microsoft's trademark, but he worked fewer hours than many people there. He wanted to do other things, too, now that he was back on his home turf. He'd missed the Seattle Sonics games he'd watched with his father on television and occasionally courtside. Newly returned to Seattle, he bought season tickets.

In Albuquerque, Allen had always been the more laid-back boss. He was the one who'd bought the big-screen TV and invited the staff over for viewings of *Saturday Night Live* or *Battlestar*

*Galactica.* In Seattle, he continued to have parties and hang out with people on staff. When everyone but uppermost management was blowing off steam on Friday nights after work at the bar across the street from Microsoft, Allen was there, too, hanging out and unwinding after a long, intense week at work. It made him a pretty likeable guy around the office.

One of the earliest employees, Marla Wood, told the authors of *Hard Drive,* "Paul was much easier to work for. He would blow up, but five minutes later it would be as if nothing happened . . . Of the two, I'd rather work for Paul than Bill any day. They are very different personalities . . . [We] were always relieved when [Bill] was out of town." Marla and her husband Steve, who were among the original 11 employees, left the company before it went public. Steve later worked for Allen at two of his companies and became one of Allen's friends.

Since BASIC, Microsoft hadn't really done much that was groundbreaking. There was no denying it was on a roll with BASIC. Revenues had nearly doubled every year and thanks to Gates's flourishing tight-fistedness, the company had no losses. It was completely solvent. BASIC had become one of the most widely used computer languages. Personal computer manufacturers from Radio Shack to Commodore, some of the leading brands of the day, used BASIC to run their machines. One company Microsoft didn't crack, however, was Apple Computer, a PC startup in Silicon Valley. It was one of the hottest PC companies, but it didn't use Microsoft's BASIC. In fact, it didn't use much of anything that other PCs used. Apple liked to keep everything in-house, or at least separate. Apple's computer didn't run on the popular Intel 8080 chip that had sparked the Altair and the PC revolution; instead, it ran on a chip called 6502 from MOS Technology.

For everyone but Apple, Microsoft had become the main game in town. Back in Redmond, Washington, the company was processing orders for BASIC for all kinds of computers. It wasn't a one-size-fits-all process, though—parts of BASIC had to be customized for different systems. Often, orders came in well before the computers were anywhere near done. Of course, this was no problem for the pair who created BASIC for the Altair, a machine they'd never laid eyes on before BASIC was finished. Thanks to Allen's handy simulator tool, in use since the Traf-O-Data days, Allen and Gates had managed to create BASIC in a computer environment they'd rightly guessed was like the Altair. Now, years later and back in Seattle, they were still pulling out the simulator again and again, to design products that would be ready when the customers' PCs were finally ready to go.

To Allen, this wasn't very challenging work. It was the same routine over and over: Once Gates got an order, the compiler that translated BASIC for a new machine needed retrofitting or translation. Allen pulled out the simulator, and off they went. Allen was anxious to do more than this.

Apple gave Allen that chance. The company was putting out Apple II, a sequel to its Apple I, and it was taking the home-computer market by storm—in fact, it was essentially creating it, since computers in the home were virtually unheard of before this. Allen and Gates weren't too enthusiastic about the Apple from a technical standpoint because they weren't excited about the 6502 chip; they thought the Intel chip was a smarter chip with more generations in its future. From a business perspective, however, they realized they had to move in on the Apple.

At first, Allen was none too happy about it. More grunt work—huge amounts of grunt work. This time, he couldn't mindlessly pull out a simulator that worked with the 8080 chip. Now, he had to create one for the 6502. But it wasn't a new kind of challenge. It was going to be a drag.

One day, Allen was griping about the work in front of him when he was struck with an idea: What if, he thought, there was a card you could put into the Apple that emulated the operating system that ran Microsoft products, but to the user it would still look like it was all happening in the Apple environment? The SoftCard, as it was called, became one of the few hardware products from Microsoft. But the introduction of the SoftCard was even bigger than Microsoft: As the world's first "emulator," it expanded the world of computing by making different machines' programs compatible with one another. It made the operating system of a specific machine available on a wholly different one. It was Paul Allen's simple idea to cut down on rewriting a compiler in the process of getting into the Apple market. No one at Microsoft thought it was that big of a deal, though. It was never patented or heavily marketed. Even so, the SoftCard sold 100,000 copies for $350 each.

Paul Allen will never go down in history as a hardware genius. He and Gates made their reputations on software, which is far more creative and esoteric than the rigid restrictions of the abilities and limitations of hardware. Software is a language; hardware is more technical. Hardware engineering is more tedious and unequivocal. Software is more malleable. Code can be designed to react in a multitude of ways to a stimulus. Allen had experienced working with hardware when he and Gates built their Traf-O-Data machine several years earlier. They had quickly learned that they were no good at it. Allen's brain was much more excited by and accustomed to software.

In spite of this, he came up with the idea of the SoftCard to change computers yet again. He began by thinking about exactly what this card was supposed to accomplish and why it should do that. Basically, the card should create a bridge between the system on which BASIC was originally created and the new system that carried this card insert. The big challenge was Apple's insistence on doing things far differently from other PCs. Whereas most PCs were running on an operating system—customized for each computer—called CP/M, Apple had its own operating system. Allen's idea was to create an emulator that would make software from Microsoft think that it was running on the CP/M, which was based not on Apple's 6502 chip, but Z-80, a chip from Intel rival Zilog—a truly "out-of-the-box" idea.

The SoftCard was complicated because it had both hardware and software on it. Allen didn't actually attempt to design it himself. Neither did anyone else at Microsoft, because there were no hardware experts on staff. Allen called in a guy who would play a crucial role in the biggest deal of Microsoft's history—Tim Paterson. For now, he was assigned the simpler task of designing the SoftCard. Paterson was an employee at a local company, Seattle Computer. They sold computers and fixed them. Paterson was a rare commodity in Seattle; he knew a little bit about how computers worked. Silicon Valley was hardware central, not the sleepy Northwest. Allen had seen Paterson knocking around the Microsoft offices. He asked him to design SoftCard.

But Paterson wasn't as much of a hardware guru as Allen had hoped. SoftCard's first appearance at an industry trade show was a disaster. Zilog threatened to pull its name off the product. Rights to the operating system CP/M hadn't actually yet been secured from Digital Research, Inc., the company that made it. But that wasn't the main problem. The problem with SoftCard was that it just didn't work. For all its promises to open up the Apple market and make products compatible with CP/M and Z-80 work, the SoftCard failed to start. It would go for about an hour and then, without warning, crash the entire system.

Allen, Gates, and the rest of the Microsoft executives were frustrated. Paterson was the outsider who was supposed to help them, but he'd failed to produce an emulator card ready for customers. So they turned to another non-Microsoft hardware expert, a guy named Don Burtis from Silicon Valley. With Burtis's help, SoftCard was made and the emulation era kicked off with the release of the product in 1981. At Microsoft, SoftCard became one of the very few things the company did that wasn't copied from somewhere else first. It was Allen's big original idea.

For as new and original as SoftCard was, it was not a mainstream, category-killer product, even if it sold well for Microsoft. Microsoft's bread and butter was BASIC, which was still selling out. The only customer Microsoft didn't have now was IBM. But then, IBM didn't have a personal computer yet. IBM was the big giant all the other computer manufacturers had feared would enter the PC market at some point. IBM had been eyeing the personal computer market, but it was too much of a lumbering behemoth to nimbly crank out a machine, like its smaller competitors Commodore and Radio Shack.

It was hard to deny that the personal computer was becoming big business, though. Apple Computer was blowing everyone away. Its computers were extremely popular, enough to excite investors, who were piling on board. On December 12, 1980, Apple raised $96.8 million in an initial public offering. If there were no other clues that IBM should get into the PC market fast, this surely showed them the world was changing.

Until 1981, IBM had always been largely a maker of mainframe computers. Now, an internal task force was set up to explore how it would enter the PC market. Things moved slowly. Everything about IBM involved a laborious process. The PC makers of the day were small and nimble and were churning out upgrades of their products before IBM had even given much thought to its own PC prospects. IBM—or Big Blue, as it was called by employees—was a 67-year-old company in 1981 with a campus in Armonk, New York. It encouraged strict corporate codes about what to wear—garters for socks were almost required for men—and how to behave. There were even company songs that most executives learned to sing. Big Blue liked to get things done through extensive research, elaborate strategic plans, and numerous reviews and votes on the plans. Only when a plan was finally, near-unanimously approved would it move forward. It was a stodgy place nothing like the fast-moving, creative companies in Silicon Valley.

Most people who worked at Big Blue were corporate order-takers, but occasionally, the company encountered some independent thinkers on its payroll. Jack Sams, Bill Lowe, and Don Estridge were among them. Working out of the company's Boca Raton, Florida, office, thousands of miles removed from corporate headquarters in Armonk, allowed them to be a little freer in their thinking. They thought that IBM would never be able to make it in the PC market if it tried to go it alone. In fact, the men had proof. In the 1970s, IBM had tried to enter the PC market with a machine called the Datamaster. It bombed. IBM was now scrambling to get back into the business, and fast. The Boca guys proposed they build an off-the-shelf PC, pulling pieces from various vendors together into a single PC and slap the IBM logo on it.

Naturally, this was blasphemy to the suits in Armonk. It was stridently un-IBM. IBM made everything itself. It never went to outside companies for a single thing. The campus in Armonk was a self-sufficient operation. It was practically sacrilegious to even suggest looking elsewhere for any part of IBM's business. Yet that was exactly what the Boca Raton office proposed.

Sams, Lowe, and Estridge didn't back down from their plans. Instead, they stepped up the pace of their work, code-named "Project Chess," to assemble a PC on the fly, almost. They obtained a microprocessor from outside; they chose the Intel 8086. Next up, they needed a software vendor. Sams was a software expert who knew of Microsoft's short history and BASIC's success. Sams told his Project Chess counterparts to let Microsoft pitch the business.

Soon enough, Project Chess was no longer a secret project by some guys hiding out in Boca. They had returned to Armonk to plead with the big bosses to reconsider. In the meantime, a corporate-approved group in Boca had been pushing ahead with plans to develop a PC internally, but they were making slow progress. The Project Chess guys showed how their plan could get IBM into the PC market in no time. The giant IBM at last lumbered into action and their plans were approved.

Microsoft was really the only option, it turned out. The guys in Boca made plans for a PC centered around a microprocessor chip from Intel that almost no one was developing products for, the 8086. This chip was a generation better than 8080. It was a well-respected piece of technology, but most computers weren't set up to handle it. The 8086 had a more complex architecture that meant it could accommodate a million characters and perform all kinds of functions. In those days, most machines used the 8080 chip, which was limited to 64,000 characters and fewer operations. IBM was going to do it, anyway.

As it turned out, Microsoft had also been keen on the 8086 chip. Even though there hadn't been a market for languages for the 8086, Allen argued for development of them anyway, and Gates agreed there could potentially be a market for it to sell to as those machines began to roll out. IBM would be the first—and for a long time, the only—machine with the 8086. This was actually good news for Microsoft, because with so few plans for the 8086 from other manufacturers, other software vendors had been slower to prepare for the 8086. Microsoft had languages ready to go when IBM called. It was a fairly easy negotiation; Microsoft got the deal.

Now IBM had a microprocessor and it had languages like BASIC and COBOL (a business language), but it had no operating system. Sams and his colleagues thought there'd be a quick fix to that at Microsoft. Allen's old SoftCard had made Apple a more versatile machine that could handle products from Microsoft and other software vendors who didn't develop specifically for the Apple. Why not use that on the IBM machine? Microsoft's Soft-Card was great because it carried a version of Digital Research's CP/M operating system on it, which, it turned out, Microsoft did not have the right to resell.

Without an operating system, IBM was stuck. Microsoft was kind of stuck, too, since IBM had decided to make the operating system Microsoft's problem. The two companies had grown closer throughout ongoing talks for a suite of languages. IBM's Project Chess group had confidence in the tiny Redmond company's ability to deliver the goods. IBM executives sat in Bill Gates's office and told him to find them a solution.

At first, Gates had no option but to direct them to Digital Research. That was directing business elsewhere, which Gates was loathe to do but he had no choice. Microsoft didn't have an operating system. What else could he do? IBM executives flew out to Digital Research immediately, but never managed to sign a deal with the company. Shortly after, they returned to Microsoft and again laid the dilemma at Microsoft's feet. They were still negotiating the finer points of the contract including the languages.

It was an exciting time. IBM, the biggest name in computers, was about to get into the PC market, and Gates and Allen thought they were going about it exactly the right way. Both sides of the table were in complete agreement on the direction of technology. "It was like they were bringing up a menu and checking off 'all of the above,'" Allen recalled later to *Fortune*. But IBM still needed that elusive operating system. Could IBM do it? Gates and Allen and the other Microsoft executives around the table knew full well there was no operating system at Microsoft. But one executive knew that Allen could pull it off, thanks to his connection to Tim Paterson at Seattle Computer. Paterson had again been tinkering around with various new products. As did Allen, he liked the 8086 chip and had requested an operating system from Digital Research. The folks at Digital Research were dragging their feet on developing one, at least in Paterson's view. So he sent away for some manuals and specification sheets and rigged up the only operating system for the 8086. He called it QDOS for Quick and Dirty Operating System. For this reason, he has often been called the "Father of QDOS."

Paterson's operating system needed customers. Microsoft lined up early on for a copy. But the company had no deal yet.

Another Microsoft executive at one meeting with IBM folks, the company's Japanese sales representative, Kay Nishi "was egging us on because he knew I had been dealing with Seattle Computer and that I thought we could probably make their QDOS work for IBM," said Allen later.

Nishi's pressure worked; Gates told IBM they could offer an operating system. IBM was satisfied and Gates signed the deal of Microsoft's lifetime to provide IBM with an operating system for its new machines.

This was huge. IBM was Big Blue. Until the federal justice department had decided it was a monopoly, Big Blue had boasted 70 percent market share. Now, its hold on mainframes and minicomputers hovered around 40 percent, but it was still impressive. It was still the 800-pound gorilla of the computer industry. And now Microsoft, the little company that was inspired by the cover of a magazine in 1975, had inked a deal to provide the part of the machine that would turn it into more than a pile of plastic and metal. Only, unbeknownst to IBM, Microsoft did not have an operating system.

It's debatable which deal was bigger in Microsoft's history; selling BASIC to MITS and launching Microsoft; or providing an operating system for IBM's big PC push, which secured its future and grew it into a sizable company. One thing is clear, though: Paul Allen was central to both events. He had been the one to push for BASIC to be created for MITS's Altair computer. Now, he was the crucial connection to an operating system the company badly needed. Allen knew about the operating system at Seattle Computer, and he would be the one to go and negotiate a deal.

Seattle Computer, on the other hand, never knew about Big Blue. Microsoft did not tell them about its plans, even though Seattle Computer had let Microsoft in on the secret of QDOS back when it was just beginning to be developed. Microsoft had found out about its operating system when Paterson had called over to see if the company wanted to develop products for it. When Allen went in to see about licensing or buying QDOS from them, he made a point of keeping quiet about which customer it was that might like to license QDOS. Seattle Computer was completely in the dark. In need of the cash, the company took Allen's first offer without hesitation.

Throughout contract negotiations, Microsoft remained mum. It included a clause that prevented Seattle Computer from trying to find out who the big customer was. Then, with an agreement of $10,000 for a sublicense of QDOS, now called 86-DOS, $5,000 for the source code, and $10,000 for signing the agreement, Microsoft had its operating system. Months later, Microsoft bought all the rights to 86-DOS for a mere $50,000 and its future was secured.

Microsoft's enduring legacy became not the little languages on which it had based its history so far; Microsoft went down in business history because of the success of its operating system. Or, rather, the operating system developed by someone else that Allen negotiated for Microsoft's long-lasting profit.

During the 10 years after IBM released its PC on the market in 1981, Microsoft established itself as a powerhouse software player. Overnight, it had become recognized worldwide as a leader because IBM had picked it to supply languages and an operating system. As Microsoft's product line grew, so did its automatic distribution through IBM. Since Microsoft's deal with IBM was nonexclusive, it could provide nearly identical products for the IBM clones that started showing up in stores in the following years.

Both Allen and Gates get credit for the IBM deal, but it appears a little lopsided—Gates took on the great computer giant, IBM, while Allen's only negotiation was with a sleepy little computer company in the northwest—without Allen, however, there would have been no deal. Microsoft might have gone down as just another software company, instead of the enormous success it became.

Although Allen was devoted to Microsoft, he continued to pursue a more well-rounded lifestyle. While Gates was working around the clock, often sleeping in his office and not going home for days, Allen would leave early (well, earlier than Gates), to catch a movie or see a basketball game. Allen wasn't nearly as fanatical about work as Gates. For Gates, it was Microsoft all the time and no excuse for missing work was good enough. Not even aerospace history.

In the spring of 1981, Microsoft employees were hard at work on a deadline for IBM. Big Blue's big PC launch was set for the fall, and there was much to be done before then. Everyone, including Allen, was putting in extra hours. But some people at Microsoft also had their minds on something else: the launch of the first space shuttle, set to take place in Cape Canaveral, Florida, in mid-April. Gates didn't give it a second thought, but Allen was a big science buff. He made plans to go. He thought, which was more important, meeting a deadline at Microsoft, or watching space history in the making? To each of the young men, now approaching 30, it was a no-brainer, and each had a different answer.

Allen and a couple other programmers left for a quick trip to Florida, but not before Allen and Gates had one of their legendary arguments. Gates was still angry about it 15 years later, when he recalled the incident to *Fortune:* "The one tiff Paul and I had was when he wanted to go see a space shuttle launch and I didn't, because we were late. Still, these guys went to the launch and I was just . . ." His voice trailed off as Allen, also present in the interview, interjected with his common-sense viewpoint: "It was the first one, Bill. And we flew back the same day. We weren't gone even 36 hours." But Gates remained resentful.

It went against everything that Gates was about. Gates rarely took entire weekends off. He had developed a penchant for doomsday scenarios and kept them constantly running through his head, thinking every year would be Microsoft's last, despite millions of dollars in the bank. Allen would fight with him over ideas, and sometimes even over money. This was just more of the Gates and Allen yin-and-yang dynamic. Though several years had passed since Gates and Allen excitedly hashed over new technology ideas on the phone and in Gates's Harvard dorm room, sparks still flew between them over new products and Microsoft's direction. The clash led to a balance that turned Microsoft into a success.

4

# FACING MORTALITY

Paul Allen was just an average working stiff when he left Microsoft. Well, maybe a little more than average. Thanks to a good idea, hard work, and a little luck, Microsoft had grown from an inspiration on one cold and blustery day in Harvard Square to a $50 million company. But Paul Allen himself was not a Microsoft millionaire when, in 1983, he moved on.

In the eight years since Microsoft arose out of the desert in New Mexico, it had grown from a two-man partnership into a corporation that was recognized around the world. Allen and Gates had had the good fortune of being aligned with MITS when Altair was the PC of the moment, and it was their continued hard work and determination—mostly Gates's—that kept up the pace of Microsoft's market share in the language sector. The company outlasted two early competitors, Processor Technology and IMSAI. As Microsoft moved to Seattle, the software market had continued to expand. But Microsoft was still a small company, even if it had gained some credibility. The software market was getting sliced up. Other companies, like Lotus Development Corp. and VisiOn, were supplying popular products like spread-sheets and word-processing programs that won them market share and much more name-recognition than Microsoft. Microsoft had been developing software products like word-processing programs and spreadsheets, too, but these products weren't as strong as the competition's. Microsoft was lucky to get the deal with IBM, which at that time had the computer industry's equivalent of the King Midas touch.

Microsoft was on its way up, but had made its fair share of mistakes, too. Allen had been behind some of those missteps. As the company's guy who was supposed to "keep us out front technologically," as Gates put it, Allen didn't always have perfect vision for what was coming next. Back in Albuquerque, he'd pushed for Microsoft to develop a version of FOCAL, but not a single copy was ever sold. According to *Gates*, even the source code became lost after such inattention to the product. In Seattle, Allen's big plan for Microsoft's expansion was to create a multiplatform version of BASIC, a single version that was able to run on many different computers, from the Apple to the IBM. But it was a complete misread of where things were going since the computer industry as a whole was moving toward standardization and wouldn't need special, customized versions unique to their systems, for long. Allen, the great "ideas" guy, had been wrong.

Allen sometimes appeared to be looking for an easier way out. He'd proved that with his SoftCard "shortcut," which turned out okay, since in addition to relieving him of more boring coding work, the product also made money. It was good for Microsoft and for Allen, who wasn't putting in the legendary Microsoft work-hours. He would sometimes take off early, or not come in for days after a Gates verbal-spar had wiped him out. He hadn't agreed with Gates that there was a problem in his taking off, along with two other Microsoft employees, to see the first-ever Space Shuttle launch in Florida in the middle of a deadline on the IBM MS-DOS project.

For the time being, in early 1982, Microsoft as a company was simply enjoying its successes. Major leaps forward were slowing.

The change-the-world ideas Allen had had for BASIC, SoftCard, and DOS were becoming more commonplace as the industry focus became standardization and incremental improvements. Microsoft itself had turned its corporate attention to growing into a big company, putting systems in place, expanding into new countries and keeping existing customers, mainly IBM, very, very happy. The future looked bright: IBM's PC had been a hit with consumers, and now other PC makers were shifting their own strategies to simply making cloned versions of the IBM PC. It meant there were now more computers equipped to handle an off-the-shelf Microsoft product.

As a cofounder of the company, Allen was involved in almost every strategic decision and in most crucial meetings with outside partners. So it was natural that Allen would be present on a trip to Europe where Microsoft executives were speaking at conferences and holding meetings with potential business partners.

The trip was planned by Scott Oki, a Microsoft employee who headed up international operations. He set the agenda to include Gates, Allen, and the new president of the company, former Tektronix executive Jim Towne. They were to start in Munich, fly to Paris, and go on to several other cities from there. Allen never made it the whole way.

He started feeling weird in Munich. He didn't think much of it, even though he'd noticed a slight bump on his neck. "I'd had little bumps before that weren't anything. But I kept feeling stranger and stranger," he recalled later to *Fortune*. Allen continued to attend meetings, but he couldn't shake off how he was feeling. He was tired, slightly feverish, and had a bit of a stomachache. But it wasn't enough to stop working. It just felt uncomfortable. "Then one day in Paris, I just felt really bad and decided I had to get back to the States," he said later.

He tried to stick it out in Paris. He thought maybe resting in his room would help. He sat out several meetings, but still he felt no better. So he went to see a French doctor, but Allen didn't speak French and the doctor wasn't very fluent in English, either. He decided to board a plane and head straight for Seattle. When he arrived, he checked into the Swedish Hospital, where he had been born.

U p to this point, Allen's life had been somewhat charmed. Un- like his parents' dirt-poor beginnings, Allen had grown up comfortably middle-class. He had parents who cared deeply about their children and provided for them well. They opened their world beyond the simple Seattle neighborhood where they lived in all the ways they could. They took them to plays and classical music concerts. They nurtured all of their hobbies and extracurricular activities. They took pains to give them the best education they could.

Allen had been lucky to go to Lakeside School, where almost every other kid was from the uppercrust society of Seattle. The teachers at Lakeside had been as open-minded as his parents, al- lowing all the students, including Allen, to pursue the things that appealed to them, even if they weren't emphasized for study, like Allen's interest in computers. There he had made an important friendship with Bill Gates, with whom he could be intellectually challenged and go on to create a successful business.

Allen had reason to believe in himself, too. It was his own wonderment with computers that drove him to keep at it. He had wisely spotted the Intel 4004 chip in 1972 as an important devel- opment, and was proved right later when he again saw that he and Gates should develop BASIC for the Altair. Microsoft had much to thank Allen for, from BASIC to SoftCard to DOS.

Outside of Microsoft, he appeared relatively happy and had made a point of filling out his life with Sonics games, rock con- certs, and the occasional pick-up band to play with, when he could find one. He had also reunited with his family once he returned to Seattle. It seemed like his life had just begun. . . .

The doctors at Swedish Hospital did not have good news. They'd looked him over the day he checked in—the same day he returned from Paris—and things did not seem right. His symptoms were serious. There were still more tests that needed to be done, but so far, all signs were pointing to a diagnosis of cancer.

Not just any cancer, but lymphoma. That would account for the bumps, the fever, and the lack of energy, they told him. Bumps tend to show up on people who get lymphoma, a cancer that attacks the lymph nodes where infection-fighting cells are produced. There are many kinds of lymphoma, from serious, normally fatal lymphoma and leukemia, to the far milder and almost always treatable Hodgkin's disease. But when medical people refer to "lymphoma," they tend to mean the most serious kind, the kind that attacks quickly and is almost always fatal. His doctors feared the worst.

Allen spent the night in the hospital with this news on his mind. He was 29 years old, just four months short of his thirtieth birthday. For someone so young, he had achieved a lot, but it was mainly in one area. Allen liked to think of himself as more than Microsoft. He wasn't like Gates, who was happy to merge his identity with the company he'd created. Allen was pleased with his successes, but the narrow nature of them left him feeling he had ignored much of life that was out there to experience. He wasn't ready to die. "It's a huge shock to realize your own mortality," he told *Rolling Stone* years later.

The next morning, the doctors came into Allen's room in high spirits. It was not the fatal form of lymphoma, they said: "You've got Hodgkin's disease and you're going to be fine." They had been wrong on the preliminary diagnosis. The chances were good that with treatment, the cancer would go into remission.

Hodgkin's disease is not an uncommon form of cancer, but its cause is unknown. It tends to show up in men more than women and almost always between the ages 25 and 35 or over 55. Some people who have Epstein-Barr get Hodgkin's disease, but aside from that correlation, no one knows where the cancer comes from. Once someone has Hodgkin's disease, it can spread from the lymphatic system to other organs, like the spleen, liver, or bone marrow if it isn't stopped. The disease is usually treated with radiation or chemotherapy, or both. Allen would have at least two five-week sessions of radiation therapy. Radiation treatment can be very wearing and sometimes affects fertility.

Despite the treatment that made him queasy and tired, Allen went back to work. He had been missed and people had been worried about him. "His absence did cast a pall on the mood of the company for awhile," says Mark Ursino, then a marketing manager at Microsoft. "When he returned, that was a relief to everyone."

Leaving Microsoft altogether would hardly have been a foregone conclusion at that point. Microsoft was very much, to employees if not to customers, equally Gates and Allen. Though Gates was involved in practically everything and seen as the real boss of the company, Allen was still its technological spiritual leader. He was getting into arguments with programmers and driving them just as much as Gates, with even more of an emphasis on what the technology did than whether it was good for Microsoft's bottom line to do it.

More practically speaking, Allen couldn't just think about quitting and, for example, live a life of leisure from then on. In 1982, he wasn't the excessively wealthy man he is today; Allen's annual salary was just $60,000. It was a good income for a single guy in Seattle. He had spent some of that money on a fast car (he and Gates each bought a Porsche 959), a house, and stuff to put in it. But he wasn't in any position to retire.

Work wasn't easy, though. "It was hard because cancer therapy takes a lot out of you," he told *Fortune.* It also gave him time to think about his life. The cancer was likely to go into remission, but until it did, it was with him, always threatening to spread and take away his life. The initial news from the doctors still rang in his ears. It weighed on his mind.

"To be 30 years old and have that kind of shock—to face your mortality—really makes you feel like you should do some of the things that you haven't done. With Hodgkin's disease or any cancer like it, there's basically a two-year window: If you can pass that period without a relapse, then it's probably not going to come back," Allen later told *Fortune.*

While he was undergoing treatment, he had thought about his interests outside of the company. He'd always loved reading science fiction books, listening to musicians like Jimi Hendrix, and going to basketball games. There were still more things he needed to see and things he needed to do. He had no idea whether he'd make it through the two-year window, but if he didn't, he wanted to have more experiences before it was all over.

Even though Microsoft's hard-driving work ethic probably had nothing to do with Allen's contracting Hodgkin's, it did have something to do with his leaving, and he wasn't the only one affected by the environment. Some Microsoft workers who had been there since Albuquerque thought the company was getting too oppressive; it was taking over their lives. While once they were thrilled by their jobs and happy to put in the long hours, they had come to feel they were being pushed out of the center of the action by newer recruits hired in Gates's image: young, supersmart, and hard-working.

Allen also wasn't the only one hospitalized while working at Microsoft. According to an account in the book *Gates,* Mike

Courtney, who had been hired by Microsoft not long after the company's move to Seattle, had suffered what appeared to be a heart attack after drinking too many caffeinated beverages during a period when he was working continuously on the early version of DOS for IBM. He was treated and he returned to work, but took a slightly less stressful post.

Allen tried to keep up at Microsoft, but finally he couldn't do it anymore. Some key projects had finally been completed—mainly upgrades to the next version of DOS for IBM—and new products like Microsoft Word and Microsoft's own operating system, Windows, were well underway. He had begun some interesting new projects in the last year, including an online service called Microsoft Network that would resurface again more than 10 years later and ultimately become a major part of Microsoft's Internet strategy. But now, he needed a break from it all, so he left Microsoft to travel the world. No one knew it then, but he wouldn't be back.

Bill Gates and Paul Allen had been friends for 15 years—half Allen's lifetime—when Allen left Microsoft to travel. For the past eight years, they had been bound by a business they started that turned out to be a hit. Their friendship had never been a sure thing or a smooth ride, but they had been compatible enough. They were each drawn to technology's possibilities, and they pushed one another along. In leaving the company, Allen would be leaving a partner who had always helped him turn his ideas into practical, money-making ventures.

Allen's leaving was a big deal for Gates, too. "It was a real change for me and a huge disappointment that Paul wasn't there. It was really sad to go by his office, because all the memos and magazines would be stacked in there," he recalled to *Fortune*.

Microsoft would be all right without Allen involved in the day-to-day operations, and later, Allen would return to join the company's board of directors, anyway. By this point, Microsoft had a strong enough reputation to hire some of the brightest minds in the country. But after Allen left, the major innovations slowed for nearly a decade. Microsoft coasted, expanding mainly by developing its software business, not creating wholly new, breakthrough products.

Gates, too, moved on. He and Allen had always had a relationship centered around exploring ideas, but Gates also preferred the business side of things. His best friend as a kid had been the business-minded tyke Kent Evans, who died in a mountaineering accident. Now, at Microsoft, Gates found a new best friend, Steve Ballmer, one of his old pals from Harvard days who had earned an MBA degree and worked in the marketing department at Procter & Gamble. Ballmer, like Gates, was heavily committed to business and especially to Microsoft. He quickly moved up the ranks from Gates's assistant to executive management. In 1999, he became the company's CEO.

In 1983, Allen was off exploring the world. The cancer treatment had ended and now he was free to travel. He visited Europe and collected impressionist paintings. He toured around; he discovered scuba diving. He loved it, he said years later, because "it takes me away from myself." Allen waited out the period when the cancer—and the threat of death—could come up again.

Death did come back, but it wasn't his. It was worse: It was his father Kenneth's, who died suddenly, changing the lives of his wife Faye and their children Paul and Jody. In November 1983, Kenneth checked into the Swedish Hospital for routine surgery on his knee, a lingering reminder of his high-school four-star athleticism (and part of the reason he hadn't aggressively pushed Paul to sign up for more sports at school). The surgery went off without a hitch and he was on his way to an easy recovery, although he was expected to have to use crutches for a while. On the fifth day after the operation, he was in the hospital practicing with the crutches when all of a sudden he collapsed. A blood clot from the surgery had broken loose, killing him. He was 62.

Being told he had cancer was hard, but losing his father was devastating. Allen had taken time off in part to become closer to his family, and now a major figure in his life was gone. His father would have been proud his son was following his instinct. He'd once told Allen to "love whatever work you do, you should try to find something you enjoy." It was wise advice Allen had pretty much followed. As further proof of their bond, Allen took to wearing the turquoise Navajo ring his father had had since high school. Then, he swore that family was even more important than ever and grew closer to his mother and sister. Later on, he would memorialize his father as a four-star athlete who served in World War II followed by an admirable occupation as a librarian working in higher education. At the end of the century, Allen hired a team to compile a celebratory biopic on his father, particularly focusing on his years in the National Guard and in Europe. Allen also paid tribute to his father's service at the University of Washington, where he had been associate director of libraries for 22 years, with a contribution of $10 million in 1988. It would go toward an expansion of the library and the opening of a new building, the Kenneth S. Allen Library, in 1990. Coincidentally, it stands across a small plaza from a building named for Gates's mother, an undergraduate building called the Mary Gates Hall. Also in his father's memory, Allen established the Kenneth S. Allen Library Endowment with a contribution of $10 million.

When Kenneth died, there wasn't much extra money, but Kenneth and Faye, Paul's mother, had done all right for themselves. Faye's husband left her three cars—Kenneth's prized 1963

Buick Electra, as well as a 1980 Toyota pickup, and a 1974 Toyota station wagon. She also had the old house on 28th Street N.E. in Wedgwood and some land on the Cowlitz River that cut through Washington state.

Faye soon became an even bigger part of Allen's life. The two loved to read books. One of their favorite things to do was to head over to Powell's bookstore and browse the shelves. Faye held an influence over Allen's reading list. She even made up a list of "160 Books for Paul," which he eventually posted on his personal Web site. Among the selections are works by P.G. Wodehouse, Harriet Beecher Stowe, Honore de Balzac, Thomas Wolfe, William Styron, Wallace Stegner, Boris Pasternak, Barbara Kingsolver, and dozens of others spanning classics to contemporary books and, of course, a good dose of sci-fi titles.

Over the years, Allen and his mother would become nearly inseparable. She would accompany him on his travels as a rich person, in his private planes to his private vacation homes. He would also build her a home on his property—with an enormous library, of course.

During this time, Allen became closer with his sister, Jody, too. They had been friendly siblings as children, playing together amicably enough; but in the years after he graduated from high school, they had drifted apart somewhat, as he pursued computing business that took him away from Seattle to the east and southwest. In the meantime, Jody had gone on to graduate from Lakeside, which had become a co-ed school the year after Allen graduated. Like her brother, she always felt a pull to be closer to home. After finishing high school in 1975, she went to Africa for nine months and when she returned, she attended liberal arts school Whitman College, four-and-a-half hours southeast of Seattle in Walla Walla, Washington. She studied drama, graduated, and went back home to Seattle.

As an adult in Seattle, Jody Allen began a career that would for the most part stick to the arts, which made sense, since she had been an active drama student in high school and college. Her first job was in the development office of the Pacific Northwest Ballet. She eventually married a golf-course manager named Brian, a native Irishman whose mother was born in Kildoney, Ireland. They had three sons, the first, Duncan, in 1989. (Duncan would ultimately attend Lakeside like his mother and uncle.) Once Allen earned his Microsoft millions and needed help managing them, he asked Jody to come on board and help out. She mainly focused on his philanthropic and arts foundations, and pretty much everything else that wasn't related to technology. She would head up the Paul G. Allen Foundation and maintain her interest in arts by overseeing the development of art endowments and other projects, like the Experience Music Project. She helped manage what would become an unruly mess of personal affairs, including the building of his house on the posh Mercer Island on Lake Washington between Seattle and Bellevue and a controversial purchase of Sperry Peninsula in the San Juan Islands.

Two years passed since Allen's diagnosis in the fall of 1982. Much had transpired. Allen had taken a break from Microsoft, seen some of the world, learned to scuba dive, and, sadly, experienced his father's death. The cancer subsided. Allen felt he was free and clear. Hodgkin's disease could possibly show up again sometime in his lifetime, but the most crucial period had passed.

Allen was ready to return to the working world—but not to Microsoft. "I took that time to step away from Microsoft and be closer to my family, and do some traveling and other things I'd always wanted to do. After that two-year period, well, I just didn't want to go back to work. I went to Bill and said, 'I want to just do something different.' I know Bill wished I hadn't decided that," he told *Fortune*. In that same interview, Gates said, "It was great Paul got better, and we wanted him back more than anything. But there was just no part-time way to come back to Microsoft. If you were going to be there, you were really going to work hard." Gates may have recalled Allen's takeoff for Cape Canaveral during a crucial work period, or even felt a little betrayed by Allen's leaving Microsoft at all.

Allen had watched as his old pal became the face of Microsoft, which was probably okay with him, since he wasn't the publicity seeker Gates was. But Gates was getting every single bit of credit for Microsoft, down to its initial inspiration. Allen took pride in his ability to see around corners and especially in the way he'd accurately predicted the future of computing after seeing that *Popular Electronics* magazine cover with the MITS Altair on it in 1974.

What Allen was after now was the early days of Microsoft— or even earlier—when he felt like he was right on the cutting-edge of technology. Microsoft was still coming up with new products, but the company as a whole had become very business-oriented. Making money had never been enough for Allen. He'd always wanted more. It was Allen who had urged Gates to build a computer with him in 1972, even though they had no business reason to do so (Gates won that argument and they held out until they did have one). Allen's development of the SoftCard wasn't to make money, or even save money. It was to try something different. Now, Allen wanted an environment that was laser-focused on new and possibly world-changing ideas, like he'd had with BASIC. He had no trouble moving on. He even left Microsoft's board of directors, although he'd rejoin several years later.

"You realize how precious life is," he later told *Business Week*. "I wanted to do something groundbreaking."

In late 1984, Paul Allen became a solo entrepreneur for the first time. He would be going it alone, without a partner to bounce ideas off. But that was okay—Allen now had experience building a company. He had learned from the Traf-O-Data experience that you have to analyze a market before you enter or else you're likely to be handily squashed by the existing competition as soon as you get there. From Microsoft, he'd learned some business basics. He'd figured out that, sometimes, products won't sell (like FOCAL); and he'd learned that accidents can turn into successes, like SoftCard. (Or, rather, all these things had happened; if Allen took them as lessons was yet to be determined.) For Allen, business wasn't as much of a draw as cool ideas were. He just wanted to make sure he was first to get them out.

In late 1984, when Allen was planning to start something new, Allen didn't have a personal stash of cash in the bank. Microsoft's plans to go public were still a good 18 months off. What he did have was his name. Paul Allen was the cofounder of Microsoft, which was gracing magazine covers and impressing people with its workforce of brainy kids in khakis pulling all-nighters fueled by pizza and caffeine. Allen set up shop pretty quickly and easily. With Microsoft's reputation, it was easy to get a loan, even though he didn't have any specific products in mind to sell. He found office space in Bellevue, near Microsoft's former home (the company had since moved to nearby Redmond). Next, he started recruiting some of his friends to help him get back to the cutting edge. He dubbed his company Asymetrix.

Asymetrix brought a lot of people back into Allen's life. He rang up his old college roommate, Bert Kolde, for one. Since graduating from Washington State University with a business degree in 1976, Kolde had earned an MBA from the University of Washington and worked in finance at aerospace firm Boeing and at the bank Seafirst Corp. He became executive vice president of Asymetrix, essentially Allen's right-hand man.

Allen also pulled in some old Microsoft employees from the Albuquerque days, including Marc McDonald, who was still a programmer at Microsoft, and Steve Wood, who'd left Microsoft disillusioned just before Allen left. He moved back to Seattle to become vice president of marketing at Asymetrix.

These people would become regular fixtures around Allen for years. For better or worse, loyalty emerged as a key component of Allen's business style. Allen thought most of his ideas for technology were inevitabilities, which meant that other people could also come up with the same idea. Pushing the envelope in technology could only be done by a loyal, dedicated team of people who could be trusted to carry out a plan to get the ideas first to market. Over the years, many people came to see Allen's insistence on loyalty as his Achille's heel—he preferred to hire the people he knew and trusted and who didn't disagree with him rather than taking a risk on a talented stranger. What he seemed not to have realized was that one of the reasons he and Gates were such a good team was because they argued and pushed each other, not because they always shared the same view.

If Asymetrix was supposed to be looking forward, its evolution was mired in the past. Allen had taken a sentimental approach to building a business. He'd stayed close to Microsoft, hired his friends, and sought to recapture the feeling he had creating Microsoft in the first place. Yet Asymetrix was supposed to look ahead, do "something groundbreaking." Allen had a funny way of getting there: Ideas, he believed, could come from anywhere, so he preferred to issue broad orders like "bring me some good ideas."

At Asymetrix, Allen's edict produced an idea that never went anywhere, followed by an accident that turned into a business that was eventually usurped by Microsoft. Asymetrix had planned to build a do-everything desktop application called Crucible that learned everything about its user and became a kind of personal assistant. But Crucible was too ambitious for its time and for the people working on the project. The company was burning through cash. Allen was repeatedly going back to the bank for more money for Asymetrix, which was having a heck of a time getting a product together. Allen grew frustrated by Asymetrix's inability to break new ground. Then, one of the top executives discovered that an engineer had been fooling around with an idea to make creating software applications easier. The executive thought it might be a good idea for a business and told Allen. In 1991, this accident became ToolBook, which became Asymetrix's long-anticipated product, six long years after Allen started out on his solo career.

While Asymetrix was figuring out its future, Allen's own future had changed instantly and dramatically on March 13, 1986. Three years had passed since he left Microsoft, where as cofounder he'd earned 6.4 million shares of stock, representing 28 percent of the company's total.

Except for his personal finances, Allen had moved on to new things. He ran Asymetrix, but he did other things, too, such as playing in a band, going to basketball games, and getting out scuba diving whenever he could.

Then, Microsoft went public. At this point, Allen was sort of a high-tech hero, nothing more. Even if the whole world wasn't completely aware of Allen's role in Microsoft, there were enough techies who knew it. He was their hero, and some people thought two camps might emerge: those who followed Gates and desired his business success; and those who admired Allen's attention to the details and his love of new ideas in technology. But once Microsoft went public, it didn't matter what field Allen was in; all of a sudden, he mattered because he was a rich guy. In a single day on the New York Stock Exchange, Allen gained a fortune—on paper—of $134 million. It opened up his world.

Microsoft never needed to go public. The company wasn't short on cash; even back in its third year in business, when sales were just $1.3 million, $233,000 just sat around in the bank. But going public would give the company some credibility and raise its profile. It would also go on to make scores of people insanely wealthy, with Paul Allen one of the wealthiest of all.

Microsoft's IPO was one of the most successful in Wall Street history. After opening at $21 a share, trading whipped into a frenzy, sending the stock soaring to $29.25 before it settled at $27.75. In the following 15 years, the stock continued to climb and split eight times to keep the price at a manageable level.

"I'm pretty happy," Allen told the *Seattle Post-Intelligencer* that day. "Everybody involved in Microsoft since the beginning has been looking forward to this day." The following year, *Forbes* put him on its list of richest people, at No. 71. Gates easily leapfrogged him to No. 25, with $236 million. Allen began spending his money in ways that rounded out his life: on yachts, a new home on Seattle's posh Mercer Island, and a basketball team, the Portland Trail Blazers.

As Microsoft's stock continued to increase in value over the years, Allen's life was dramatically impacted. Through the wealth that was piling up every day from Microsoft stock options, he became one of the most watched entrepreneurs and investors in the high-tech world. As time passed, occasionally Allen became frustrated by all the money. There was just so much of it, and it brought him attention he had never sought. But thanks to that March day in 1986, he could count on being stuck with publicity, money, and the shadow of Gates and Microsoft for a very, very long time. He had better make Asymetrix work.

5

# ON HIS OWN

B ehind his low-key exterior, Paul Allen is a nostalgic fellow who pours money into things that remind him of the past. He bought the property in Albuquerque where Microsoft used to be. In Seattle, he had his favorite old movie theater, the Cinerama, renovated. He gave $1 million to the Oregon Shakespeare Festival he used to attend with his family every summer growing up. In 1988, he paid tribute to his late father with a $10 million grant to the University of Washington library where his father worked for many years.

Sentimentality is sweet, but it's not always good for business. Allen should have known that. He and Gates had been secretive and self-interested since the days of Traf-O-Data and the beginnings of BASIC. Even the purchase of the operating system from Seattle Computer had been secretive and solely within Microsoft's own interests. But ever since became ill, he gave more thought to the things that were important to him. He relished meaningful things in his life, like the excitement of that day when he came up with the idea for BASIC, and the creative, early days of Microsoft. He wanted to bring back a company built around ideas that was always at the cutting edge of technology.

Asymetrix was his first try. For the first six years of that company's history, nothing happened. Engineers labored over a pie-in-the-sky, dream concept that Allen had been thinking about since 1977, when he mentioned to a trade magazine an idea for "the kind of thing that people carry with them, a companion that takes notes, does accounting, gives reminders, handles a thousand personal tasks." Six years passed. It never came together. The company had to move on.

The first product out of Asymetrix wasn't the end-all-be-all portable personal assistant that Allen had envisioned, but it was an exciting product in its own right and just as focused on making computers do more. It got people excited about software and rejuvenated Allen's image . . . for a while.

The product finally ready to ship in 1990 was called Tool-Book. It established Allen as someone who had always been thinking about a world in which computers were the norm, not the luxury they were in 1991. ToolBook was relatively easy to use. It made computers friendlier and potentially open to more people. ToolBook was meant to work with Microsoft's still-fledgling operating system, Windows, to aid hobbyists in building software applications. Using readymade, drop-and-drag parts, ToolBook would help them assemble things on their computer screens, like a calendar, for example, or a way to organize a CD collection, or even more complicated business applications. ToolBook would be the first exciting chapter in Allen's new, post-Microsoft life.

But all did not go as planned, beginning with ToolBook's launch on a spring day in 1990 at the New York Public Library in midtown Manhattan. Allen prepared to step into the technology spotlight for the first time since he'd left Microsoft seven years earlier. He'd been very quiet about his company, as were his loyal employees. Asymetrix was a big mystery to anyone paying attention to the Microsoft cofounder. He was very unlike Gates, who promised things well before they were ready to go, in some cases, before they'd even been discussed. Allen was the opposite, he hadn't wanted anyone to know he'd even started a new company, but word had leaked out in 1985, and his vice president of marketing, Steve Wood, had confirmed to the *Seattle Times* that the company existed. That's all he said.

Many tech trade magazines wondered occasionally what Allen's company was up to and why it was taking so long to produce anything, but the company shied away from commenting each time. Allen was insistent on secrecy, believing as always that ideas could too easily be copied. Many people in business have a healthy dose of this kind of paranoia, but Allen's total and utter lack of communication in cases like these made it seem excessive. Besides, his concern was pointed in the wrong direction; the person he should have been most wary about was one he called a friend, or at least an ally.

On this day in New York, Allen was about to show the world his latest good idea. He stood before trade reporters and tech executives, a large screen behind him. Soon, the audience would see a demonstration of ToolBook, followed by a videotaped endorsement of ToolBook by Bill Gates, whose every word techies and finance gurus hung on. ToolBook had the distinct privilege of being the first and only product created for the highly anticipated third version of Microsoft's Windows, which was expected to be generations better than the previous two versions, offering a pleasant interface, a trend carried over from Apple's graphical screens. ToolBook relied almost entirely on graphics and would show off some of the features of Windows nicely. It was a good deal for both Asymetrix and Microsoft.

It should have been a perfect launch for ToolBook . . . but it wasn't.

The screen lit up with the tagline for ToolBook: "Opening Windows for New Tools." The audience waited for what would come next. They were there to see ToolBook, but mainly to see Allen, who had been such a mystery since leaving Microsoft.

"People were just assuming Paul would compete with Microsoft," says Pam Miller, who was an outside public relations consultant to Asymetrix. "We had to keep some of that at bay."

For now, nothing was happening at all. Allen stood there. The screen didn't move. Windows had crashed and the video prompter was frozen. No one knew what had happened. Eventually, an embarrassed Allen and his staff tinkered with the computer enough to get it working. But it was too late. The event was a dud.

No one really noticed, though, because the next day, the whole world was caught up in news from Microsoft. Not only was Allen's fumbling debut forgotten, but the company, itself, was lost in the headlines that were to follow about Gates and the long-anticipated, new version of Windows.

Even after the debacle in New York, ToolBook all but froze up on its own launch. After some excitement from technology reviewers who gave it high marks for how easy it was to use, it sputtered. ToolBook was a handy tool, but it had been loaded up with so many features, hardly anyone had a machine that could handle it. It moved as slow as molasses and most people lost patience. Sales initially spiked to several thousand in a single month, but slowed rapidly. "There was this white board by my office that had sales figures. They were selling several thousand in the first three months. Then one month, it was only a thousand," says Jeff Day, a former product manager at Asymetrix. By the end of the year, only 50,000 copies of ToolBook had been sold and revenues were just $10 million. Not bad for a first product, but more was expected from Allen, who himself expected more. "When Microsoft was the size of Asymetrix we had 10 or 11 products and two guys working on them," Allen told the *San Francisco Examiner.*

Allen had had such high hopes for ToolBook. "Paul's vision was to make ToolBook the new BASIC," says Day. That was fair enough. Just like BASIC was an easy-to-use programming language for its day, ToolBook was a very pedestrian way of programming.

If anyone was getting in the way of ToolBook's progress, though, it was Allen. He was acting like a "feature freak," the term used to describe techies who get all caught up in the nifty things software could do, while losing sight of the big picture. Allen was doing that. He wanted to load up ToolBook with all the cool ideas that ever came his way. Some managers tried to tell him that this was why ToolBook was so slow and having so many problems in the marketplace. But Allen's attitude was, "Get it in there. Worry about the other things later."

Allen wasn't an easy boss. He was frustrated by employees who weren't able to respond to an order to come up with "ideas" that "knocked his socks off," according to a former Asymetrix manager. He sometimes thought they were slacking off on the job and once went so far as to drill engineers about how they were filling their days. (The manager says they weren't slacking, as Allen had suspected.) Other people weren't doing their jobs, either, in Allen's view. He needed them to come up with something revolutionary. He knew he'd spot it when he saw it; they just needed to keep at it. Each time they presented ideas, Allen was nonplussed. He'd send employees away and tell them to try again, but gave little specific feedback on how, or even why, their ideas hadn't worked for him.

Many reports over the years have described Allen as shy, but that's not quite right, say the people around him. "He was extremely *publicity* shy," says Miller. "But he'll absolutely tell you right or wrong what he thinks." But he also will refrain from saying things for a while. He doesn't mind waiting for good ideas to come along, but he will wait only so long.

He finally blew up. One group of employees had presented ideas to Allen several times, but Allen hadn't liked any of them. The employees were extremely demoralized. They didn't know what to do next, but they really wanted to please their boss. Mark Ursino, a former Microsoft manager who became general manager at Asymetrix, went to Allen in the hopes of fixing the situation for his staff. "These guys are dispirited," Ursino told Allen. "They're working hard and I think it's a good plan they have. At the least, it would be good to give them some strokes. The last thing they need is [for you] to shoot them down." Allen listened. "Oh yeah, I'm not gonna yell at them," he told Ursino, who believed him and sent his group back in. They returned shaken by the experience. "He ranted and raved," says Ursino. "I was floored."

Allen's top two lieutenants, Wood and executive vice president Bert Kolde, weren't helping the situation. Lower level managers like Ursino and Day were arguing back with Allen, but Kolde and Wood, the top guys, were mainly just carrying out Allen's orders. Allen hadn't learned along the way that what made for successful business wasn't simply his ideas; it was also good business smarts. Without the balance he'd had from Gates, Allen struggled as an entrepreneur.

Gates was still in the Allen picture, though. At first, he helped his old friend by making ToolBook the first product available for Windows 3.0. Then, he turned on him. Not long after Gates's ringing endorsement of ToolBook on launch day, he told his own staff to start working on a Microsoft version of the product. Within six months of ToolBook's launch, Microsoft announced that it had developed a similar product, called Visual Basic. Gates's Visual Basic quickly leapfrogged ToolBook in sales and popularity. Back at Asymetrix, Allen set about turning ToolBook into a Visual Basic-killer. He frustrated managers and engineers by insisting that the ToolBook team focus solely on beating Microsoft's product—mainly by throwing in more features, naturally. Thanks to the tension between Allen and the staff, and the time it took to add the new features he wanted, it was three years before a new version of ToolBook was out the door—not the one year that was expected.

With a new version of ToolBook delayed and sales not nearly as robust as hoped, Asymetrix tried other products to stay afloat. Over its first few years, the company rolled out one product after another in what looked like a haphazard attempt to stay in the game. There was a clip-art product, a database program, and a computer-based slide-show product called Compel. Compel looked like it might be the one that stuck—it was receiving rave reviews and winning over customers—but then Microsoft came out, about six months after Compel, with PowerPoint. It obliterated Compel in the marketplace.

Allen kept pouring money into Asymetrix. Since the first starter loan in 1984, he'd been back to the bank for a $7 million line of credit personally guaranteed by himself. As the company's debt climbed toward $50 million in 1995, Allen finally had enough. He brought in an old pal from Microsoft, Vern Raburn, and told him to fix things. Raburn restructured the company, reduced staff, and brought in a new CEO, Jim Billmaier from Sun Microsystems. They prepared to take the company public to help Allen get some of his money back and lessen Asymetrix's dependence on Allen for cash.

For the next eight years, Asymetrix struggled as a company that made learning software, the one market where Asymetrix's ToolBook had had the most success landing customers. The company finally went public as Asymetrix Learning Systems in 1998, 14 years after it was first launched; by contrast, Microsoft went public 10 years after Allen first had the idea for it. Asymetrix opened at $11 per share, hit a high of $19.13 in July 2000, and plummeted from there. It continued to languish around or below $5 per share. Microsoft, meanwhile, was doing all it could, including splitting its stock several times, to keep its ever-ballooning valuation in check and its shares below $100 apiece. In 1998,

Asymetrix restructured a second time, now becoming an online learning company called Click2Learn. It continued to struggle, reorganizing and raising outside funds several times. It was not a good first showing for Allen.

If nothing else, Asymetrix was headquarters for what would become a sprawling Allen empire. Here, he built a strong, loyal following of executives who remained with him for years and moved on to other Allen efforts. It was also a place for him to workshop ideas and prep them for launch, possibly, into their own companies. In the end, ToolBook itself really hadn't been so bad. Techies all over the world liked its easy-to-use design and hundreds of them would gather each year at Asymetrix conferences to prove it. They still do.

But it hadn't been good enough for Allen, who had long since pulled his great hope from Asymetrix.

There is much to admire about Paul Allen: Despite his failures and missteps along the way, he has never given up hope in the future potential of technology. Asymetrix didn't work out the way he had wanted it to. He wasn't happy about it at all, but it didn't stop him from moving on. He still believed he had good ideas for where technology was headed; he believed he had a strong grasp of how it all worked and could be the one to deliver it to people. He always had the end user in mind.

But now it was 1992. The world had changed a lot since 1984, when he launched his first company. Asymetrix was rooted in that past, which was exclusively about what software could do to improve the lives of the people who used computers. In 1992, computing had become a bigger story. Now, it wasn't just about the computer, but about connections to the computer and even transforming the machine into something else, possibly resembling television. Interactive television and the so-called information superhighway had arrived.

Not long after ToolBook's launch, Allen had become interested in this bigger story through an investment he made in a local start-up called SkyPix that was supposed to deliver television channels to people's homes over a broadband network provided by satellite. This fascinated Allen, who recalled a conversation he'd had over lunch with Gates at Shakey's Pizza in Vancouver, Washington, in 1974, when they were working at TRW. It had occurred to him then that computers might be a way for people to be connected to one another. Entertainment and services might be delivered over these connections. It would open up a whole other world.

It wasn't such a stretch, really, to imagine such a thing, even then. Allen and Gates both knew that computers could connect to one another over telephone lines; that's how they'd plugged in to the powerful PDP-10 computers in downtown Seattle from the junky little Teletype machine up at the Lakeside School. Still, Allen's idea on that day at Shakey's became the start of an inspiration for him.

When Allen learned about SkyPix in 1991 and that it needed money, he put up an investment in the company. Later, he put in more. Then, near the end of 1992, he opened up a new company to provide the very things he'd talked about with Gates at Shakey's that would make the connections interesting in this other "world." He called the company Starwave.

From an entrepreneurial perspective, Starwave got off to a start not unlike Asymetrix. Allen tapped a friend, his reliable lieutenant Steve Wood, to head the new business, which had an open charter from Allen to do things for SkyPix's channels. Basically, the company would create the user interface for the set-top boxes that would be in the homes of people who subscribed to the SkyPix service. It was up to Starwave to determine what was on the box in data form: interactive shopping channels, interactive television shows—anything Starwavers dreamed up. Allen, of course, simply wanted them to come up with "something groundbreaking," as he always wanted to do in his post-Microsoft years.

SkyPix went bankrupt in 1993. For Starwave, it was the equivalent of Crucible never working at Asymetrix; it left the company with nothing else to do. What now? Allen could have closed up shop and moved on, but he didn't. He kept Starwave open because he wanted to find another delivery system for the interactive multimedia products that Starwave was supposed to generate. He thought about buying cable systems, but ultimately decided against it.

Starwave managers thought briefly about providing content and services for the online services of the day, companies like CompuServe, Prodigy, and America Online. Microsoft had begun serious development of a consumer online service called Marvel. But the really hot thing of the moment was the CD-ROM. The CD-ROM could transform the sleepy PC from mainly a data experience with some occasional graphics into an interactive, dynamic experience that was as good as video games and sometimes almost as good as television. Even executives in Hollywood were excited about the CD-ROM and started developing titles. Allen told Wood to get Starwave into CD-ROMs. And, then, almost immediately, he pulled Wood out of Starwave. "It wasn't my idea," Wood said at the time. "The fact is Paul decided we needed a change here."

Allen had another assignment for Wood: His third start-up was to be an idyllic environment where Allen's beloved "ideas" would grow and be nurtured in an intellectual greenhouse. It would be a lab called Interval Research, based in Palo Alto, California, near the famed computer research lab, Xerox PARC (Palo Alto Research Center). While Allen had someone else in mind to run the day-to-day operations at Interval, he wanted Wood to be the vice chairman and focus on grabbing the best ideas from Interval's researchers and bring them back to Starwave, where they would be turned into commercial products. That plan ultimately never played out, and Wood moved on to a career in wireless services outside of the Allen world.

Back at Starwave, a new guy was taking over and he was nothing like the usual Allen loyalist, who tended to be low-key. Mike Slade was outgoing, smooth, and publicity seeking. Allen knew him from Microsoft days, when Slade was a marketing manager there. He had since moved on to Apple and back again to Microsoft. In the fall of 1992, Allen recruited Slade to Asymetrix and put him in a holding pattern while he figured out where he wanted him to go. When Starwave's mission changed, he picked Slade to shape its new direction. "I decided Starwave needed Mike's leadership to aggressively move this company forward," said Allen in a company press release.

Slade was fine for the job at hand. Allen had pretty much lost interest, anyway. "Paul's m.o. at the time was, write the check and check in once a month," says a former Starwave executive.

As Slade took the reins, Starwave was making CD-ROMs, mainly for big-name entertainment stars like Clint Eastwood, Peter Gabriel, and the Muppets. These clients would be really big coups for any multimedia company, but Starwave was a nobody company with no track record and no star executives from either Hollywood or the CD-ROM world. What Starwave had was Allen's name behind it. Getting meetings with the biggest names in New York and Hollywood was a breeze. Need to see the vice president at *TV Guide?* No problem, but why not see the CEO, instead? Need Barry Diller? Okay. "At Paul Allen companies, all the doors are opened," says former Starwave engineer Paul Budak, who was one of the company's first nine employees.

The CD-ROMs turned into a bad business, though. In what was emerging as a trend among Allen-backed endeavors, the

CD-ROMS were praised for their elegant design and high quality, but they were huge money-suckers. It was just like the top-notch ToolBook that never earned revenues for Asymetrix. Starwave sold the CD-ROMs to consumers for $50 apiece, but the company needed to sell millions to make any money from them. The deals they did with the stars were really bad deals, too: Starwave picked up the production costs—which tended to run into the millions—and paid the entertainers for the rights to their names, likenesses, and other assets. Sales were lackluster; Gabriel's CD-ROM sold only 100,000 copies in two years. Starwave's debt climbed quickly into the tens of millions.

Allen didn't seem to notice. But then, many Allen companies run up debts long after other companies would have had their efforts slowed by anxious investors. Allen, because of his great wealth, has great patience with the companies he starts and invests in. It takes a long time before he decides that he has spent too much money or has been taken advantage of. At that point, however, he's furious, and pulls out fast.

Slade might have known this when he decided Starwave needed to find a new line of business with greater potential for making money. But it's more likely he just wanted to make sure he got out of the deal with enough money to line his own coffers. He made it no secret he wanted Starwave to IPO. One day, Slade arrived at work saying, "We're *gonna* go public this year," according to the former executive.

Starwave did find a new business, but not because a bunch of employees sat around and tried to come up with "ideas," as they'd done at Asymetrix. Just as BASIC, SoftCard, and ToolBook had happened coincidentally, so did Starwave's new business idea. It came from an engineer who was just trying to help his bosses see some of the work that was being done for an online service that Starwave was going to provide content to: He uploaded the content to the World Wide Web and told them where they could find it. It was simply easier and more efficient than putting it on disk and circulating it through management.

"It was as if there was this collective 'ah-ha,' " says Jeff Day, the former Asymetrix manager who had since moved over to Starwave. Starwave decided to become a Web company. It was the best accidental decision the company could make.

Allen was really only peripherally involved in Starwave. Asymetrix would be the last company for a long time that he put in many hours for. It wasn't just that he wasn't interested; by the 1990s, he had too much going on. He was the owner of the Portland Trail Blazers basketball team; he had investments in several dozen companies; he had homes all around the world; and he was doing all he could to live a well-rounded, meaningful life—the mission he'd set out for himself after his father's death and his own bout with cancer.

He might have been more involved, though, if it weren't for Slade, who, according to one of his top executives at the time, "was running interference, because [Allen] was so erratic."

Starwave was also very un-Allen. It wasn't software, and it wasn't even all that much about technology. Once Starwave became a Web company, it was really more like a magazine publishing company in the old style. Starwave employees put up "pages" with stories on them. They would occasionally add some nifty interactive features, like a scrolling ticker with sports scores on a sports site, for example. But for the most part, Starwave was made up of many content people and a few technology folks. This wasn't where Allen preferred to play.

Occasionally, Allen tried to change Starwave into something that interested him. Every month or so, Starwave executives expected Allen in the office. Pizza would be ordered from Domino's with ham and pineapple, the way he liked it. They'd sit around a large table in a conference room, fire up a presentation screen, and give Allen a look at their latest work. "He'd grumble and leave," recalls a former senior executive. "Paul would never do the 'tell them what you like' part. He'd say, 'It's all garbage. Here's what you should be doing.' If he said positive things, he would say it to Mike Slade after. Slade would sometimes come back and say, 'Here's what Paul liked.'" Allen was as uncommunicative as he'd ever been, but at least he wasn't tearing the heads off this group like he had at Asymetrix. He aimed the brunt of his dissatisfaction at Slade. "You didn't want to be Mike Slade. Sometimes he was a confidante; other times, he was treated like dirt. Like, maybe the pizza's not there on time and he's pissed at Mike about it," says the former executive.

Allen did occasionally make suggestions to the group. He didn't love the publishing model, but he did like its celebrity-centric site, Mr. Showbiz. "He said, 'Search is really the key. We should really give a way to find any celebrity you want.' That was really perceptive, to make that statement in 1994, 1995. Paul pushed us in that direction," says the former senior executive.

Having Allen as the boss was always about mixed messages. He didn't say much to anyone on staff, but then, out of the blue, he'd have his assistant call someone and invite them to fly down to Portland for a Trail Blazers game with him in his jet, for no apparent reason.

He also opened up his home to employees. In what became a tradition at Allen-backed companies, Monday nights were employee nights at Allen's estate on Mercer Island. Executives and staff could play basketball on his NBA-regulation sized court, or watch movies at his 12-screen cineplex, the Allen Estate Theater, which was complete with a concession stand. Allen wasn't always around, but now and then, he'd show up and chat with some of the employees who were a little more techie, like him.

"He would chum up with Slade and Patrick [Naughton]. He could talk technology with Patrick; he liked him," says the former executive. (Starwave chief technology officer Patrick Naughton later gained his own notoriety when he was arrested on the Santa Monica Pier in Los Angeles in 1999 for the intent to solicit sex from a minor. Naughton was ultimately sentenced to a $20,000 fine, nine months' in-home detention, and five years' probation.)

Meanwhile, Starwave had become a sensation. It was a content company in the earliest days of the Web when there weren't many companies dedicated to producing high-end, expensive content. It produced several sites, including Mr. Showbiz, Family Planet, Outside Online, and ABCNews.com. Its biggest site, however, was what later became known as ESPN.com. Though a coup of a deal with ESPN, Starwave boasted one of the most visited sites on the Web, ESPNet SportsZone, which it produced and which was the company's main revenue-generator. It was also its biggest liability, since it didn't own the rights to the brand forever.

Starwave was turning out to be a hit, for sure, but not where it mattered, on the balance sheet. By 1996, Allen had poured some $96 million into the company, but it was still in the hole. Starwave's sites were supposed to make money from advertising revenues and subscriptions to members-only portions of its sites, but aside from the ESPN site, none of the others were drawing enough traffic to convince advertisers to spend their money. ESPN pulled the weight for the other sites. It wasn't much. In 1996, there weren't all that many advertisers on the Web, and none of them had special budgets for that kind of spending. Management and Starwave's board briefly considered an IPO— they even hired investment bank Alex.Brown, which drew up the registration papers—but when another option came along, Allen took that one.

The bidder was Disney, which was paying attention to Starwave ever since it acquired the cable sports channel ESPN in its 1995 purchase of ESPN parent Cap Cities. Disney noticed ESPN's site wasn't managed by ESPN, and that wasn't how Disney did business. Disney kept everything in-house. Executives at Disney Online suggested to Starwave they might try to pull out of their existing deal, or at least not renew when the contract's term was up. But the Disney folks knew they needed Starwave for its sophisticated Web publishing systems. At the time, Web publishing systems as sophisticated as Starwave's were rare. They weren't available on the shelf to buy, and they were difficult to build from scratch. Without Starwave, Disney couldn't do anything about ESPN online, and as more advertisers got hip to the Web, it was beginning to look like a real money-maker.

Allen got wind of Disney's feelings and rang up some of the top management. "I'm interested in getting another investor in," said Allen, according to a former senior Disney executive. Disney considered his offer, and in the spring of 1997, paid Allen $100 million for a 37 percent, noncontrolling stake in Starwave, with the option to purchase the rest of the company at a later date. A year later, Disney took that option, paying $250 million for the rest. Allen made a profit of at least $200 million. Compared to Asymetrix, Starwave was a true hit; it actually gave Allen a return on his investment. It was a bittersweet win, though. Allen hadn't really cared as much about getting his money back; he was a techie and that's where he wanted to do "something groundbreaking." Starwave's publishing model wasn't it.

Allen's plan for generating ideas wasn't progressing well in the purely commercial ventures he set up, so he took a different tack with Interval Research, his next company. He told Interval to focus exclusively on ideas, thinking that might do the trick. It didn't.

Allen didn't want to start a company that just cranked out some basically useful products and focused mechanically on revenue targets. He wanted an entity that could handle long-term development. Microsoft had locked up the short-term space, often by mimicking successes it saw at other companies (which had put in their own years of development). But Allen was also genuinely inspired by the long-term view. He recalled how his idea of a computer-filled world in 1973 had taken years to come to fruition. With Interval Research, Allen hoped to capture ideas early on and make them the property of Interval. "There are a number of interesting technologies just over the horizon, but they aren't ready for a typical two-year product cycle," said Allen in a company press release.

The plan was that Interval would get $100 million over 10 years to brainstorm randomly and explore even the wildest concepts in the hopes of finding something revolutionary. But Allen also expected the new firm would produce ideas that could eventually become commercial products. Interval would make money by retaining intellectual property rights and charge licensing fees for the use of products it developed; or it would spin-off companies and retain an ownership stake.

David Liddle was hired as Interval's CEO. Liddle had started on the ground floor at Xerox PARC when it opened in 1970. After 13 years, he grew frustrated that a lot of the great ideas generated by the researchers at PARC were slipping into the hands of outside companies who turned them into commercial products. Liddle left PARC and formed Metaphor Computer Systems to develop visual programming tools, much like Asymetrix. In 1988, IBM took a minority stake in Metaphor and gradually upped its investment and influence to a point where Liddle and his partner, Charles Irby, felt squeezed out by Big

Blue. The two sold Metaphor to IBM in 1991 and left. Now, Liddle was hiding out in Silicon Valley, looking for his next opportunity. Interval sounded right to him.

Once he was on board, Liddle set about building an idyllic research and development center. More than 100 researchers were hired with backgrounds in science, digital media, music, psychology, journalism, cinematography—the point was to pull together people of various backgrounds, group them around an idea and see what happened. Liddle said that researchers should be allowed to "follow a good idea wherever it goes." Soon, Interval filled up with people like Rob Shaw, co-creator of the chaos theory; Joy Mountford, designer of high-speed tactical-fighter displays for the F-16; Jim Boyden, who created the inkjet printer; and Donna Hoffman, a professor at Vanderbilt University who, along with her husband Tom Novak, were among the first to study e-commerce in the early 1990s.

Scientists and academics, accustomed to tight budget constraints, reveled in the generosity of Allen's coffers. They set to work on a range of projects. Some researchers worked on a watch that would be embedded under the skin, while others created the musical "stick" played by the singer Laurie Anderson. Then there was the Electric Carnival, a traveling multimedia tent that accompanied the alternative-rock tour Lollapalooza in 1994. Researchers hastily filed patents on their ideas, while observers merely mocked them. *Harper's* magazine showcased the seeming absurdity of the projects (or the overly academic approach to the seemingly banal) by printing outtakes from an internal Interval memo about the upcoming Lollapalooza event:

Who are the 15,000 to 30,000 people per concert who are the audience for the Electric Carnival?

They include "zippies," "cyberpunks," "head-bangers," "wannabees," the younger "Rave" audience (mostly youth from eleven to seventeen), and older "weekend warriors." The large majority are sixteen to twenty-four.

What do we know about the majority group (sixteen to twenty-four), and what does it imply for a successful exhibit?

Their common preoccupation is the question of personal identity. . . . They feel marginal to mainstream society. . . . The majority of them will be drunk, stoned, tripping, or otherwise chemically altered.

Interval Research was a playground for ideas, all of them pointed toward the far horizon of technology, where Allen liked it best. At least once a month, he would fly down to Silicon Valley in his $15 million jet to review projects underway. While researchers made presentations, he would sit and listen. Unlike at Asymetrix or Starwave, he did not rant, rave, or insist on his vision of how things should be. He didn't say much at all, in fact. Allen tended to have one measure for approval, according to Michael Naimark, a researcher in media and the arts who was on staff at Interval: "The one thing that is more true than metaphor is that it used to be that the currency of Paul Allen was how many times he said 'cool' [during a project presentation]. In the latter part [of Interval's history], it was when he said 'currency.' Interval evolved into 'how can we monetize.' That was the first sign of change," says Naimark, "then he closed [Interval]."

Allen had always been somewhat erratic, changing his mind as he became distracted by "cool" new ideas. After Interval was several years old, he changed his mind about just how much "research" he wanted to emphasize in this new company. It didn't take a genius to figure out that Interval didn't exactly have a patent hold on innovation. Silicon Valley was heating up with new products and services backed by deep-pocketed venture capitalists, but it was also a time when even the biggest companies were innovating. One of the big new ideas that came out of the 1990s was a Web language called Java, and it came from the $6 billion computer company Sun Microsystems. Allen's idea that new concepts came only from research labs was turning out to be somewhat of a bust.

"When Interval began, we just did cool things. It was 100 percent research, 0 percent development," Naimark told *Wired*. Vanderbilt professor Donna Hoffman says it was simply a "well-funded sandbox. If you wanted a toy, you could get it."

Gradually, the free-form environment came to an end. Allen wasn't involved in the day-to-day operations of Interval, but he pushed Liddle to get products ready for public consumption. Instead of releasing products into the marketplace, Interval began releasing entire companies. In a single day in November 1996, Interval unveiled three that were ready to go: Purple Moon, a developer of video games for girls in a $6 billion market dominated by games for boys; ePlanet, which aspired to replace keyboards and mice through technology that read human gestures and expressions through a digital camera; and Carnelian Software, Internet software that made Web publishing easy.

None of these fared well. Carnelian closed in July 1998 after it failed to raise any venture capital. Purple Moon managed to land other backers, including Institutional Venture Partners, where Liddle's wife, Ruthann Quindlan, worked and the esteemed Allen & Company (run by Herbert S. Allen, no relation to Paul Allen). Purple Moon ultimately closed its doors in February 1999 after selling only 139,909 games in 1998. The company's assets were sold a month later to market leader Mattel, which had sold 1.4 million games in 1998. ePlanet landed $3 million to $5 million from Intel at the end of 1998, but failed to close future rounds. On September 30, 1999, the company scaled back to a technology licensing company.

There were so many failures. Allen, the "ideas" man, was losing confidence in his third attempt to build his own company after Microsoft. At Interval, three failures and no successes proved to be too much. Interval's struggle to come up with "groundbreaking" ideas had worried him for a while, anyway. In late 1997, he said, "I'd like to see Interval . . . have an ongoing experience beyond 2002, but you make judgments as you go along. You know, paradigm-shifting ideas don't grow on trees." With the closure of ePlanet, Allen made a judgment. He sent a memo to staff that issued new marching orders: Interval could still be a research-and-development facility, but it needed to emphasize the "development" aspect. He also gave Interval researchers a target for their research for the first time: broadband cable, since Allen had begun to buy up cable companies like Marcus Cable and Charter Communications and wanted to do something interactive with them. For some researchers, Allen's new dictum was good news. "For the first time, he has articulated broadly what he'd like to hear from us," researcher Bonnie Johnson told *Wired* in 1999. Allen had grown impatient with his research lab and now he was becoming more involved.

Interval never made it to 2002. In April 2000, Allen pulled the plug, saying it wasn't a good environment for pure research. Interval's closure didn't do much to prove that Allen was an "ideas" man on the path of groundbreaking technologies. Some of the brightest minds had come on board and there was little to show for it. He was trying to find a formula for groundbreaking ideas, but it was proving difficult. But Allen's problem wasn't coming up with ideas. It was doing something productive and profitable with those ideas. That's where Gates had always been an asset to the dreamy Allen. He never again found that balance, but his money allowed him to wander and stumble for years without it.

For a long time, Allen stopped trying to start new companies. Instead, he would invest a little here and there to keep an eye on what other people were doing. Sometimes, he'd go back for more, and eventually buy up the entire operation.

He also began to give some true focus to what he was trying to do. It was more than "something groundbreaking." With the SkyPix investment, he'd shifted his thinking to a connected world. Now, he had an updated technology strategy. He called it the "wired world." He even had it trademarked.

*Top:* Paul Allen in his
Asymetrix office, 1985.
(*Photo:* Peter Liddell/*Seattle Times.*)

Bill Gates with Allen in
discussion at a Sonics
game, 1993.
(*Photo:* Mike Siegel/*Seattle Times.*)

*Top:* Allen with his mother, Faye.
(*Photo:* Richard S. Heyza/*Seattle Times*.)

*Right:* Sperry Peninsula, the tip of Lopez Island purchased by Allen for $8 million in 1996.
(*Photo:* Greg Gilbert/*Seattle Times*.)

*Bottom:* Allen in his element, jamming with friends, 1997.
(*Photo:* Benjamin Benschneider/*Seattle Times*.)

Top: With his sister Jody Patton at his side, Allen describes his vision for the Experience Music Project.
(*Photo:* Harley Soltes/*Seattle Times.*)

Allen a là Hendrix, preparing to smash a ceramic guitar to bits at the opening of the Experience Music Project.
(*Photo:* Jim Lott/*Seattle Times.*)

Allen's second sport: On the field with Seahawks president Bob Whitsitt, left, and coach Mike Holmgren (right) preseason, 2002.

(*Photo:* Rod Mar/*Seattle Times.*)

Animated Allen, cheering for his own home team as a Trail Blazer teammate scores on the Seattle Sonics, 1998.

*Photo:* Harley Soltes/*Seattle Times.*)

Allen with Monica Seles, often rumored to be more than just a friend, at a Sonics game, 1997.

(*Photo:* Harley Soltes/*Seattle Times.*)

Allen with David Geffen at the 2000 Golden Globes.

(*Photo:* Rose Prouser/Reuters.)

Allen at a party he co-hosted at the Cannes International Film Festival, 2002, with Jack Nicholson and Gina Gershon.

(*Photo:* Evan Agostini/Image Photo.)

Mr. Hollywood: Allen at the star-studded Cannes party, 2002.

(*Photo:* Evan Agostini/Image Photo.)

6

# PAUL ALLEN, VENTURE CAPITALIST

I n 1990, Paul Allen's Microsoft money was like Monopoly money; there was so much of it, its value became abstract. He spent some of his $1.1 billion fortune the way a lottery winner might: He bought a mansion on Mercer Island; he added cars, planes, and boats to his transportation stable; he traveled and played a lot. But he was also just as serious about technology as he had always been, so, in addition to starting his own company in the years since leaving Microsoft in 1983, he also set up an organization to handle the rest of his money. He called it Vulcan Northwest. Thus, Paul Allen became a venture capitalist.

Vulcan sounds like the perfect name for a firm started by a sci-fi lover who screened *Battlestar Galactica* for Microsoft employees back in Albuquerque days, but Allen picked the name not for the home planet of *Star Trek's* Mr. Spock; Vulcan was the Roman god of volcanoes. As Allen has explained it, Vulcan represented change, fire, and creation, though Roman mythology also calls Vulcan a god of *destructive* fire. For Vulcan, the venture capital firm, the many losses over the years made it seem more like the god of destruction was keeping watch over the firm's work.

At first, Vulcan didn't do much. It was mainly looked after by Allen's sister Jody, who'd been working in the development office at the Pacific Northwest Ballet. Now, she ran Allen's finances, somewhat. Her main interest was the arts. As a high school student, she had starred in and directed many of the plays at Lakeside, participated in local theatre, and gone on to study drama in college. The Pacific Northwest Ballet job was a natural step for her. A general investment job wasn't, however, so she focused on the things that interested her.

Vulcan Northwest quickly became mainly philanthropical under Jody's care. She set up three foundations in the arts and medical research. Allen focused on the business side of his firm, but he was involved with his start-up Asymetrix when he wasn't off enjoying life. For its first four years, Vulcan Northwest really wasn't much of a technology investment firm.

Allen's college roommate Bert Kolde served a dual role as executive vice president of Asymetrix and an advisor to Vulcan. Kolde brought investment ideas to Allen as they came up. In 1987, he was running operations at Asymetrix when he noticed Layered, a company he thought worthy of Allen's attention. He talked it over with Allen and then made a call to Layered, a Boston-based company that pretty much had a lock on the market of accounting software for the Macintosh.

Allen wasn't interested in getting into the Macintosh market, but he liked the graphical user interface on the Mac. At Microsoft, Allen had begun several initiatives to move the company out of text-based programs and applications into those with graphics. His ToolBook application was all about using graphics to make programming easier. Allen liked what Kolde showed him in Layered; maybe that company could develop a version for Windows, the operating system from Microsoft that was becoming the standard on the PC.

Layered's focus was the workplace, just as Asymetrix's was in 1987, when that company was trying to build the business product

Crucible. Allen had always been as interested in making computers easier to use in the office as he wanted them to be at home. When Kolde brought Layered to his attention, he thought it was a good company to be involved with. He told Kolde to go ahead and do some kind of deal with Layered.

The three-year-old Layered was a $10 million company that sold accounting software for the Macintosh to small-business customers through retail chains like BusinessLand and ComputerLand. The accounting software, Insight, was the company's flagship product, but Layered's CEO, Stephen Burakoff, wanted to expand the product line, either by developing new ones internally, or acquiring them and rolling them under the Layered banner, kind of the way Microsoft acquired products and made them its own. Layered had strong distribution channels that Burakoff wanted to exploit. That was his pitch to the Boston-area venture capitalists who were ready to put up $3 million when, late on a Wednesday night, everything changed.

It was two days before Burakoff was going to close his deals with the venture capitalists. He was happy enough with the money. The venture capitalists were fairly blue chip, and anyway, he was glad to have the money so he could grow Layered into a larger company, maybe move its product line beyond the Macintosh. At eight o'clock, Burakoff sat at his desk reviewing the term sheets. The phone rang.

"This guy says, 'I'm Bert Kolde, I represent Paul Allen. I'm at Asymetrix. We love your products and we want to invest,'" says Burakoff. He showed no signs of shock that the cofounder of Microsoft had taken an interest in his little company; Burakoff played it cool.

"Great," Burakoff replied. "But I'm about to close a round, I'm not about to disrupt it." After a second of thought, he said, "If you can get out here tomorrow, we can talk." They showed up the next day. Burakoff was impressed. Not only was this Paul Allen, the cofounder of Microsoft, but the entire group seemed to be a very reliable bunch. He pushed them once more, telling Kolde that if he could get $500,000 by Friday afternoon, he'd disrupt his ongoing financing. A check arrived at 4 P.M. Friday; Burakoff halted his other plans and accepted Allen's offer instead. "We thought it was smarter money," says Burakoff. "Now, I'm not sure it was."

Getting Allen's money was the easy part. Working with him and his top lieutenants wasn't. Over the following few years, Layered slowly disintegrated from a promising young company with a leading product into one mired in a culture of indecisiveness and ultimatums that has marred many Allen companies and investments.

At first, Burakoff was grateful for and thrilled by Allen's interest. Burakoff had wanted to expand Insight onto the Windows platform and here was a guy who really wanted to do that, too. It was a marriage of common interests. Layered engineers got to work on a Windows-based version of the accounting software.

Meanwhile, Burakoff still wanted to throw other products into Layered's lineup and take advantage of the powerful distribution channel. But soon, it became clear that Allen didn't care about any of that. He only wanted the accounting software product. "There were other ways to grow the business, but he was absolutely insistent on the Windows product," says Burakoff.

Burakoff and Allen butted heads. Allen pointed out to Burakoff that the small-business market for the Macintosh version was dead, now that many businesses were moving to PCs. Burakoff agreed, but he suggested they position the company as a broader firm. "We had thousands of retailers. All were intimate customers of ours," he says. But Allen said no. "He had a temper. I remember him slamming his fist down on my desk one day," Burakoff recalls. "Our arguments were perpendicular. He saw it one way, I saw it another." By the end of 1988, Burakoff had left Layered, but he never blamed Allen for wanting it his way: "A hugely rich guy doesn't have to take shit from anyone," he says.

Allen had put $3 million into Layered at first, but he'd also opened his checkbook to the company, which started burning through cash as it failed to take in revenues. It was truly turning into an Allen kind of company.

With Burakoff out of the picture, Layered came fully under Allen's control. He installed Kolde's brother Velle at the top. Bert Kolde and Steve Wood were around occasionally. None of them managed to get Layered going in any direction—either Allen's way or Burakoff's way. The engineers failed to produce a Windows version before Allen decided in 1990 that he'd had enough and sold Layered to Peachtree Software in Atlanta. Allen's first foray into venture capital was a harbinger of what was to come; he almost always pushed his companies to do things the way he wanted, even if it might have been to their detriment, like with Layered.

While Layered was a failure for Allen, it wasn't for one Layered executive. Thanks to Layered's troubles, one executive rose to the top—ultimately—of Allen's empire. His name was Bill Savoy.

Savoy was 24 years old when he joined Layered as a controller. He'd grown up in New Braintree, Massachusetts. He left his family in 1980 at age 16 because home, he told *The Wall Street*

*Journal* 18 years later, "was a place that didn't value anyone who wanted to better themselves."

Savoy was pretty much on his own after that. He finished high school, enrolled in a local college and graduated with a business degree. He took a finance job at Polar Beverages and became a municipal bond analyst at State Street Research. Then, he joined Layered.

He was fairly well liked. "He's a straight-shooter," says former Layered executive Thomas Youngman. After Burakoff left Layered, Kolde and Allen began hammering through top management until pretty much no one was left. All of a sudden, Savoy was one of the most senior people in the company and the guy in control of its dwindling finances. Kolde turned to Savoy with the charge to fix Layered for Allen: Find a buyer, or something, to help him get out of this mess.

Savoy was ambitious and hard working and faced this task with enthusiasm and a sense of duty. There wasn't much left of the company to sell, but Savoy managed to find a buyer in Atlanta-based Peachtree Software. In the eyes of the Vulcan group, Savoy had done well. At least, he'd gotten Allen out of Layered.

Once Layered was sold, Savoy, then 26, went home and started thinking about his future. He had no job. He didn't even have any severance. He'd done good work at Layered, but it hadn't gotten him anywhere. Or so he thought at the time.

Before too long, Vulcan was calling for Savoy. Allen began a habit with Layered that he continued through his myriad investment adventures over the years: He discovered new executives who he asked to join him on his journey. Savoy was one of them. Allen didn't have a job for him at Asymetrix, but he did need some help with Vulcan Northwest, where no single person was heading up tech investments. Savoy moved to Seattle and, at the age of 26, found himself in the position of handling much of Allen's $1 billion fortune.

Savoy did not prove to be a winning financial forecaster, but he was a helpful aid to Allen, who until now hadn't had anyone focusing exclusively on his business investments. Savoy went into Vulcan Northwest and started cleaning things up. "It's not like receipts were in shoeboxes, but they definitely needed to be organized," he later told *Bloomberg*. With Savoy's help, Allen launched Vulcan Ventures, a venture capital arm that would focus solely on his investments in businesses. Allen's sister Jody would manage the rest of his money.

Generally, venture capital firms get their money from a variety of sources and focus on a return on investment. They build up teams of investing partners who have hands-on experiences in the fields where the firm intends to invest. Vulcan Ventures was different. It was made up of Savoy and a few other folks, they did not have a specific investing mandate, and getting a return on investment wasn't the name of the game.

There really wasn't much of a game of any sort in 1990, when Savoy joined Vulcan. Investing at Vulcan was about putting money into the companies that caught Allen's interest, which was broad. He was interested in computers, but he really just wanted to find the coolest kinds of technologies out there. He found a local company called Virtual Vision that made a pair of goggles with built-in TV screens. You could look straight ahead and see everything, but if you looked down, you could watch a movie. (Truck drivers were one of the biggest groups of consumers at first, but many of them became distracted while driving. The company ultimately found greater success selling to dentists for patients who donned the goggles during treatment.) Another company that caught Allen's eye was Egghead, the software retailer. But the company that captured Allen's imagination and transformed Vulcan was a local Seattle company called SkyPix, which planned to beam interactive TV channels into people's homes. Now this was an idea that knocked Allen's socks off.

SkyPix was extremely futuristic. At a time when cable TV was 30 channels or fewer on some systems, this company promised to deliver 80 channels. What's more, the connections could be two-way, which meant it was the beginning of interactive TV, a ground-breaking notion that was just beginning to pick up followers in major media companies, where their leaders talked about a "500-channel universe."

Cable was looking passe, with all its heavy wires and maintenance issues. SkyPix had a different plan to get more channels into people's homes: satellite. The company owned one satellite and another transponder. But the really big deal was its technology, which could take digital TV signals and compress them so that six channels could be fed through a single channel, where only one could go before.

Big names lined up to get involved with SkyPix. GTE inked a deal to provide uplink and playback services for its direct-broadcast satellite service (as it was called) in exchange for use of SkyPix's compression technology. Mitsubishi wanted to finance the production of its receivers. Home Shopping Network wanted to invest $30 million, as well as assume responsibility for back-office operations like customer service.

A demo version of SkyPix was ready for the 1991 Consumer Electronics Show in Las Vegas, and it was one of the biggest crowd-pleasers the show had ever seen.

SkyPix was so hot that cable operators were downplaying its advantages. Cable titan John Malone called it "an early, primitive, hard-wired form." Cable companies had teamed up to launch their own direct-broadcast satellite service called Primestar, and NBC and News Corp. prepared to launch a $1 billion

DBS venture called Sky Cable. SkyPix was exciting because its technology compressed video and added interactivity.

The company had been started by Frederick and Richard Greenberg, two brothers from New York. In the 1980s, the Greenbergs had run their own bank, First City National Bank & Trust. They had also been investors in a variety of areas, including media, entertainment, and real estate. They were involved in Hollywood finance several times, pulling together partnerships to back movies. When they stumbled across this video compression technology, they decided to buy in and built a company around it, adding some 100 employees in Seattle and New York.

The brothers Greenberg didn't pay their SkyPix employees well, but instead bestowed on them huge amounts of stock options that, with all the buzz, was expected to be very valuable in the near future. Employees happily set about putting together the SkyPix service. Rights to movies and videos were secured; a few services were set up like ordering pizza over the SkyPix connection; the engineers got to work on the set-top box that would receive it all. There was a lot of excitement around the place. "We all worked so hard," says one former SkyPix engineer.

But SkyPix had many troubles. First, the technology was never ready on time, and it was expensive—it cost $500 to build each box. The Greenbergs needed to raise more money, but were having trouble. Investors were skeptical since the launch date kept getting pushed back, but they were even more troubled by events around the Greenbergs. In 1991, word leaked out of an ongoing grand-jury investigation into their activities in the 1980s. As heads of their bank—which had been quietly shut down in 1989 by government officials—the brothers Greenberg were accused of lending money to partnerships and companies they controlled in violation of insider-trading laws. The news all but scared off investors and new sources of funding seemed hopeless for SkyPix by the fall of 1991.

That's when Allen stepped up to the plate with $15 million. To Allen, the investment gave him entree to SkyPix to have a look around.

The Greenbergs continued to try to raise more money, but they were having no luck doing that. Even with Allen's $15 million, unpaid bills were piling up. Finally, frustrated employees and creditors banded together and sued the company in the summer of 1992, demanding payment. SkyPix was forced to file for bankruptcy protection.

That didn't throw Allen. By now, he'd decided he liked what he saw in SkyPix and was prepared to rescue it. SkyPix represented something truly innovative to him. But Allen was no better for SkyPix than the Greenbergs. In fact, he was worse, since his interest had given demoralized SkyPix employees new hope that their great big experiment was going to finally see the light of day. During the bankruptcy proceedings, Allen submitted a restructuring plan to the courts in the hopes of gaining control of SkyPix. If all went according to his plan, he expected SkyPix to turn a profit of $42 million by as early as 1994. But Allen didn't get it. The Greenbergs got their company back, but turned again to Allen for help. Under his plan, Allen was going to put in $150 million, an amount the Greenbergs still wanted. Allen agreed to give the company the money, but he demanded control of the company in exchange; the Greenbergs said no. In the end, nobody won. When Allen found he couldn't run it himself, he walked. With no other hope, SkyPix folded.

Allen has often abandoned situations in this manner, and he's earned a reputation for it. His money has allowed him to automatically get what he wants, but even before he became rich, Allen was always pretty sure of himself. He had been right about BASIC, after all. He still believed he knew best where things were going. It made him difficult to get along with, as Stephen Burakoff found out at Layered.

Savoy managed to do okay with him, though. Now that Allen had the SkyPix experience, it was a different world at Vulcan. SkyPix had been a bust, to be sure, but for Allen, it was a turning point. With SkyPix, he became really excited about a new technology for the first time in years. He began to think only about a connected world and the technologies that could bring that world about. "TV will basically become a hybrid of television and the computer," he told the *Seattle Times* in 1992. "Eventually, there'll be a worldwide network that's a combination of existing phone companies, broadcast satellites, fiber optics and cable TV." Allen called it a "wired world."

Savoy took this as his cue. He told *Business Week* his job was to "listen very carefully to 'wired world' ideas articulated by Paul and invest in companies that fit with that vision." Allen kept thinking about this connected world with a hybrid machine in the home. He wondered aloud about what that meant. "Once everybody's wired up to this, what will they use it for? For archival purposes? Do you want to have a video pen pal in India? Do you want to track worldwide commodity prices? Do you want to sell some consulting service somewhere else in the world? Maybe we can create virtual-reality interfaces where you can take on different personalities, or just walk through huge sets of data looking for information about Paul Allen or [Trail Blazers guard] Clyde Drexler or whatever you want. . . . I'm trying to figure out what comes next," he said to *Fortune* in 1994.

By the end of 1992, he had it figured out. Computers, televisions and all those connections were headed toward a wired world. It was a theory that gave shape to a general vision he'd had. In 1974, he'd talked about a connected world with Bill Gates over lunch at Shakey's Pizza in Vancouver, Washington. Now, it was almost here. Not only was it really exciting that this wired world was unfolding, but it gave Allen another reason to believe he knew best about where technology was headed. The idea, after all, had been his two decades earlier.

Wired world could be a science fiction concept or a comic strip title, but Allen gave it his own definition. On his Web site, he set aside a special section to introduce visitors to the wired world, described as "millions of organizations and individuals connected through their computers." Rather broad, but it breaks down a little. There are four components needed to bring about the wired world: software "that searches, filters, and customizes information to make it useful"; hardware, like servers, phones, personal digital assistants; infrastructure like cable or satellite; and content, like music, movies, sports, or games.

Allen has never been a very vocal person publicly. But when it came to his wired world theory, he was suddenly loquacious. Thoughts raced through his head. He was eager to spread the word about the wired world and let people know it was coming. He took pains to describe exactly what was happening and give it all some context. He told *Fortune*, "Periodically, you have the potential to marry a couple of different technologies in a way that will really change things. It doesn't happen very often. The ability to use the microprocessor in a general-purpose computer was one of them. Another was the development of the graphical user interface at Xerox PARC. Microsoft's Windows operating system sprung out of that. The marriage of video technology, computer technology and networking is another sea change, where you try to ride the incredible wave that's coming. That's the core convergence of ideas for the information superhighway. So you say, 'Okay, we're getting a whole new medium here. What can we really do that people haven't thought about in their individual areas?' It's not just showing movies on demand. What wholly new applications and user interfaces and products and services can you deliver?" When it came to the wired world, the publicity-shy Allen was a chatterbox!

The wired world remained broadly defined, but, at least, it gave Savoy something to do with all those billions left in his lap. Allen's wealth by 1995 had accumulated to $6.1 billion, two-thirds of it in Microsoft money. Microsoft's successes had cleared one hurdle after another, each time sending its stock soaring. In 1995, excitement built up behind Microsoft's forthcoming launch of the operating system Windows95, its most ambitious and highly anticipated product yet. Already Allen's shares had increased in number through three 2-for-1 and two 3-for-2 stock splits since Microsoft went public in 1986. The performance of Allen's Microsoft shares alone vaulted him from the No. 16 spot on *Forbes*'s list in 1994 to No. 4 in 1995. Allen badly needed these gains; his other investments weren't performing nearly as well.

As an investor, Allen wasn't out to make money; he didn't need to. "I can afford to do riskier things than most venture capitalists," he said. "I can just swallow hard and say, 'Okay, if I lose $50 million on this, then fine. I've got three or four other things going, and some of those came in.'" Of the hundreds of proposals that crossed Savoy's desk each year, he recommended dozens to Allen and maybe a few would get funded. Together, they set out to build the wired world. Savoy would negotiate on behalf of Vulcan. For Allen, Vulcan was about the "psychic rewards of making products that people enjoy, and have fun doing it." He was blatantly less concerned about pushing companies to profitability.

Even if Allen wasn't out to make money, he often had a magic touch. The simple knowledge of his investment could increase a company's value overnight. When Vulcan invested in wireless services company Metricom in 1993, for example, that company's shares surged 29 percent in a single day. Allen took a 14.6 percent stake in online financial data provider Telescan in November 1993, when shares were trading at $1.75; by the following July, shares had increased to $6. Egghead Software, the retail chain, saw its shares climb thanks to Allen's investment; and America Online, back in 1993 an also-ran in online services, got a boost from Allen's 18 percent stake.

To some degree, Allen was proving a better investor than entrepreneur. In 1994, Vulcan invested $20 million in the direct-broadcast satellite company United States Satellite Broadcast Co. (USSB) for a 3.9 percent stake. Allen turned that into $46 million. A 6.4 percent stake in information technology security company Certicom doubled his $18 million investment.

With all of these investments, Allen was pulling together various pieces that he hoped would combine to create a wired world. Metricom provided the wireless connection; Telescan offered a service accessible through these connections; Egghead was the place where some of the hardware and software was purchased; AOL was both the connection and the services. USSB extended Allen's initial interest in satellite delivery of interactive communications; Certicom was a way to keep it all protected. For the most part, Allen invested in small companies where he'd have a better chance of integrating his wired world idea. Allen was gaining a reputation as a dabbler, while he insisted it was all part of a wired world strategy. "The unique thing I look for in investments is breakthrough technology that can tie in or benefit from the things I'm doing in the other organizations I've invested in," he said to *Fortune.*

Part of his grand plan was to have the various companies he invested in work with each other, though that wasn't the only goal. He was also just placing bets in companies that represented elements of the wired world as he envisioned it. To the extent that he encouraged some sort of cooperative building of that world, Allen created an annual conference for the top executives of his companies and called it the "Synergy Summit." Each summer, Vulcan-backed executives descended on some up-scale place like the Phoenician Hotel in Scottsdale, Arizona, as they did one summer. Allen was there; so was Savoy. The CEO of one former Vulcan-backed company recalls arriving at the hotel and, passing the basketball courts, spotted a rather large man playing basketball with a very small one. They were Allen and Savoy, putting in a game of hoops before the conference events started.

The event usually began with a few words from Allen; nothing special, just a welcome to his executives. Days were filled with presentations from his myriad holdings giving updates on what they were doing. Nights featured sumptuous spreads and live entertainment. Often, Allen, a passionate amateur guitarist who held on to his childhood enthusiasm for Jimi Hendrix, would take the stage with the band. Allen said he was out to bring his various holdings together into one big picture, but he didn't give them much direction on how that would happen. He just threw them all together and hoped "ideas" would spark.

On rare occasions, Allen invested in mature companies. Generally, he wasn't as interested in these companies, because he couldn't see how they could move quickly into his wired world. But in 1994, Ticketmaster fit into the wired world because it was a service that people might want to get over their computers, instead of going to a ticketing booth. They were already ordering tickets over the phone; why wouldn't they want to order them online?

In a stock deal that valued Ticketmaster at $300 million, Allen acquired an 80 percent stake and control of the company. "Ticketing just naturally seemed like something you'll want to do in this wired world," he said.

For Allen, the stake in Ticketmaster also brought entree into a world he was enamored of. Located 1,000 miles-plus to the south of Seattle in Los Angeles, Ticketmaster was in the heart of Hollywood, maker of the movies he adored. By controlling

Ticketmaster, Allen became the newest member of the Hollywood elite, owner of one of the most powerful companies in the live-events business. He was invited to affairs where he began meeting stars in the music and movie industries.

Ticketmaster was very important to Allen, but he didn't run the company; he never ran his companies, although he usually had a huge influence. Not so, here. The operations of the company fell under the purview of 15-year Ticketmaster CEO Fred Rosen. Rosen had been with Ticketmaster since it was owned by the Chicago-based Pritzker family who sold it to Allen. Rosen had never wanted the Pritzkers to sell out—his suggestion had been to go public. He didn't have any ownership stake in the company, so a sale would mean nothing to him financially, despite all the years he'd put into the company. When the Pritzkers decided to sell, Rosen planned to leave.

Allen asked Rosen to stay. Rosen wanted full control of the company. After some negotiation, Rosen agreed to stay and Allen steered clear. Occasionally, he gave Ticketmaster ideas, and even put some pressure on Rosen to use some of them, like launching a magazine (which it did) and a TV show (which never materialized). Allen was also helpful in mediating at least one situation, when Ticketmaster and Microsoft scuffled over an unauthorized link to the Ticketmaster Web site from Microsoft's Sidewalk site. Another time, Allen arranged for Starwave to help Ticketmaster build its Web site. Naturally, Ticketmaster executives were invited to attend his annual Synergy Summit.

To the hoi polloi at Ticketmaster, Allen was a guy who knew computers. On one visit to Ticketmaster offices, Allen helped Rosen figure out how to work his computer. (Rosen hadn't had a computer before.) Another time, one former senior executive nearly mistook Allen for a tech-support staffer. During his first few weeks, the executive was having trouble with his computer and popped his head out of his office to call for help. Looking down the hall, he spotted Allen. "He was dumpy. He was wearing navy Dockers, a tattered shirt, and this scraggly beard," says the executive. "I was new to the company and I thought he was the IT guy." The executive stopped himself before asking the chairman of Ticketmaster into his office for IT assistance.

The staffers at Ticketmaster never really got to know their big boss. He wasn't around much, and when he was, they didn't realize who he was.

Clearly, Allen was an awkward fit at the nontechie Ticketmaster, but he tagged along on one company retreat at a resort in Santa Barbara, California, anyway. While the senior executives knew full well who Allen was, the rest of the staff didn't. Allen preferred those people, who were less obsequious. "He wanted to hang out with mid-level people," says the former Ticketmaster executive. "Everyone was sitting by the pool, and when he heard they were going shopping, he said he wanted to go, too. Those people were too young to be intimidated." They thought nothing of Allen's position in the company relative to theirs and let him tag along. At another event, Ticketmaster's annual retreat in Aspen, Colorado, Allen had former Eurythmics guitarist Dave Stewart along with him, to the bewilderment of other company executives, who were still trying to figure him out. "He seemed to cultivate the 'cool rich guy' thing," says a former Ticketmaster executive.

After four years of controlling Ticketmaster, Allen got out. He had never been all that involved in the company, aside from a few moments of synergy, here and there, and it hadn't ever really connected with his other holdings. By this time, May 1997, Allen was also very secure in his Hollywood standing. In 1995, he had become the primary backer of the new Hollywood studio DreamWorks SKG, so he now had a regular table at the hotspots in town. Allen bailed out of Ticketmaster once a suitor came calling.

The sale of Ticketmaster was a money-maker for Allen. In November 1996, seven months before Allen agreed to sell, Ticketmaster pulled off an IPO that valued the company at $494.2 million. Allen held 12.3 million shares, trading at the time at $12.75 each.

The interested buyer was media mogul Barry Diller, who saw Ticketmaster as an opportunity to grow his own empire, which then included QVC and the Home Shopping Network. He offered Allen 7.2 million shares of HSN valued at about $209 million. Allen made $40 million on the deal.

Allen's obliviousness to business, his inability to get a standout success behind him after Microsoft and the fact of his accumulating fortune coming almost entirely from a single source inspired one publication in 1994 to famously dub him the "accidental zillionaire," a tag that has stuck with him ever since. Some executives who have worked closely with him say that for Allen, the title is as much of a nag on his conscience as his frustration that Bill Gates sometimes gets all of the credit for Microsoft, while Allen is overlooked.

A story, in the popular, glossy tech magazine *Wired*, was the first real scrutiny of Allen as a businessman. It gave him full credit for his role in co-creating Microsoft, but pointed out that he had less luck starting companies, and his returns on investment were just so-so (Virtual Vision, Egghead, and others—Lone Wolf Technologies, Trilobyte, Medio Multimedia—ultimately folded after Allen had given them several rounds of cash). Allen wasn't happy about the article. So unhappy, went one rumor that spread through the *Wired* offices, he was preparing to buy up every copy of the issue with this story. He never did. He did, however, carry a grudge against the magazine and everyone associated with it. "He became mortal enemies with *Wired*," says a former top executive at the magazine.

At an industry party a few months after the story was published, his grudge was apparent. He'd just been introduced to Charlie Jackson, cofounder of the company that developed multimedia software Flash. Jackson's first company, Silicon Beach, had been sold to Aldus Corporation for $25.5 million in 1990.

Jackson was a rich-guy tech investor and, Allen was about to learn, also one of the first backers of *Wired* magazine. As soon as he heard that, Allen's demeanor changed from pleasant to prickly, according to Jackson. "Oh—*Wired's* not my favorite magazine," he said. With that, he turned abruptly away from Jackson and took up conversation with others in their circle. He never spoke to Jackson again.

A couple of years later, Allen's office turned on *Wired*. The magazine had launched a Web site, www.wired.com, and Allen's office felt the domain name was too close to Allen's trademarked wired world. They suggested to *Wired* executives that they might sue, but never followed through.

The "accidental zillionaire" moniker was something that irked not only Allen, but his top financial lieutenant, Savoy, too. In an interview with *Bloomberg* many years later, Savoy said he was seeking vindication for his boss. "Ten years from now, I want people saying we were right in seeing the coming of the 'wired world,' and we knew what to do when it arrived," he said.

7

# THE AOL EXPERIENCE

I n 1992, America Online was a scrappy little start up. It had $21 million in revenues and a $66 million IPO behind it, but it was still very small in the big world of media. Among other online companies, AOL was nearly an also-ran, compared to two others, CompuServe and Prodigy, which had far more subscribers and, importantly, many more deep-pocketed backers.

But AOL was intriguing to Paul Allen. Allen had learned about the company through Interval Research CEO David Liddle's wife, Ruthann Quindlen, who was among the people at investment bank Alex.Brown who handled AOL's IPO. She and Liddle convinced Allen that AOL was an interesting company and a wise financial play, so on IPO day, March 19, 1992, Allen scooped up 50,000 shares at $11.50 apiece.

AOL was at a turning point. The seven-year-old company, formerly known as Quantum Computer Services, had recently provided customized online services for computer makers like Apple and Commodore. These companies would bundle the online services with the rest of the software on their machines; Quantum would be paid a fee for its work, or earn income when people subscribed to the services. In 1991, Quantum branched out aggressively into a new area by creating its own service, called America Online, to go after Prodigy and CompuServe, which had been in the market since the early 1980s.

Little AOL had formidable competitors to beat. CompuServe, which was owned by tax company H&R Block, boasted 1.1 million subscribers who paid $7.95 per month to use the service. Prodigy was a joint venture of IBM and Sears, Roebuck & Co. It was a powerhouse with 1.75 million who paid $12.95 each month for access. AOL, with just 180,000 subscribers, didn't really play in this space. It was more like some of the other lower-tier Internet services of the day, General Electric's GEnie and Delphi Internet Services, which had just started up and were looking for customers.

But AOL had gone public to pay off debts and grow AOL into a bigger player in the online services area. Now, AOL had shareholders to please. They needed more subscribers and fast, either through their own service, or through deals with other computer makers. They'd put more of an effort behind the AOL service and brand name, but also expanded the distribution strategy to include going back to the computer manufacturers and asking them to bundle AOL's branded service alongside the customized versions AOL had created for them in the past. It really was the only choice, anyway; both Prodigy and CompuServe had already found distribution through computer companies, too. AOL needed a strategy to keep up.

To consumers in 1992, subscribing to an online service meant getting content like news and information, shopping opportunities, and message boards. It was all about subscribers interacting with other subscribers on the same service. These services were usually completely separate from the Internet, meaning subscribers to an online service could only do or read as much as was available on that service. The practice led to the coining of the phrase "walled garden" to describe AOL and other services.

Of the two market leaders, Prodigy was very consumer-oriented, with many shopping services; CompuServe targeted the business community with financial data and related information. AOL decided to be a really easy-to-use service, since some people complained that Prodigy and CompuServe were difficult to navigate. In 1992, personal computers were an increasingly common household appliance, but most Americans weren't using them everyday. AOL wanted to make computers and modem communications less scary and technical, so they offered no whiz-bang features and rigged a service with clickable open-and-close screens, like the word-processing applications many people were using. It was very basic. Subscribers could find magazines and some shopping on the service; then they would go to chat rooms and type in messages in real-time, almost as if they were talking on the telephone.

The future was never certain at AOL. The tiny Vienna, Virginia, company had high hopes and just 136 employees. A young and ambitious senior executive named Steve Case was in charge. He based his decisions on his vision: He believed that the world was going to want to get connected through their computers. AOL could provide an online service where everyone would want to be. It didn't sound all that different from Allen's wired world.

Steve Case had come to AOL by way of a marketing job at Pizza Hut. He was low-key and casual. He wore khakis to work and didn't say much. He quietly observed other people, markets, and the way his online service was being used by customers. He wasn't a brash CEO or a big salesman. He was a genuinely shy man. He was nearly the opposite of the tech industry's mascot, Bill Gates, except that he was fiercely driven and devoted to his company. But Case was also like Paul Allen; he loved technology and the way it could be used by consumers. He had early visionary experiences like Allen. In 1983, he'd seen a demonstration of an online service and became hooked on its potential. Unlike Allen, he wasn't a feature-freak; he pushed for simplicity in AOL. He wanted lots of people to be able to use it, and he listened to their feedback and observed their habits. People were spending a lot of time in communications areas like e-mail and chat. He built up those areas and made them the main draw to AOL.

Case kept things simple with customers, but he pushed the envelope behind the scenes. It was a balance that worked. In 1987, he inked a couple of risky deals with Apple, Commodore, and Tandy that left the balance of the expenses in Quantum's lap. Quantum's board of directors wasn't happy to learn about the deals and almost fired Case. But he remained and the deals ultimately paid off. Case established a tradition of giving products away up front with expectations of future profit, like when AOL later earned a reputation for mailing out free copies of its software to get customers to sign up for the service.

It helped that Case wasn't the end of the line. He had shareholders and a board of directors, who kept him in check. It was a balance that served AOL's success in the 1990s. With Case as its fearless, visionary leader, AOL also had a board and other executives to give Case a dose of reality when he began believing a little naively in the future. It was the board that stepped in when Case began believing in one particular preying shareholder: Allen.

In its earliest days as a consumer online service, what AOL needed more than anything else was aggressive growth. It needed customers and a higher profile. At first, Allen's interest was greatly welcomed.

In 1992, when he invested in America Online, Allen was caught up in SkyPix and Starwave and piecing together his grand wired world vision. He had figured out that the connections between people—whether satellite, cable, fiber-optic, or telephone—were key to bringing the wired world together. He really wanted to be the guy who made the wired world happen, so he had bought SkyPix. He had good vision; he should have been given the reigns, he believed. He had a good gut about these things and when it told him to do something, he felt he should act fast. When he had seen the *Popular Electronics* cover in 1974, he urged Bill Gates to get moving *pronto* on BASIC. It had been the right move. Now, he wanted to get going on the wired world—before it was too late.

He had acquired shares in AOL partly as a favor to Liddle and Quindlen, but once he did, he started thinking more about this little company in Virginia. Online services weren't something he'd really pursued so far, but maybe there was something there. They were the connections into people's homes, and they controlled everything consumers saw on the service. In some ways, these online services had created their own wired worlds.

Allen's wired world was far more interesting than theirs, though. In his view, our connected universe was more than just some static pages with stories on them, or online catalogs offering goods and services. Those were important features, and he'd even considered having Starwave create catalogs online, but he had bigger plans for the wired world. He wanted to send movies and music to people over two-way connections that let people from all over interact with each other and with the things they received over the service. The wired world was also very open; it wasn't a "walled garden" at all. That perception would prove troublesome when it came time for Case and Allen to tango.

One thing Allen did like about the online services of the day was the fact that people were congregating there. Subscribers were creating communities on the online services. AOL's chat rooms were among the most popular and they ultimately drove the company to success, as subscribers told their friends about the service and wanted on, too.

But that wasn't the only reason AOL was appealing. Allen liked AOL also because it was fairly small, and it was independent. The company had shareholders to serve, but it wasn't at the mercy of a huge bureaucratic structure, the way Prodigy and CompuServe were. AOL was a company he could influence and possibly control fully. Allen doesn't get involved half way with companies he finds interesting. If he's turned his attention on a company, it's because he sees a grand plan for the company and wants it implemented.

AOL was a perfect component of his own vision. AOL was developing strong relationships with its customers; Allen had ideas about how to expand those simple communications into bigger, more interactive relationships over open, broadband connections. A major thing he objected to with AOL was its proprietary technology. He had always focused on making technologies available to the widest group of people possible. That's what BASIC had been about: an easy-to-use language that could become a standard. Asymetrix's ToolBook was also meant to be available to anyone. AOL's closed environment bugged Allen. It was the one big thing he would change if he were in charge. He would push AOL to get out onto the Internet and move into broadband as quickly as possible, before anyone else got there. Cable and satellite companies were hungrily eyeing high-speed connections and Allen thought they might be the first to deliver the much-hyped 500-channel universe if he didn't act fast. He told Savoy to buy more shares in AOL.

At first, it looked to the passing observer like Allen was just being a rich-guy investor who had a knack for technology and had picked AOL as a company with a bright future. But less than a month after AOL's IPO debut, Allen bought an additional 248,000 shares for between $11 and $14 each. With some other shares picked up along the way, Allen now had around 365,000 shares out of the company's 5 million or so outstanding shares; it gave him about a 7.3 percent stake in the company. In the fall, he went back for more. Between October 1 and October 5, 1992,

Allen spent $1.9 million for 150,000 shares. Prodigy and Com-puServe were considered the stars of the online services sector, but Allen had chosen to back tiny little AOL.

Allen's investment activity was very exciting for AOL. In-vestors on Wall Street sat up and took notice of Allen's interest. He was the cofounder of the hugely successful Microsoft and the country's tenth richest person worth $2.4 billion. As an investor in tech firms, he had begun throwing very large sums of cash around—or at least threatening to, in the case of SkyPix—and was considered a visionary in technology. When it came to AOL, Allen said it looked like a good investment to him. With a stake greater than 5 percent, he was required to report his intention to the Securities & Exchange Commission. In a filing, he said he held the shares as an investment only. Investors started lining up.

"Paul validated the company," says a former financial analyst. "He took it from a $20 stock to a $60 stock."

As AOL's share price went up, people started believing in the scrappy online service, which had just 5 percent of the online ser-vices market, compared to the 30 percent that Prodigy and Com-puServe each boasted.

AOL still needed the help. Besides their two existing competi-tors, AOL executives were growing anxious over news from Red-mond, Washington, where Microsoft was getting serious about its own online service, for now called Marvel. By this point in the game, Microsoft had earned a reputation for overcoming the com-petition in markets it entered. Allen himself had experienced that firsthand with two of Asymetrix's products, first ToolBook and then the slide-show presentation software Compel, which were each handily beat by Microsoft's Visual Basic and PowerPoint. At AOL, the executives' main strategy was focused on keeping Microsoft at bay. Becoming a higher profile company would help. They looked on eagerly as Allen continued to buy in and lend further credibility to their company.

By fall, Allen held 746,000 shares in the company (he'd made other, smaller transactions along the way, via Savoy). It gave him a 13.5 percent stake. As the months wore on, he picked up more shares. All of a sudden, AOL's board was a little nervous: Was Allen really just in it for an investment? He'd become very aggressive, buying up many shares in just a matter of months. Soon enough, they'd learn more about his real interest—the wired world—and the way he operated. When Allen saw the way things should be, he usually paid little mind to the interests of other parties. He just pushed ahead with what he wanted, and, since he was concerned about being first with an idea, he often didn't tell people his plans, just as he'd kept mum about Asymetrix and Crucible. It made a lot of people uncomfortable, but it was the way Allen liked to get things done: his way.

As the board started asking questions about his investment, Steve Case and Paul Allen arranged to meet at tech conference PC Forum in early spring 1993 to get to know each other better. They planned a more formal meeting later, where Allen and Savoy presented their ideas for AOL. They wanted AOL to forget about its "walled garden," low-tech approach and start thinking fast about broadband. Allen's wasn't the wrong approach, since, ultimately, that's where it was all headed. But if AOL had abandoned its easy-to-use approach at a time when many modems were just 9600 baud over telephone connections (very, very low-speed), it probably never would have made it through the 1990s to become a dot-com success story with a market cap big enough to dwarf major media companies like Time Warner, which it acquired in 2000. (AOL's own story eventually played out like a dot-com failure, though, after its acquisition of Time Warner.)

AOL executives disagreed with Allen and made no plans to change course.

A llen couldn't get anywhere with AOL. He had all these great
ideas for the company, and they weren't listening. But AOL
executives weren't just afraid of Allen. Like him, they were
nervous people, too, and they thought perhaps he was doing
Microsoft's bidding to either strangle AOL or surreptitiously
merge it with Microsoft. In their eyes, Allen's role in creating
Microsoft made him just as much a representative of that company as Gates.

Despite the meeting's outcome, Allen had become really interested in America Online for his wired world. He told Savoy to
buy more shares. Throughout March and April 1993, Allen acquired another 12.4 percent of AOL's shares in a number of separate purchases. In the first 10 days of May, Allen sold off 700,000
shares of Microsoft, which made many people think he was building up cash reserves to acquire AOL outright.

The sale gave him about $65 million, which would have been
enough to buy a third of AOL's 6.7 million outstanding shares to
add to the 24.9 percent he owned at that point. AOL's stock
jumped $4.50 to $30.50 as hordes of investors hastily traded
shares in anticipation of a takeover by Allen, which they viewed
as good for AOL, since he was a solid investor with an endless
supply of cash to pour into the company. But on May 3, 1993,
Allen said in an SEC filing that he had no intention of doing so;
he again said his interest was merely as an investment.

But Allen also wanted to influence AOL executives and he
wanted to pair AOL with some of his other holdings. The only
thing he managed to get done was a deal between AOL and
Ticketmaster to develop ticketing services online.

By now, AOL executives were almost too late to prevent Allen
from gaining a greater role in the company. He now had 24.9 percent. If he held more than 25 percent, he was automatically due a
board seat. That was the last thing AOL executives wanted. They

didn't like Allen's ideas, and they did not like the way they felt misled about his interests. A board meeting was called to begin a "poison pill" defense. A "poison pill" maneuver is not something companies like to do. It floods the market with shares, but it also devalues those shares held by an unwanted shareholder, like Allen. It worked. Allen got the message, but he still tried to reason with AOL executives. "He did originally want to get more involved in the company and for a variety of reasons, [such as our] strategic alliance strategy, we just didn't think that was appropriate," Case told the *Washington Post* a year later. Among the few things Allen told AOL executives directly was, in a closed-door session that excluded Savoy, "This is America and I should be able to invest in AOL if I want to. What is wrong with that?"

Allen had a point. AOL executives insinuated to the press that they were caught off-guard by his investments, but in reality, AOL was no dummy company. It had savvy executives with years of corporate experience behind them on its board, including Silicon Valley venture capitalist Frank Caufield of the esteemed Kleiner, Perkins, Caufield & Byer, and a member from the Tribune Company. Former Secretary of State Alexander Haig was also on the AOL board.

"AOL wasn't totally blindsided by Allen, but they were apprehensive about his intentions," says the financial analyst who worked closely with AOL at the time. "But it's not surprising what happened. Here's Paul Allen. He's a visionary." And AOL needed his interest.

Besides, Case didn't really blame Allen as much as he blamed Savoy. In all the time that Allen's stake had grown, Savoy had personally insisted to Case and others that the moves were innocent. Case felt betrayed. He was hardly the only person ever to bristle from Savoy, but Allen's dalliances with AOL were the first high-profile example of how some people felt about Savoy: They thought he was arrogant in his post and they didn't trust him. Sometimes he bullied people and other times he didn't give them the full story. Savoy believed that his job was to make sure deals were structured in Allen's favor, sometimes at the expense of other investors. Eventually, this habit earned him a bad reputation. But in 1992, Steve Case, like most people, knew little about Savoy. He found out the hard way.

Allen finally got the message that AOL wouldn't be swayed and backed down. He seemed to go away for a while and became a passive investor in the company. Meanwhile, AOL soared. Through the end of 1993 and into 1994, AOL tripled its subscribers to nearly one million and saw its stock hit a high of $92 a share. Through deals with just about every major media company, AOL raised its profile. It was on its way to becoming a leading online service.

Allen grew tired of being a passive investor. If he couldn't do something with it, he didn't really want to be involved. Allen didn't pull his entire stake in one fell swoop, though. It took two quick hits in the summer and fall of 1994 and then he was finally rid of AOL.

On July 29, 1994, he halved what had become an 18 percent stake in AOL (after the poison-pill defense changed the proportion of his 24.9 percent stake) by dumping 733,000 shares. He made a $27 million profit, but other AOL investors weren't so lucky; shares lost 8.25 percent of their value that day and closed at $55.63 each. His next move was a sale of 150,000 shares during the week of September 12, 1994, lessening his stake by 2 percent. He was all but done with AOL. On September 19, he sold his remaining 548,000 shares and wiped his hands clean of AOL. The entire experience had gained him a $100 million profit.

Allen's pull-out was just as surprising to outside investors as his initial interest. "I got calls from every institutional investor asking me, 'Did we get bamboozled?' 'Does he know something we don't?' and Paul refused to discuss it," says the former financial analyst. It was typical Allen not to comment on anything he did—his aversion to publicity. His spokeswoman alluded to the wired world when she told reporters at the time why he pulled out: "A key criterion of Mr. Allen's investment strategy is to work with companies that can contribute to or benefit from the technology and strategy of other Paul Allen companies," the spokeswoman said, explaining Mr. Allen's exit. "The desired synergy was not realized with America Online."

The entire experience kept Allen's image as a respectable technology investor intact. The *Wired* story hadn't yet appeared calling him an "accidental zillionaire," and no one had really noticed that he wasn't getting very far with Asymetrix. Starwave and Interval Research were fledgling companies in 1994 and hadn't had time to prove themselves. Allen's investment track record was a new phenomenon, and his wired world theory wasn't as widely known. He was still very much of a mystery, and it worked in his favor.

By the time Allen pulled out of AOL completely, online services were starting to look antiquated, anyway. The World Wide Web had arrived, along with the popular browser company Netscape (which AOL later bought). Many analysts thought Allen looked smart for pulling out.

But if he'd held on, he could have been a billionaire by virtue of AOL stock. Thanks to the dot-com boom and six stock splits, AOL stock really began to pick up in value at the end of the decade. It hit a high of $175 in January 1999 after five stock-splits. Allen's pull-out looked wise enough at the time, but as the stock soared, it only made him look like even more of the "accidental zillionaire," since he lost a chance for a windfall of his own.

Allen's Microsoft earnings were constantly piling up, and he was having a hard enough time spending much of it before another deluge came in. The fact that he lost out on a couple of billion dollars only proved to anyone who was paying attention that Allen was never very interested in the machinations of Wall Street or finagling his finances to earn more billions; he was no Warren Buffett with a keen eye for valuable stocks, or even a passing interest in them. Allen was on a different mission: He was out to build the wired world . . . and have a little fun in the meantime.

8

# HOLLYWOOD, HERE HE COMES!

For a guy who said "cool" quite a lot, Paul Allen seemed more like his other favorite phrase: "huh." There was his appearance, for one matter. He was out-of-shape, his weight dragging low around his middle like a programmer who sits at his computer all day long. An overgrown beard hid the lower part of his face and the rest was nearly covered by large, wire-rim glasses. His clothes were not just uninspired, they were far from what you would expect from a billionaire: lumberjack-plaid shirts, department-store khakis, and brown loafers. He was a frumpy, unattractive guy, made worse by his height—over six feet—and the wide girth of his droopy middle.

It wasn't enough that Allen didn't look cool, he didn't act cool, either. People commented on how "nice" he was, but others said he wasn't very interesting, that he could be dreadfully boring, and sometimes even rude. He had a hard time making small talk, so in social settings, it was difficult to engage him. Once he did start talking, it was usually about something he had an interest in already, not necessarily anything that mattered to the other person. It made him a bore, though he didn't seem to notice it. For the most part, in social conversation, Allen said little.

Not a bit of it really matters, though, when you are the 13th richest person in the country, as Allen was in 1994, when he met

David Geffen, one of the "coolest" guys in Hollywood. Geffen had worked his way up through the corporate ranks of the entertainment business and partied his way through the social strata, dating Marlo Thomas and Cher before eventually coming out as a gay man. Geffen began as a mailroom clerk at a New York talent agency, became a favorite son of legendary Warner chief Steve Ross, and launched his own record label, Geffen Records, the most successful startup in American music. By the time he met Allen, Geffen was stylish but subdued, enjoyed buying and selling practically anything, and had never lost his love of doing business deals and making money. To Geffen, Allen probably didn't seem very hip, but that didn't really matter, since his $3 billion alone made him a very attractive potential deal partner. The two men met in 1994 at Herb Allen's annual mogul getaway, one of the most prestigious business events of the year. (Herb Allen is no relation to Paul Allen.)

Herb Allen was at the center of media and entertainment investment banking through the 1970s, 1980s, and 1990s. His firm, Allen & Co., had managed mergers, acquisitions, public offerings, and other major deals for some of the most important brands in business since the 1960s, beginning under his father. Allen, was a genuine Hollywood insider, having helped launch the studio Savoy Pictures in the late 1980s and managed the public offering of Imagine Entertainment, the studio started by the director Ron Howard. Back in New York City, where his firm was located close to Wall Street, Herb Allen had played a part in helping the Seagram Co. take a stake in Time Warner. He counted as past and present clients Coca-Cola, Blockbuster, Matsushita, Columbia Pictures, General Electric, and many more. Herb Allen was at the top of the list when anyone wanted to raise money, buy or sell a company, or float a company on the public stock market. Having Herb Allen involved lent cachet to a deal.

It wasn't hard for Herb Allen to draw people to his ranch in Sun Valley, Idaho, as he began doing in 1983. Since then, he had played host to a cadre of giants of the business world each July, and the get-togethers had grown in prestige and importance every year. Part tee-time, part deal-making, and only a small part a conference featuring presentations, Herb Allen's schmoozefests became the hottest ticket around, especially as deals began to take root on the greens of his property. The ball got rolling there on Disney's acquisition of Cap Cities/ABC in 1996, and so did an earlier deal between Turner Broadcasting and Castle Rock Entertainment. So popular were Allen's events, *Vanity Fair* dispatched photographer Annie Leibovitz to Sun Valley in 1994 to capture and make celebrities out of the moguls in attendance.

By dint of his role in Microsoft, Paul Allen had every right to be there, but it really was his money alone that made him more influential. In the 10 years heretofore, Allen had poured more than $1 billion into tech start-ups, and with that kind of money being thrown around, he was sure to have some say in the direction of media and technology. Herb Allen saw fit to invite Allen that year, as well as people like Disney CEO Michael Eisner, News Corp. chairman Rupert Murdoch, billionaire investor Warren Buffett, and then-powerful agent to the stars Michael Ovitz, who was chairman of the Creative Artist Agency. Naturally, Bill Gates was there, too, along with other tech stars like Andy Grove of Intel and Michael Dell. That July and every July before and since, Sun Valley becomes the epicenter of the American business network.

Allen wasn't just going through the motions in Sun Valley, but neither was he a maniacal deal-maker like many of the other guests were. So when he was wandering around the Sun Valley Lodge, where most of the guests stayed, or mingling near the golf course or tennis courts, he didn't eye his guests as deal targets, he didn't see the field as a chess board, as other moguls did. Allen was, after all, an "ideas man," as he once told a reporter. If anything, he was looking for some company. Geffen could do that. A master salesman, Geffen wove his way through a slew of topics until he found one that interested Allen. "We initially talked about art and struck up an instant rapport," Allen later recalled.

It wasn't long before David Geffen was a major influence in Allen's life, leading him through the glitzy world of Hollywood and helping him spend his money and put to good use his billionaire-boy's toys. Allen began flying his jets down to the Santa Monica Airport, landing pad of the rich and famous in Hollywood. Geffen would then lead him on a tour of dinners and parties, introducing him to stars like Jeanne Triplehorn and Carrie Fisher, producers Penny Marshall and Howard Rosenmann, all of them friends of Geffen's. Sometimes, Allen would sail his yacht, the Meduse, down to Los Angeles, dock it in Marina del Rey and the parties would begin there. Allen had stars in his eyes, and later giggled when he talked with one magazine reporter about meeting the celluloid of Los Angeles.

It appeared to some that Geffen didn't expect much of Allen. Allen would come to small, private dinners at Geffen's with movie stars and moneymen in attendance, and he wasn't counted on to contribute much. At one gathering, one of Hollywood's main financiers had joined Geffen, Allen, and another business partner for dinner at Geffen's home in Malibu. "We were talking about business, and Paul just sat there. He was very quiet, he never perked up," says the financier. Was Allen being shy? Maybe. But to this guy, Allen's lack of interest came off as rude.

Allen was enamored of Hollywood and knew he had Geffen to thank for it, but he had also been moody in the past with his investments. "He's so hard to know. He's introverted," says the financier (the financier says he would never do business with Allen because he's like this). In the past, Allen had resentfully pulled his money and influence from America Online and SkyPix when he didn't get his way. If Geffen wanted a deal from Allen, he was being wise to keep quiet about Allen's introverted demeanor.

In March 1995, eight months after they first met, Geffen and Allen became more than friends; they became inextricably joined through business when Allen sunk $500 million into Geffen's latest start-up.

The new venture was sparked by the departure of Jeffrey Katzenberg from Disney after he lost a bid for promotion to president of the company, a job that ultimately went to the talent agent Michael Ovitz. Katzenberg was out of work and looking for his next opportunity when he and pal Steven Spielberg decided to start their own film studio. They asked Geffen to join them. The launch was kicked off with a press extravaganza in Beverly Hills and the media quickly dubbed the three the "Dream Team."

The Dream Team had talents, connections, and influence, but they were short on cash and hadn't even named their new venture yet. Spielberg, Katzenberg, and Geffen had each put up $33 million for a total two-thirds stake in the venture. They needed far more if they were really going to get the studio going. They figured one billion dollars was the right figure, and offered up the remaining one-third of the company for that amount. Sometime in the winter months, Allen heard from Geffen. "He said, 'Hey Paul, Jeffrey Katzenberg, Steven Spielberg, and I are thinking of starting a new venture. If you'd like to look at investing in it, I can send you up some information,'" said Allen.

It wasn't the first time a movie studio had eyed Allen as a potential investor. Those looking for Allen's money had to get past his investment chief, Bill Savoy, who had seen many proposals from the entertainment industry. Savoy knew that the financial details of the movie business weren't very good. Studios spent millions to produce a film, its budget padded with the exorbitant salaries of stars, star directors, and costs for the latest technologies. Most films exceeded their budgets. Studios' best hopes were to cover their costs—forget about profit—and most of the income tended to come from international and video markets. Savoy wasn't very impressed by Hollywood. "Since 1990, I've looked at every movie studio opportunity that's been available in the marketplace but every company looks the same if you sit down and run pro formas," a ho-hum Savoy told the *Red Herring*. "What it comes down to is having a group of people that can deliver what the spreadsheet says."

Allen gave Savoy Geffen's "information" to look over, but he was really only going through the motions. Since meeting at Herb Allen's in Sun Valley, Geffen and Allen had developed a friendship that superceded the normal new-business motions. In March 1995, Allen became an investor, with an 18 percent stake, and the Dream Team unveiled their new name, Dream-Works SKG.

Allen invested his money (borrowing against Microsoft stock for the stake, per his usual style of investing) and DreamWorks got its name. But unlike the earlier press event, this news received little attention, despite the sizable amount of Allen's investment or that it meant DreamWorks could become a reality now that it had padded its coffers. Instead, Bill Gates, Allen's foil, came along and stole the show, snookering Allen yet again. Not one week after Allen's investment had closed with almost no fanfare, Gates and the three partners were sitting high on director's chairs before yet another troupe of fawning press, announcing a Microsoft relationship with DreamWorks. Microsoft would put $100 million into the company for a very small stake, and the two would form a joint venture to develop multimedia titles called Dream-Works Interactive. Media the world over covered the event, and the DreamWorks partners gained credibility for their new venture, with the great business success story Microsoft behind them. Allen's investment was occasionally mentioned in these articles, usually only as an afterthought.

I n four years, DreamWorks turned out several films, but many were duds, including the Nicole Kidman/George Clooney film

*The Peacemaker,* DreamWorks' first feature, and the animated film *Small Soldiers.* The TV unit produced bombs, too, including a much-hyped but short-lived show starring Ted Danson and Mary Steenburgen. DreamWorks Interactive wasn't having much luck, either, and found itself buried under competition from Sony, Nintendo, and Electronic Arts. The company was in financial shambles. In the summer of 1998, investor Cheil Jedang, a South Korean food company, pulled the $320 million stake it had put into DreamWorks. (Allen came to the rescue, quickly picking up half of Cheil Jedang's stake and increased his holdings in the company to 24 percent, making him the largest shareholder in DreamWorks.) By the measure of hordes of reporters, DreamWorks wasn't looking like much of a success. It looked more like an abominable failure.

But Allen was having fun, despite the poor performance of DreamWorks. He had always loved movies; he was a movie junkie. In his home, he had built a plush, 20-seat cinema with an actual concession stand in the lobby, calling it the Allen Estate Theater. More than 2,000 titles were available for viewing at any time. He often invited employees over for a "movie night" and he made the theater a regular, proud stop on the tour of his home on Mercer Island for his visitors.

However, Allen the movie junkie was also Allen the self-professed "ideas man." He had many ideas for entertainment with a technology twist. "What if the hero made decision B rather than decision A," he suggested during an interview with the *Los Angeles Times.* "Maybe it's a dynamic virtual experience where you are in there with a bunch of other people who are representing other roles in the story and you are making rules in real time."

But no one in Hollywood was listening to Allen. Allen would fly down to Los Angeles for meetings at DreamWorks for presentations. Even though DreamWorks was a star-studded Hollywood studio, it was still a Paul Allen company, and therefore just as obligated to keep Allen posted on what was happening with his money . . . sort of. "Paul would come down and talk to the partners and some of the employees. There were meetings with the senior staff. And then there would be time set aside for people to ask Paul questions about what was happening in technology," says a former DreamWorks executive.

DreamWorks execs listened, but they didn't do much more than that. When Allen brought some of his specific ideas to Spielberg, Katzenberg, or Geffen, they didn't go any further. There was never any mandate to DreamWorks executives to push the digital envelope in their work, or any internal pressures to think about other Allen companies and what they were doing. Maybe Allen didn't put more pressure on the partners because he believed in them more than any other group of people he had ever backed. Says the former executive, "Paul looks at Steven, Jeffrey, and David, and he knows they know how to run movies, TV, and music." Or maybe those three didn't want someone without any entertainment experience telling them how to run their business, even if he did happen to have a lot of money and was a big shareholder in the company.

Geffen continued to be an influence on Allen. He suggested Allen reconsider his facial hair and trade in the glasses for a pair of square-frame, hard-rim specs. "I did mention to Paul that he might look better without a beard," Geffen told *Rolling Stone*. Off came the beard, more clearly revealing Allen's placid face; the glasses highlighted his translucent blue eyes. Geffen's entertainment-biz friends had front-row seats in the transformation of Paul Allen from technology nerd to, well, technology nerd who hangs out in Hollywood. Howard Rosenmann was one of Geffen's friends who saw it happen. "It was just like Candide," he said, "in which David played the role of Dr. Pangloss, the sophisticated man who teaches the humble Candide how the world works."

DreamWorks wasn't working out very well as a business, but the investment was otherwise paying off: Allen was learning about "cool."

DreamWorks eventually turned a corner and earned itself an enviable reputation in Hollywood. Part of the problem with the shoddy film releases had been that DreamWorks' star filmmaker, Steven Spielberg himself, was wrapped up in commitments he'd made before DreamWorks was formed. In 1997, he freed himself up and began work on *Saving Private Ryan*, which DreamWorks produced. The next year, in 1998, *Saving Private Ryan* put the new studio on the map as it won over moviegoers, earning millions at the box office. A film the following year, however, really gave DreamWorks' partners and investors reason to gloat. *American Beauty* was released by DreamWorks and not only earned a place in consumers' hearts and wallets, but also won an Oscar in 2000. *American Beauty* gave DreamWorks an Oscar (well, five of them, including "best picture"), a necessary prize for any respectable studio.

For Allen, it was Oscar-schmoscar. He loved his Hollywood parties and his Hollywood friends, but the navel-gazing importance of the Oscars was lost on him. Sure, he showed up at DreamWorks' post-Oscar party at the swank Spago restaurant in Beverly Hills, where he mingled with California governor Gray Davis, the astronaut Buzz Aldrin, and of course the cast of the movie and the three DreamWorks principals. But Allen, who normally appeared stoic, again stood poker-faced in a chat with Geffen when a reporter from the British magazine *Empire* came up to the two moguls with the question, "How does it feel to win your first Oscar?" Allen failed to offer much of an answer so Geffen jumped in to cover for his friend. "This is his first film company," Geffen said with a chuckle.

Geffen knew well enough that it wasn't Allen's first film company and that Allen was no stranger to the artifacts and accoutrements of Hollywood. But by this point, March 2000, Allen may have become somewhat skeptical of the rituals of fame by his own brush with a little too much attention where he really didn't want it.

Paul Allen's first business deal in Hollywood wasn't Dream-Works. By the time he was signing checks for Geffen, Katzen-berg, and Spielberg, Allen had already set up shop in Los Angeles, on trendy Robertson Boulevard, next door to New Line Cinema, the edgy independent film studio, and across the street from the Ivy, restaurant-to-the-stars. But DreamWorks, though at first a money-loser, would turn out to be a more stress-free investment.

This first Hollywood venture, called Storyopolis, was a company backed by Allen to the tune of $1.25 million to develop children's books, movies, and TV shows. It was part art gallery, part entertainment studio, and all about children's stories. The company set up a storefront on Robertson to sell classic and popular works of children's literature and showcase art by storybook illustrators, while behind the scenes, Storyopolis executives optioned children's stories and turned them into films, TV programs, and multimedia. Immediately, Storyopolis began developing plans for movies and TV shows for *Bloom County* illustrator Berkeley Breathed's *Red Ranger Came Calling* and Ralph Steadman's *I, Leonardo*. Warner Bros. signed on for the rights to a first look at anything Storyopolis produced. After a splashy launch party, Storyopolis began shaping up to be a solid business with a bit of star quality. Said Storyopolis's spokeswoman, "It's Paul Allen's first toehold in Hollywood." Soon enough, however, Allen would find himself swept under a current by the force of drama at Storyopolis.

The new company was the brainchild of Abbie Phillips. Phillips, a married mother of two, was a former biologist who, with two partners, had launched an art gallery-cum-bookstore in 1988 in Los Angeles that was dedicated to children's books and their illustrators, called Every Picture Tells a Story. After a falling out with one of the partners in 1994, Phillips took her original concept for an art gallery/bookstore and added a Hollywood twist. When, through mutual friends in Hollywood, she managed to present her proposal to Allen, he liked the idea; put in for up to $1.25 million; and brought in another partner, Megan Taylor, with whom Allen was romantically involved and who had been an executive at Realworld Multimedia, the production company owned by the singer Peter Gabriel, one of Allen's celebrity pals. Phillips and Taylor became co-founders and co-presidents.

Fortunately, Storyopolis hired two other people to run the company, Dawn Heinrichs and Fonda Snyder, because before long, Taylor had been fired after breaking up with Allen. Phillips was busy traveling around the world looking for authors and artists to sign to Storyopolis deals. She and Allen continued their professional relationship, and Phillips soon became somewhat of a regular on Allen's trips around the globe, to places like Fiji and Hong Kong. For business, of course, but she had come to fancy herself a "special" friend of Allen's.

Soon enough, that relationship, too, fell apart, amid cries of misappropriated funds and sexual harassment.

Paul Allen, his mother has said, "isn't a mama's boy," but the apron strings do seem tight. His mother Faye lives on his estate in a separate building that houses her 1,800-square-foot library (Faye, a former schoolteacher and widow to a librarian, is an advocate of reading programs); she is a regular fixture on Allen's travels for business and pleasure; and family vacations are a norm in the Allen family, even now.

Someday, he has alluded, he would like to settle down and marry—he's just "looking for the right woman," according to an account in the Los Angeles Times. At 49, in 2002, he still hadn't found her, but fame and fortune, he discovered, afforded him some very high-profile and exciting women as companions.

Allen had had serious girlfriends ever since he graduated from high school, and one former high-school classmate recalls lots of double-dating back then. His relationships after school were fairly serious. One girlfriend drove across the country with him when he dropped out of college and went to Boston to be with Gates and ultimately form Microsoft. Another was a steady in the post-Microsoft years, but the relationship ended and she said that Allen's wealth was turning him into a more suspicious and less pleasant person than he had been before. His last girlfriend had been a computer engineer. When Allen began entering celebrity circles, he started finding new romantic interests in that world.

Monica Seles was Allen's most serious celebrity girlfriend. In 1997, Seles was a 21-year-old tennis pro who had been through the rigors of fame. As a teen, she'd become known for grunting her way through games. In 1993, on her way to her next championship, she was stabbed in the back with a knife and dropped out of tennis for a few years. When she returned to the courts, she was struck with another round of sad news. Her father, who had been her coach and biggest supporter, had been diagnosed with cancer. He died in 1998.

Though Allen, at 44 in 1997, was far older than Seles, they had some things in common. They each showed up regularly in the sports columns and were very private individuals. They had each been through a serious health situation and recovered, and each of them knew the pain of losing a father. Allen has never disclosed a romantic relationship with Seles and neither has she (although one of her spokespeople defended the relationship at the time as "just friends"), but people who attended his parties and knew him professionally believed he was truly crazy about Seles. "He was really in love with her," says a journalist who spent time with Allen for a story in a major magazine. In 1997 and 1998, Allen and Seles made regular appearances at Portland Trail Blazers and Seattle Sonics

games, and were spotted in local Seattle restaurants dining together. The relationship eventually fizzled. Those who have spoken with Allen about it say he was disappointed by its ending. "He
was very broken up," says the journalist.

"I remember your warmth next to me, the sound of your
breathing, like the sea." So wrote Allen in the months and years
after his relationship with Seles, and some people believe that the
album "Grown Men," on which these lyrics appear, featuring his
band by the same name, was inspired by their break-up. This
song, called "Rhythm of Hearts," is poignant and aching and can
only be about some long-lost love. The song's lyrics dwell on
memories of two lovers' time together and ends with a plea to
take him back.

The album in general is full of loneliness, misunderstanding,
mistrust, and a lot of pain. His words almost cry out for understanding: Everything he does seems wrong.

Underneath the lyrics, the band plays pure light-rock with a
sweet, melancholy guitar twang over a thoughtful, plodding bass;
a moody saxophone gets a solo in one refrain. But it's not certain
that the album; which also contains songs written by Allen such as
"Kingdom of the Lonely," "Lost in a Maze," and "Time Has Its
Reasons"; was meant for Seles. Seles's own reasons for being in the
relationship are unknown, but in 2000, she did say that Allen had
helped her through the loss of her father. A more sinister view of
Seles's interest in Allen was mentioned in *Sports Illustrated* writer
L. Jon Wertheim's book *Venus Envy: A Sensational Season Inside the
Women's Tour*. According to Wertheim, Seles had a keen attraction
to money.

It must be fun being Paul Allen's girlfriend. He's got boats,
planes, houses all over the world, and friends and acquaintances
in almost every social circle. There's almost no need ever to leave

his houses or yachts, though, since they're all equipped with enough musical, literary, artistic, and cinematic entertainment to last for years. At his home, he has an art gallery, swimming pool, tennis courts, basketball court, and an underground garage—full of really expensive, really fast cars in which to take drives around Seattle's Cascade Mountains. He's got a Ferrari and a Porsche 959—but that one's in a warehouse somewhere, along with a twin owned by Bill Gates, since neither meet American anti-pollution requirements. When the cars aren't fast enough, there are always the planes in Allen's personal hangar at Boeing Field in Seattle (the Challenger 601, the Boeing 757, another Boeing 757 for his sister Jody, and sometimes the fighter plane he shares with Microsoft executive Charles Simonyi).

It was from one of Allen's yachts that another rumor of romance sprang, this time involving a woman well known to go after men with money. She was the leggy Texan supermodel Jerry Hall, who in 1999 was just breaking up with her husband of 13 years, Rolling Stones' Mick Jagger. Hall, being something of an attention-seeker, probably leaked word about her decision to join Allen on his yacht off the south of France. The information hit newspapers the world over on August 11 and August 12 in 1999. For the next few months, tabloids and gossip columnists pried into the relationship between Allen and Hall. They came up with little, and Hall eventually moved on to millionaire banker-polo player Tim Attias and billionaire property developer Guy Dellal.

Celebrities probably suited Allen. Like Allen, they lived in glass prisons, where their entire lives were ogled at and picked over by vulturous reporters, fans, and the public in general. This constant prying has made some celebrities skittish, skeptical, and often immune to intimacy. But perhaps two famous people could possibly live with some sort of mutual understanding.

Allen's noncelebrity girlfriends, on the other hand, were treated to a lifestyle of the rich and famous, but were dumped in the most classless style imaginable. The movie producer Jennifer

Todd was involved with Allen for a while in 2001. It was easy to understand this match. Todd, 32, was much younger than the 52-year-old Allen, but since she moved among movie makers and stars, she brought that world to Allen, which he was still entranced by. (Ironically, Todd also produced the film *American Psycho*, which featured the actor Jared Leto as a stock broker named Paul Allen who is brutally killed by the main character.) For months, Allen sent Todd gifts and invited her along on family vacations. Then one day, suddenly and unexpectedly, according to a close girlfriend, Todd was cut off. He no longer called her and wouldn't return her calls. And it wasn't the only time he did this. Friends of one female music executive say that she also dated Allen for a while, before Todd, and he broke off the relationship in a similar manner. "That's happened several times," says one friend of the music executive. "I guess he's so used to having his own way that he can just let things drop off."

These dumpings created a confusing impression of Allen and his style of romance. The subject was never cleared up, exactly, but it became the focus of close examination in court in 1998.

The depositions were nearly disastrous. There was Allen's sister, Jody Allen Patton, on the stand being asked whether she had "any belief that your brother has been or is celibate," or "that your brother had sexual relations with Megan Taylor," the cofounder of Storyopolis. Allen's litigation attorney, employment specialist Nancy Abell, objected and Patton never answered the question, but the damage was done. Allen's jealously guarded privacy and his personal reputation were being bandied about before a courtroom of press and current and former executives at his companies.

They were all here because Abbie Phillips, the other Storyopolis co-founder, had accused Paul Allen of sexual harassment.

Her side of the story, according to court filings, went like this: On May 24, 1996, Phillips and the cinematographer Peter Gilbert flew to Seattle to have dinner with Allen at a restaurant. They enjoyed an evening of good food and good conversation. After, Gilbert returned to a hotel in Seattle and Phillips and Allen went to his estate. Phillips' presence at Allen's home wasn't out of the ordinary, since it wasn't unusual for Allen to invite guests back to his house after business dinners, and often to have them stay the night in one of his many guest bedrooms. Phillips had stayed over in similar situations in the past. This time, however, she says Allen tried to pull some moves on her. According to Phillips' testimony, in a meeting (at 3 A.M.) in his bedroom—"Paul often sees visitors in his expansive bedroom," Phillips explained in court—Allen held Phillips down and fondled her breasts. "You don't want to go there," Phillips told Allen and wriggled away, running off to her bedroom. The next morning, the harassment continued, according to Phillips, who told lawyers that Allen entered her bedroom the next morning in a robe and got into bed and tried to have sex with her.

Over the course of the trial, a pattern of bad behavior by Allen was put on public display. It wasn't the first time Allen had treated women badly, Phillips claimed, and cited four other women who had been mistreated. Her lawyer, David Yardley, accused Allen of "developing crushes, lavishing gifts and vacations on, and then firing married female employees." Yardley asked Patton why Allen would invite illustrator Berkeley Breathed's wife Jody along on many trips and to many basketball games, often without her husband. Allen had also lavished gifts and vacations on his married administrative assistant, Pia Vanhanen. Patton said she thought all of these actions were innocent gestures.

Phillips also said that Allen's sister and executives at Vulcan had bullied her, that they put pressures on her, "gang-style," that ultimately led her to resign "under duress and threats." In her complaint, she noted that after the May 24 incident, they began requiring her to document her time in 15-minute segments and asked her underlings to spy on her by reporting back about what Phillips did all day. Yardley also tried to show how naturally suspicious Allen could be when he put Allen's former assistant Vanhanen on the stand and asked her why she'd been fired. Allen, she said, thought other people might be able to get information out of her, without her knowing, and he was desperate that his travel and work schedule—the things he accused of her accidentally leaking—not be known. "Paul could no longer feel confident about my functions. He was afraid that Megan Taylor [who no longer worked at Storyopolis] . . . would somehow get information from me about Paul that I was giving [her] without knowing that I was giving information," said Vanhanen in her deposition. "Paul couldn't be sure of my confidentiality. . . . So, you know, he has to do what he has to do." Sometime in October 1995, Vanhanen was fired from Vulcan.

Whether Allen was a sexual predator or not, he and his team must have been somewhat confused by Phillips's behavior. For a year after the alleged incident, Phillips continued to work for and travel with Allen, as if nothing had happened. It wasn't until a year after she was fired and two years after the May 24 event that she filed the suit against Allen. Meanwhile, Phillips had a mixed reputation herself. Though she had made a success of her first business, Every Picture Tells a Story, she had been sued by her former business partner, Lois Sarkisian, who claimed Phillips owed her $100,000 for several works of art that she had acquired for herself through the gallery. In Allen's counterclaim to Phillips's suit against him, he said he believed Phillips had misappropriated $29,623 in personal expenses. Phillips's lawyer Yardley said those funds had been approved by Allen in advance to cover the cost of litigation in the suit with Sarkisian, and that it predated May 24, 1996. For reasons that are still unclear, Phillips was dismissed from Storyopolis on April 2, 1997. Her claim against Allen was filed a year later.

The truth is hard to find in the haze of counterclaims. When Yardley threatened to put Allen's mother Faye on the stand and question her about her son's sexuality, Allen's attorneys began discussions about a settlement. Yardley and Phillips had believed his mother was key to the case, since she and Phillips had once talked about "her son's difficult relationships with women and his sister's role in extricating him from these relationships." But that's exactly when Allen promptly instructed his lawyers to work out a settlement with Phillips. What really happened between Phillips and Allen remains a mystery. Those who knew Phillips couldn't believe she would have made up such a story, while some who know Allen don't think he could ever be so aggressive with women.

Being sued for sexual harassment must have been unnerving for a man so private he makes his personal life a legal matter, brandishing nondisclosure agreements at every opportunity. Employees of Allen's personal holdings, from Vulcan Ventures to his flight crew, are all required to sign documents saying they will never tell anyone about their work for Allen. The same goes for his social activities. Since 1996, Allen had been throwing elaborate, world-renowned parties for the famous friends he'd made, along with his regular crew of business cronies and members of his family; no guest was admitted without their signature on a legally binding agreement to keep all details of the affairs secret. But can you really expect hundreds of limelight-seeking celebrities to keep quiet? Hardly.

"It's the best party I've ever been to, bar none," Geffen told *Rolling Stone*. Added Howard Rosenmann, Geffen's producer friend, "No one entertains like that anymore. He is like a Medici, a grand seignior, someone who entertains in the old style."

Allen's first star-studded party was at his Cap Ferrat villa on the French Riviera in 1996. The following year, invitations went out for a masked ball at Cipriani in Venice. To celebrate his 45th birthday in 1998, Allen planned a week-long luxury cruise to Alaska. The cruise cost about $9 million. In 2000, he invited celebrities and very important people on a trip to St. Petersburg in Russia, traveling by former Soviet spy ship-turned-luxury liner from Helsinki. The entire affair cost Allen $13.8 million after flying his 200 guests by chartered plane to Helsinki, hosting them on the $1,400 per-head-per-night ship and offering them activities like tall-ship cruises, helicopter rides, private museum tours, and day-long sauna retreats. Every event featured a musical performance by some of the celebrity guests.

Hosting such affairs may inculcate one into celebrity society, but for Allen, it failed to make him any less frumpy or any cooler than he had ever been. It certainly didn't make him any more charming or better equipped to manage social conversation. Allen tended to avoid topics he didn't like to discuss, or people who disagreed with him, the same way he abandoned companies that didn't follow his plans. One Hollywood screenwriter recalls speaking with Allen at one of Allen's favorite eateries in Los Angeles, Ago, about Allen's Portland Trail Blazers. As soon as the conversation turned against his team, Allen simply turned and walked away from the screenwriter without explanation. Other business associates say he's done this in the past; it's Allen's way of dealing with subjects he'd prefer not to discuss.

Allen continued his tour of the famous and rich. In 1995, in a swank flat in a hip northeast neighborhood in London, he had come to hear Gary Brooker croon the lyrics to "A Whiter Shade of Pale" as he strummed the chords gently on his guitar. Allen sat like a teenage groupie with eyes bugging and mouth hanging open at the feet of the rock stars he idolized. He wasn't alone. All around him sat celebrities, cross-legged and otherwise reclined, on the floor. "It was incredible," recalls one of the party guests.

These were the evenings of "Partially Plugged," the name given by host Douglas Adams, the late author of *The Hitchhiker's Guide to the Universe*. Every few months or so, Adams would invite musicians, celebrities, and people he deemed interesting to join him and his wife Jane Belson in their home for an evening of music in a takeoff of MTV's "Unplugged" series (because the musicians at Adams' affairs, if they liked, could plug in to an electrical outlet.

Allen had met Adams through Berkeley and Jody Breathed. Allen had taken to Adams, asking him along on various jaunts around the globe. Allen's wealth was a little overwhelming for Adams, say friends. Allen told Adams he, too, was a bit burdened by his wealth. On one occasion, he told Adams, "I've spent money on jets, boats. I don't know what to do next." Adams, who liked to find creative solutions to a problem, had a thought: "What if I get seven of the most brilliant thinkers and we come up with something that is fabulous and a way of doing something good. Would you write us a $1 billion check?" It was an idea that never came to pass.

Meanwhile, Allen was enjoying "Partially Plugged." Regulars to Adams' events knew the drill. Adams would assemble about 80 people of fame and interest with the expectation that absorbing conversations would spark. Ideas would fly. Above all, sycophantic behavior or schmoozing was forbidden. The evenings would be a safe haven for this group of important people to casually linger and intensively engage without the pressures of their status.

Despite the established ritual, Allen came off as a little perturbed on one particular occasion. Bodyguards had been installed throughout the apartment and in the backyard because one celebrity in attendance required it: the author Salman Rushdie, who, at the time, was moving around, on the run from officials in

Iran. "I think he [Allen] was slightly miffed," says one guest who was there.

Miffed or not, Allen was a horrible conversationalist on that occasion and other "Partially Plugged" events. "He's completely hopeless at small talk, but fair enough, so are a lot of people. But he's not particularly gracious or particularly witty or particularly funny," says one of Adams' party guests. "I remember Paul being very enthusiastic about his boat he was building. That was a subject he'd be quite enthusiastic about. But he's not good at being desperately interested in what other people are saying."

In fact, Allen may have been distracted. His $3 billion was growing, and he couldn't spend it fast enough. He threw it at start-ups and charities, but it wasn't enough. He was realizing that he could use his money selfishly, too, to create experiences and environments for himself that had lived only in his mind since he was a kid: Where thoughts of basketball and Jimi Hendrix lived virtually, he'd now make them a reality.

9

# "ALLENTOWN"

I t really didn't take long for Paul Allen to get used to being a rich guy. He already knew he never wanted to punch a clock or sit behind a desk. He had learned that in his year away from Microsoft in 1983, after being diagnosed with cancer. On his time off, he grew quickly into a dilettante, traveling, learning to scuba dive, collecting art, watching basketball games, and playing the guitar as often as possible. His health scare had made him realize that he should do more in life than just work, and he seemed to be out to prove it.

After Microsoft's successful initial public offering in 1986, Allen finally had the means to do all the things he'd ever wanted to do. On that day, he amassed a fortune worth $134 million. He didn't go about spending it all in one place, and rarely cashed in his valuable stock options, perhaps knowing they would appreciate in value. For the most part, he let his options grow, using them as collateral for loans when he needed large sums of money. Those occasions started happening in 1988, just two years after his financial windfall.

Allen's first big buy as a millionaire was a sports team: Basketball, of course. Since he was eight years old, Allen had been in and out of love with the sport, playing with friends on a neighborhood team, where, he later recalled with a chuckle, his position was "last man off the bench." His father Kenneth, who had played many sports successfully in high-school, realized he didn't have an athlete on his hands in his son, but the two of them bonded over their love of basketball and other sports, spending hours in front of the television watching games. But Allen really became hooked as a spectator when he returned to Seattle from Albuquerque in the late 1970s, thanks to an engaging winning streak by the Seattle Sonics.

Perhaps in part because of his love of watching basketball, Allen's first purchase once he started earning an income of his own at Microsoft in Albuquerque was a large-screen television. Gates, who spent his own early Microsoft money on a Porsche 911, once joked that "watching all those basketball games on [the TV] may have gotten to Paul."

Allen truly had the basketball bug. In 1988, it occurred to him that since he had all this money, why not get a team of his own?

The Sonics were the team he really wanted. He knew their record and playing style intimately. But what really meant a lot to him was that they were based in his hometown, the city where he had insisted Microsoft relocate from Albuquerque in 1978. Allen loved Seattle about as much as he loved basketball, but the Sonics owners weren't selling.

If he couldn't buy his hometown team, Allen really didn't want to go too far for another. Just three hours south of Seattle (by car—only an hour when you travel by Allen's jet), was Portland, Oregon, which had a team called the Trail Blazers.

The Trail Blazers had been incorporated 18 years earlier and won just one championship, in 1977. In the mid-1980s, the Trail Blazers had begun to look a bit ragged, and the tiny arena in which they played, the Portland Memorial Coliseum, seated just 12,666. Though the team had sold out games for 12 seasons, the capacity just wasn't enough to make much money. It was a team that needed an overhaul. Even so, the Trail Blazers weren't officially for sale.

"I said, 'I can't put a price on the team,'" the team's owner, Larry Weinberg, said at the time. But the idea had been planted. Weinberg spent the following weekend talking long and hard with his wife about what they might do. The two ultimately decided that there were other things in life to enjoy besides owning a basketball team, so if Allen offered the right price, they'd take it. He did: $70 million. "The decision to sell was one of the most agonizing decisions of my life," Weinberg said. "However, there comes a time when it's appropriate to move on."

The Weinbergs moved on, and Allen moved in. At first, he did little. He schmoozed with the players. He invited two of them, Kiki Vandeweghe and Clyde Drexler, out to his Mercer Island estate for dinner. The event stirred up a small commotion in the league. In the days before the get-together, Vandeweghe had been packing his bags for New York state. He'd grown tired of warming the bench in Portland, and the New York Knicks had offered him playing time. In return, Portland would get New York's first-round draft pick position.

After Allen got to know Vandeweghe over dinner, however, he didn't want him to go. No formal deal had yet been signed, but the Knick's Al Bianchi was furious when he heard that Allen wanted to keep Vandeweghe. "We had a deal and it was vetoed," he said at the time. Vandeweghe ended up staying (a few months later, though, the deal was back on and Vandeweghe went to New York).

Players, Allen loved; coaches were another matter. One of the first things Allen did was swap out the coach, Mike Schuler, and replace him with assistant coach Rick Adelman. Adelman led the team to the Finals in the next two years, but by 1991, he was slipping. Allen kicked him out in favor of Seton Hall coach P.J. Carlesimo.

In the first five years after Allen bought the Trail Blazers, they improved as a team. But eventually, their reputation began to sully. Thanks to Allen, they had become very spoiled. He loved his players and showered them with gifts. He bought them a plane to travel in to away games. He gave them a private, luxury health club in the new arena he had built, and each year, he hosted a week-long retreat at his home. He paid them such exorbitant salaries that the Trail Blazers earned the dubious reputation of having the biggest payroll in the entire National Basketball Association. All of it had the effect of making the players act like spoiled children. Two of them were arrested in Chicago in 1994 for getting into a scuffle with a truck driver. On the court, referees regularly ejected or fined star players for aggressive, arrogant behavior. The players were hardly remorseful, but then, why would they be, when no one was keeping them in check.

For Allen, it mattered little. He was happiest when he was courtside, whatever the price. "Owning the Blazers has provided me with some of the most enjoyable times of my life," he said. He was a fixture at most games, usually with his mother Faye, or an executive from one of his companies, or the occasional Hollywood celebrity. In Portland, some longtime season ticket-holders came to call their new owner, "big, fat Paul," because his usual stance was to gaze stoically onto the court from behind his beard. That is, until Vandeweghe or star player Clyde Drexler made an unexpected shot, and then Allen would be on his feet, pumping his fist into the air and cheering along with the rest of the crowd. He often led the fans in the wave, and sometimes stood up, turned around, and, still poker-faced, led a cheer to support the team.

In the back office, things were just as out of control as they were among the players. Allen was padding the management ranks left and right with old friends and their friends and relatives, making it the most bloated management staff in the league. It was old Allen habits at work again, hiring those he believed loyal, without planning for a well-run organization. Allen started to see that the company wasn't running as efficiently as he felt it could. In 1995, he sent in his old friend Bert Kolde to clean things up.

Since he and Allen had reunited in 1985, more than a decade after they were college roommates, Kolde had helped Allen run Asymetrix and manage some of his investments in other companies. Kolde was a loyal aide to Allen at Asymetrix and Vulcan. Now, Allen was trusting him to go into the Trail Blazers organization and make order out of the mess, which partly meant slashing the staff. It made Kolde somewhat unpopular.

It wasn't just that people didn't like Kolde, or disagreed with his decisions. Some of the Trail Blazers executives (and some of the players) didn't trust him. The team's former physician, Robert Cook, called him "the Rasputin of the royal court." Kolde simply dismissed these comments as sour grapes from people who had been let go and made no apologies. "We are a performance-oriented company. We don't give lifetime jobs," he told the *Seattle Post-Intelligencer*.

Maybe they weren't handing out lifetime jobs, but everyone knew full well that Allen could afford to spend as much money as he wanted on his team. He'd already put up the bulk of the cash on the new Rose Garden in Portland. The fancy new arena cost $262 million and seated 21,000. Allen being Allen the high-tech baron, he made sure the Rose Garden, opened in 1995, had some features other arenas didn't have. The ceiling was created with a flexibility that allowed it to absorb or reflect sound, depending on the event. The place would carry 750 television monitors so that fans wouldn't miss a moment of the game while in line for snack food or in the bathroom. "This was unheard of at the time," says John Lashway, public relations director for the Trail Blazers until he was fired by Kolde in 1995. People like Lashway, the rest of management, coaches, and players were all loaded up with the latest computer technology available. They were a very wired team. "We were always ahead of the curve," says Lashway. "We had game stats and game-night operations on the computers. Paul's background added a lot."

Allen thought his beloved Trail Blazers should be as much a part of his wired world as anything else. In 1995, he put a bug in Starwave's ear to build a Web site for the Trail Blazers; they became the first NBA team to have its own site.

When Allen couldn't make it to the games, he had another option in the wired world he'd created for himself. He rigged his yacht to receive a direct satellite feed from the Rose Garden. Naturally, the feed didn't come from any ordinary broadcast sent out to stations, but from cameras and a control room set up to create and transmit a special video broadcast just for him.

For Portland, Allen had built the Rose Garden, bought the Portland WNBA team Fire, and given $1.25 million to the Oregon Shakespeare Festival he attended every summer as a child with his family. But back in Seattle, Allen was just beginning to expand his land holdings, for good and for bad. Some people derisively dubbed it "Allentown."

You get the first glimpse of "Allentown" on Interstate 5 from the north. From this elevated view of Seattle, the Experience Music Project (EMP) bursts into sight like a brightly colored plastic lump sitting in a heap at the foot of Seattle's elegant, slender Space Needle. It could be a giant version of one of Jimi Hendrix's famously smashed guitars left to melt in the sun. That's also one way to think about the events that led up to the EMP.

The EMP is a museum created to celebrate the history of rock and blues with exhibits of the music and musicians from the Pacific Northwest, with a special section for Seattle's homegrown grunge tradition. There's also, naturally, a roomful of Hendrix memorabilia, because of Allen's longtime passion for Hendrix's music. Another room is set aside for hands-on experience with musical instruments, where visitors to the museum can enter private booths and learn through an interactive system how to play the drums, guitar, or keyboard. Near a concert stage in the main hall, a towering display of famous guitars and guitars once played by famous people serves as the centerpiece to the museum.

But to Allen, it was all wrong. It was originally supposed to be a museum dedicated entirely to Jimi Hendrix, his idol since Allen was thirteen.

"Paul Allen's a guitar groupie. He loves playing the guitar more than anything," says one business associate. It really is a toss-up whether Allen prefers basketball over music, and he once joked that as he put the finishing touches on his *Grown Men* album, he had kept "one eye on the mixing board, and one eye on TNT, watching the draft."

In 1990, he began investing in his passion for Hendrix. He spent tens of thousands of dollars on items once belonging to or touched by Hendrix, including a shard of a Fender Stratocaster once famously smashed by Hendrix on stage at the end of a performance. Allen plunked down $50,000 for it. Soon, he had a collection of 5,000 Hendrix memorabilia. But he wanted to do more; he wanted to build a tribute to Hendrix and share all of this with the world. He approached his sister Jody with an idea for a museum. "I really like this stuff, I get a kick out of looking at this stuff. I think other people will, too," he told her. How about we call it "The Jimi Hendrix Experience," he suggested.

Not so fast. Though to him it might have seemed otherwise, the world wasn't Allen's for the right price. Unlike a willing sports team, he couldn't go out and buy himself a museum and slap Hendrix's name on it, nor could he simply acquire Hendrix's music, as he now also wished to do. There was the matter of the surviving members of Hendrix's family, as well as an attorney named Leo Branton Jr. in Los Angeles who didn't just roll over for Allen.

B ranton was a prominent Los Angeles attorney who had repre-
sented black entertainers such as Nat King Cole and Lena Horne. In 1971, he talked the Hendrixes into letting him take care of Jimi's music rights, asking Al Hendrix for permission to do so. In the process, Al Hendrix lost all control of Jimi's music, but he eventually earned lump sums of $500,000 and $50,000, and in the 1980s, began to earn a $50,000 yearly stipend through Branton for Jimi's music.

Hendrix later claimed he had no idea how his son's music was being distributed, and when he found out in 1993 that the rights were about to be sold to MCA for $30 million, he called a halt to the deal he had with Branton and sued him for fraud. Branton had controlled the overseas distribution companies that handled Jimi's music, but, according to Hendrix, he'd never told his client that. Hendrix had enough of Branton and wanted to bring Jimi's music back under family control.

Paul Allen also wanted in; he needed to spend his billions; owning and distributing Hendrix's music seemed like the right thing, especially since he was also considering a museum in Hendrix's honor. Allen took his plan to Branton: Allen didn't own any distribution companies himself, but he planned to set up a deal through a nice little U.S. company that he'd be able to keep tabs on. Branton said no. Jimi's music sold throughout the world, so it made more sense to go with a multinational company like MCA, not Allen's little vanity corporation.

But you don't tell a No. 1 fan to go away and expect him to listen. Allen remained involved, but instead of working with Branton, he took a position against him. Allen backed the Hendrixes in their suit and put in for a $5 million interest-free loan to cover legal fees. Allen's camp claimed the gesture was done in goodwill, because of Allen's passion for Hendrix's music. But the loan wasn't completely free. In exchange, Al Hendrix gave Allen a handshake agreement to endorse a Jimi Hendrix museum. With Allen's help, the Hendrixes won their suit. In 1995, all rights went back to the family.

Allen wanted more, though. He still had his eye on Hendrix's music. He dispatched his lawyers with the order to get the rights to distribute Jimi's music. They'd spin their pitch around the museum, which Al Hendrix had already endorsed. How about letting the museum have global, royalty-free rights to license the music? Hendrix gave them a flat "No." Hendrix had just spent years fighting for the rights to his son's music and now he had it back. He wasn't about to give it away! One newspaper report at the time said that Allen may have responded by cutting off any further financing and demanding repayment of his loan. The museum, denied unlimited access to Hendrix's music, was forced to expand beyond its original scope to include Pacific Northwest musicians. The Hendrixes and the Allens have spoken little since.

Through it all, Allen and his staff tried to maintain a clean image. "Mr. Allen's motives were never sinister," said his spokeswoman Susan Pierson Brown. "His intentions were always absolutely altruistic. Mr. Allen never set out to and never will end up making a dime off this museum project. Anyone who knows him realizes that it was always love, not money, that drove this dream from the start."

Once the aim of the museum changed, Allen seemed to lose interest and let his sister Jody Allen Patton handle most of it. Allen was occasionally involved, though, particularly in the design.

Thinking about the design was kind of fun for Allen. It was creative. He had to think over how Hendrix's music, and music in general, could be described in physical terms.

Well, music moves, he thought. It flows. It's like—water. "Make it swoopy," he told the architect.

Naturally, this wasn't just any architect. It was the famous, inventive architect Frank O. Gehry, who built the stunning Guggenheim Museum in Bilbao, Spain. Gehry, however, wasn't Allen's choice. "Jody had to convince me," he told the *Seattle Times*. "Frank's architecture is very much on the cutting edge," which was too much for Allen at first. Jody insisted, though. In the end, said Allen, "I think we actually pushed Frank to be even more extreme, and he's usually pretty extreme."

The final outcome left a lot of people scratching their heads. One local Seattle paper called it "a gigantic successor to the Queen Anne Blob." But Allen was used to people misunderstanding what he was trying to do. He'd been frustrated by public perception of his actions ever since he became a public figure. *Wired*, for one, had lost patience with his investing strategy, dubbing him the "accidental zillionaire." Investors hadn't understood his activity in AOL. About the EMP, Allen told the *Seattle Times*, "Anything that's at the cutting edge, it takes a lot for people to get used to. To me, it's just breathtaking and beautiful. If you can't find part of that building to like, that would really, really surprise me. But there are always going to be people who don't like something like that because it's that exuberant."

Allen was more concerned about the inside of the museum than the outside, anyway. He wanted his Hendrix collection perfectly displayed, and it was important to him that visitors get the hands-on experience of playing music. The distribution of design was split up according to the outside and the inside: Gehry handled the external features, while the interior went to a group that had just designed the interactive "Newseum" in Washington, DC. From an architect's point of view, it's almost like designing just half a building. This didn't work so well for Gehry, who occasionally grew frustrated over the project and his client's inaccessibility. Allen and Gehry met just a few times, and at the groundbreaking ceremony in 1997, they said few words to one another. "He wasn't really that involved," Gehry told the *Seattle Weekly*. In the beginning, Allen had envisioned the museum as a special tribute to his rock hero, but when it turned into something else, he left the project to other people, for the most part.

A local architecture expert once suggested that Allen's civic impulses were "kind of a modern equivalent to the Medici in Florence." The Medici were not a titled family, but grew into a powerful family through banking and commerce; they were always seen as a friend of the common folks. It's a good way to think about Allen, but not exactly right.

It's true, Allen felt strong ties to his birthplace. Seattle had a magnetic pull that tugged at him when he was working with Gates in Albuquerque in 1977. By that point, he'd been away from Seattle, Washington, for three years, and wanted to go back. He suggested to Bill Gates that Microsoft had run its course in the desert and that they should return to the place they grew up. Gates argued that if Microsoft were going to go anywhere, it should be to Silicon Valley, which was shaping up to be the center of the most significant technology developments. But Allen had to be back in Seattle and refused to see it any other way. Eventually, he won. In 1978, Microsoft relocated permanently to the Seattle area and Allen came home.

Paul Allen has never left since. He built a mansion in Beverly Hills and bought homes in New York, London, and France, but Seattle is his home. His mother and sister are there, as are all the memories from his childhood. Allen has even held on to the family's old home on 28th Street N.E.

Allen has invested in his hometown. And it might look like he has the public's interest at heart when he makes his moves around the city, but ultimately, he's just a billionaire who throws money at things he wants changed. "There are threads that run through these things, but there's no singular master plan," Allen said of his civic investments. "There's the desire to be fresh, to incorporate high technology, to do things in high-quality ways. What we're doing downtown kind of reflects the breadth of my interests in all these different areas, all the way from music to sports to high-tech to movies and so forth."

Seattle's "Allentown," is about "my interests," according to Allen. Still, it's nice to have a billionaire around whose own interests occasionally dovetail with the rest of the population.

If it weren't for Allen, the city would be short one NFL franchise. In 1997, the Seattle Seahawks were in danger of leaving town if a local owner couldn't be found. Allen stepped in and bought a majority stake. Next up, he raised support to build a new stadium for the team. Some local taxpayers objected to Allen's insistence on sharing the cost with them, even after he'd ensured they wouldn't lose the whole team. Allen, for his part, objected to their objections. "People need to appreciate that this is a business, a sports business, and you have expenses, mainly for players and coaches," the veteran sports franchise owner told the *Seattle Times*. "For this to work out in the long-term, we need to find ways to increase revenue that would allow us to put a better team on the field and give the fans a better experience."

Allen's purchase wasn't instantaneous; he had to be convinced to take on a football team. He liked football, and he'd once considered buying a Canadian Football League team, but by now, the Trail Blazers took up too much of his time. When the city of Seattle couldn't find any other way to keep the team in town, Allen agreed to buy in. Eventually, Allen had the existing Kingdome stadium rebuilt, and made the city share the $450 million cost.

With the Kingdome—a partially covered, glimmering structure along the water near Seattle's downtown—Allen added a
tract of land to his holdings. He used it to build a green-glass
office building for Vulcan Ventures and some of its holdings. The
EMP building sat to the north of downtown. Allen also hoped to
develop a public park for $21 million, but when local shopowners
on the property protested, he called a halt to the project. But
when the Cinerama Allen attended as a child looked like it was
closing, it was he who swooped in to rescue and refurbish it. It
was no wonder some people called his hometown "Allentown."

For all Allen did for the city, though, some people still thought
he was occasionally selfish and not always forthcoming about his
motives. In 2000, Allen backed a local initiative for a new education program with a $200,000 contribution that became the sub-
ject of a scandal when some people pointed out that Allen's stake
in Edison Schools, an East Coast company, could benefit from the
initiative. The campaign he backed had been designed to bring
charter schools—publicly funded but privately run—to the city.
Edison Schools was trying to make a business out of running charter schools. Allen claimed his stake in Edison was too small to matter and was unrelated to his interest in charter schools, but it still
made some people uncomfortable. The initiative eventually
passed, however, and the controversy died down.

Allen managed to walk away from many of his dust-ups without any noticeable scars, since most people just piped down and
moved on. Sometimes they did so because they were impressed
by Allen's wealth, and wanted to be able to appeal to him again in
the future. But as he had already found out, not everyone was
afraid of Paul Allen.

A 10-year-old boy rode up the long drive that led to the front
gate of Allen's Mercer Island estate. His bike was dusty from

the road, but he didn't care. He was on a mission: He had to save his summer camp, Camp Nor'wester, which had just lost its home to Allen, who bought the property where it operated.

Behind those locked gates lived Allen and his family, who held the fate of Nor'wester in their hands. In their possession were the baseball bats, bunk beds, basketballs, canoes, and the rest of what made Camp Nor'wester popular for 50 years with kids between the ages of nine and sixteen. "All I want is to talk to Paul Allen," the boy pleaded with Allen's security guard on a fall day in 1996. "Sorry," said the guard. The next day, people around the world heard about the incident. Paul Allen had refused to see a 10-year-old boy who was trying to save his camp. Allen looked like a selfish billionaire who was more concerned about buying himself a nice piece of land than about a beloved kids' camp.

The world came to hear about it because the whole thing had been choreographed. The boy was part of a demonstration held outside of Allen's house. A few dozen campers and their families were there, too, singing camp songs. It had all been arranged by a group calling themselves the Friends of Sperry Peninsula, an area on Lopez Island in Seattle's San Juan Islands that Allen had just acquired for $8 million. His purchase would displace the camp, which had few options for relocation.

The group had been set up to try to convince Allen to let the camp stay on Sperry, where it had resided for 50 years. Allen had other plans, though. He wanted a respite for his family. Friends of Sperry Peninsula thought that was wrong. They coached the boy and alerted the media about the event. Everyone from the local television stations to the *New York Times* were on hand to capture the moment.

It didn't work. Instead, the Allens were pissed. They were so mad, in fact, they went back on some of the few promises they'd already made to the camp. They decided the boy and his camp not only wouldn't get their land back, they wouldn't get their equipment any time soon, either. They'd have to wait through a "cooling off period," wrote Allen's sister Jody in a letter to camp officials.

The Friends' plan hadn't worked, but they didn't stop there. They recruited the local Native American group of Samish Indians to their side. They appealed to the local San Juan Preservation Society and tried to have the property declared historical by the state, so that Allen couldn't develop the property. They even tried to get Allen evicted from the island by raising legal concerns about the development he'd begun on the property.

The Friends tried all avenues to appeal to the Allens. They tapped a source in Los Angeles to win over Steven Spielberg's support for their cause (it didn't work). The group even dispatched several people Allen's mother's age to appeal to her. "I had them loan her a book and said, 'At least, she'll have to return it to you,'" says Richard Carter, who headed the Friends group and was a former assistant director at Nor'wester. Eventually, Allen's mother Faye did get in touch with her peers and agreed to meet them. Over lunch, they told her all about Camp Nor'wester. They brought along photo albums and shared their memories. She listened to their stories. "I'm lobbying for you," she said at the end of the meeting. But Allen's mother couldn't make a difference. When she asked them back to lunch, she told them: "I made your appeal—and I lost."

Nothing worked. Allen and his sister—some say mainly his sister—fought with a battalion of expensive lawyers every step of the way, and won. Even when they were barraged with written, spoken and sung appeals to keep the camp on the island—or at least pay a visit to see what it was all about—they kept their focus: In the spring of 1996, the Allens had bought a piece of property, and it was theirs to do whatever they liked with it. They wanted a home, not a kids' camp.

The San Juan Islands weren't a big part of Allen's childhood, as they have been for many Seattle residents, but he was still sentimental about them. With wealthy friends from the

Lakeside School, he'd occasionally traveled as a child to one or another of them. Now that he could afford to live out there, he wanted his own island. So in 1995, he made his first purchase, buying Allan Island.

It was a sucker's purchase. Noisy, lying beneath the path of planes headed for nearby Whidbey Naval Air Station, Allan Island was also full of jagged, rocky cliffs that made development difficult. It wasn't nestled amidst the rest of the San Juan Islands, but out on the open seas, an unfriendly place to be. Then there was the matter of actual survival; it would take years to get the paperwork sorted out to get drinkable water to the island. Allan Island was entirely unlivable. When Allen learned in the fall of 1995 that Sperry Peninsula was available, he jumped at the chance to buy that as a replacement.

To the people at Camp Nor'wester, Paul Allen was a mystery. His only visit to the Sperry property was in the winter of 1991, when all the campers and counselors were gone. He never heard the children's camp songs wafting through the trees, or their cries of laughter coming back from the shore as they paddled by in canoes. "In summer, the place comes alive. The sound of children's voices is what's magical about this place. We could have taken 'No' better if he had come to see the camp," says Carter, who was assistant director of Camp Nor'wester when Allen bought the property.

Carter, who is also a playwright, became somewhat of a public figure during the controversy. "Don't mention Richard's name to the Allens, they hate him," jokes his wife. For two years after Allen closed on the property, Carter led the Friends of Sperry Peninsula and their futile attempts to get Allen to change his mind, and let Camp Nor'wester stay on the island.

In the beginning, most people involved thought Allen was just buying the land, but not to do anything with it. It was a logical assumption based on the camp's ownership history. Since the camp relocated to Sperry Peninsula in 1945, ownership of the land changed hands several times, but each time, the new owners allowed the camp to remain. The last owner, a commodities broker named Chuck Curran, had eyed the island for a summer home when he bought it in 1980. After seeing the camp in full swing, he agreed to vacation elsewhere and let the camp stay. For this reason, the board saw no reason to question Allen's interest as a buyer.

Carter and a few others thought differently. From the beginning, Allen's bid was marked by mixed messages that raised flags. There was the odd timing of his offer on the property, for starters. Though the camp was never put on the market, Allen had somehow found out about it. The only notice of Curran's plans to sell had been written about in the camp's newsletter, sent to patrons along with an appeal to help the camp raise money to buy Sperry Peninsula. The property was valued at $8 million. The camp director wrote in the newsletter that Curran was backing out of the property and appealed for help to raise $3.5 million in six months. According to Carter, Curran had offered the camp the chance to buy back the peninsula themselves, and said it would be theirs if they could raise at least $3.5 million. The message was an appeal to the camp's supporters to help the camp become its own landlord. It wasn't intended to spread the word about the land's availability. Allen, says Carter, "found out through the camp's advertising it needed help," but instead of helping, he decided it was an opportunity to buy the property himself.

The camp made considerable strides toward becoming the new property owners. Within six weeks, donors had contributed $2 million to the cause, and some patrons were offering to write checks for the balance. "Then all of a sudden, things changed," recalls Carter. People involved in the sale were acting strangely. Curran wasn't returning calls. He wouldn't deal with the camp. Through the local rumor mill, Carter learned that there was another bidder, who had offered to pay the entire $8 million at once.

Allen can't be entirely to blame for the camp's plight. Curran, the former owner, was also quick to take his offer. Though he'd offered the camp the opportunity to buy back the island, he never really thought they'd be able to do it. "There was absolutely never any indication to me ever in the history of the camp that that was realistic," Curran said at the time. With this in mind, he snatched Allen's offer.

Carter and others were outraged. They told the board to act quickly and appeal to Allen to keep the camp. The other directors thought Allen would come to see the camp's merit on his own and not to worry. They were wrong.

A llen wasn't entirely unmoved by the camp's pleas. He had never attended summer camp himself, but he wasn't as cold-hearted as some painted him. He offered all kinds of support to the camp. They could have Allan Island, he said, and he would give them $100,000 to cover relocation costs. In the transaction, he'd acquired everything but the camp's name, including the teepees, the paddle oars, the horses, and boats. They could have all of it back, he said. "Really, he's being very generous," his spokeswoman, Susan Pierson, insisted to all media who called.

But Allan Island was no kind of fair trade. The island was a bad place for Allen and his family to set up their summer home, but it was even worse for a bunch of kids who hoped to wander through woods and paddle up streams. It wasn't safe, and the naval station didn't want them there. "Please, we get enough complaints already," wrote the base's admiral in a letter to Nor'wester.

Allen eventually built a huge home on Sperry, with 22 bedrooms, and two guest houses, one each for his mother and sister. The camp was permanently displaced. It was another instance of Allen wanting his way and making sure he got it, or else.

Just because Paul Allen reveled in his billionaire-boy status, spending his money on sports, music, and vacation homes, didn't mean he was an entirely self-involved billionaire. In 1990, he had separated his business investment arm, Vulcan Ventures, from the group that would handle his personal investments and charitable contributions, Vulcan Northwest. Vulcan Northwest set up three foundations in Allen's name, all run by his sister Jody, and began doling out cash to groups in the arts, medical, and charitable organizations in the Pacific Northwest. By the end of the decade, three more foundations had been added to give money to forest protection, virtual education, and music.

But it wasn't enough to earn Allen a solid reputation as a philanthropist. That's partly because his contributions were aimed at the sleepy northwest, where they failed to attract much national attention. But mostly it was because he just wasn't spending all that much money, for all his fortune and status. Allen was consistently among the top 15 billionaires on *Forbes* magazine's annual list throughout most of the 1990s, yet he never cracked the top 20 in the rankings of philanthropists. Bill Gates was also a laggard, but by the end of the century, he quickly caught up. In a ranking of most-generous Americans in *Worth* magazine in 2000, Bill and Melinda Gates ranked No. 4 with $846 million. Allen came in No. 22. He had a poor track record: From 1987 to 1998, Allen gave away $26.4 million, according to the *Chronicle of Philanthropy*, while the Gates's, in just four years, from 1995 to 1998, gave away $5.3 billion.

Occasionally, Allen would become personally involved in his charitable giving, like when he hooked up with his Microsoft friend Nathan Myhrvold, the former Microsoft chief technology officer. In August 2000, Allen put up $11.5 million and Myhrvold added $1 million to a new telescope for the Search for Extra-Terrestrial

Intelligence Institute that would look even further into space for signs of life. "To say it is a long-shot would be an understatement," Allen told a reporter for the *Seattle Times*. But it was fun, it was geeky, and he got to pair up with a buddy to do it.

This was more like what Microsoft millionaires did, and Allen was akin to them and their dot-com descendants. Well before any of these other nouveau, high-tech rich came on the scene, Allen had already set the trend for how they lived. He spent his money on the things he liked and built himself a world to live in. Those who followed were like Allen. Mark Cuban was one. The founder of an Internet company called Broadcast.com, Cuban sold it to Yahoo! for $5 billion in 1999 and became an instant billionaire. Cuban cashed out, went home to Dallas, and bought himself a basketball team, just like Allen.

With Allen as their captain, loads of newly rich appeared on the scene and had fun spending their money in the 1990s—until the good times fell apart in one disastrous plunge of the stock market in April 2000. Then, only those like Allen—the "old" high-tech money—were left standing.

# THE OTHER
# WIRED WORLD

When the World Wide Web came along, it looked like this would be Paul Allen's time to shine. The Web, after all, was Allen's wired world vision laid out in clear view for all to see. It connected everybody, everywhere. It was practically word for word what Allen had suggested to Gates over pizza at Shakey's in Vancouver, Washington, in 1974. "Eventually, everyone is going to be online and have access to newspapers and stuff and wouldn't people be willing to pay for information on a computer terminal?" he told Gates. Now, here they were online, with access to newspapers, "and stuff," and occasionally willing to pay for things.

Allen plunged right in. While Web mania was in full swing, he brainstormed new ideas and backed nearly 200 new companies, eventually plowing billions of dollars into new ventures. But when it was all said and done, the "Internet economy," as it was dubbed, went down in flames of its own overexcitement and Allen had little to show for it. A pitifully small portion of his companies became enduring successes; dozens even went out of business altogether. He was not as prescient as he wanted to be nor as smart an investor as many people expected one of the creators of Microsoft to be. But Allen was more concerned about "cool" ideas than the huge financial windfalls of the dot-com days.

In many ways, the Internet phenomenon was just a faster version of what Allen and Bill Gates went through with Microsoft. The start up experience was the same—lean, mean, and based on a dream. With the advent of the personal computer, hordes of hobbyists set up shop with new products and services around it. When the World Wide Web arrived, a business sector similarly spawned that moved fast. Little companies sprang up headed by recent graduates from places like Stanford University and California Institute of Technology. These entrepreneurs had wild, esoteric ideas and worked around the clock to prove them. They were very much descendents of Allen and Gates. Like Allen, they pushed ideas ahead of their time, and like Gates, they had the chutzpah to push products and make claims before they were ready. Soon enough these new entrepreneurs had many people believing in them—people with money. Venture capitalists on Sand Hill Road in Silicon Valley lined up with millions of dollars to spend. Wall Street bankers angled for the opportunity to take these little companies public. For these companies, the expectation of great wealth was a big part of the process. For Allen, the start-up dream had never been about money. His old friend Steve Wood, who had remained part of Allen's circle socially since moving out of his business holdings in 1992, explained in 2000 to *Bloomberg* that Allen's interest in the Internet, technology and the wired world was about one thing: "Paul Allen's primary motivation and I'm serious is to change the world."

When it came to the Web, Allen was intrigued by two kinds of sites. The search engine made sense. He once said to a reporter for the *Seattle Times*, "Say you've got all human knowledge available online. How do you browse it? There are some really interesting problems to be attacked there." If you did that, he thought, a vast, untamed place like a wired world, or the World Wide Web, would need a search engine to make sense of it all. He thought regular people would like it. It was what he had pushed for at Starwave with its CelebSite Web site. (In 2001, he did launch the other part of that idea with plans for a Web-based "Final Encyclopedia" a term coined by sci-fi novelist Gordon Dickson that refers to a place where all human knowledge is centered.)

Naturally, because he hoped people would "be willing to pay for information on a computer terminal," Allen also thought e-commerce made sense. E-commerce was the new term for selling goods and services over the Internet. In Allen's wired world concept, e-commerce was the rule, not the exception.

Right in Allen's backyard in Seattle, one little company was doing a bang-up job of e-commerce. Amazon.com was the brainchild of a former investment banker who, legend has it, had driven across the country in 1995 and written a business plan along the way. Amazon.com sold books and won over the hearts and minds of investors, Wall Street, and consumers, reaching a $5 billion valuation in 1998 and attracting millions of people to its site. Amazon was one of the great get-rich-quick stories of the "Internet economy" (for the principals of the company, at least), and it proved that people would buy things over the Internet.

Simple e-commerce as defined by Amazon and mimicked by thousands of others seemed a little pedestrian to Allen, however. It was also already well underway when he eventually got involved. Allen didn't like to fall in line; he had his own ideas for how things should be. Allen fancied himself master brainstormer for his companies and consumers in general. In 1998, he told the *Seattle Times,* "I'm an idea person."

For the Web, Allen had one incredibly big idea: "everything." The first thing he did was buy the Web site name, www.everything.com. But now, Everything.com was just an empty domain name. There was nothing on it, and no plan behind it. Everything.com needed a reason for being and it had to be new, different, and seriously "ground breaking" (Allen's goal for his post-Microsoft years). Allen was still out to change the world and prove his post-Microsoft value. He had high hopes that Everything.com would do it.

Allen's business m.o. wasn't unlike the dot-com generation of entrepreneurs. Like them, he'd always had a build-it-and-they-will-come mentality. His wired world theory was based on the premise that he would create it and people would come to experience it. Bill Gates, on the other hand, had a hard time in the Internet economy, at least at first. Gates was good at identifying markets to move Microsoft into; Allen was about having good ideas that other people should recognize. Many Web sites, at first, were created with that kind of view in mind. If it was a good idea, thought the sites' founders, why wouldn't people want to show up?

For Everything.com, Allen plucked a guy from Asymetrix, his first start-up. Tom Van Horn was married, 35, and a graduate of the Wharton School of Business who had done a tour of duty as a consultant with McKinsey & Co. before he entered the Paul Allen family of companies in 1996. He came in through Asymetrix, where he ran InfoModelers, the database company. Van Horn quickly learned the ropes at Asymetrix: Please Allen, do what he wants, don't argue back too much, and you'll do fine. In other words, Allen's de facto loyalty policy. After two years, Van Horn was named CEO of Asymetrix spin-off SuperCede, which had plans to go public (but never did). Now, Allen had a new assignment for him.

"Do something in e-commerce," he told Van Horn. It was Van Horn's chance to really prove himself to his wealthy career benefactor. If he got this one right—if he piqued Allen's interest—he'd land a spot in the Allen inner circle for a very long time. Or, if he came up with a really good idea, he could take the company public and get rich. Either way, a lot was riding on this challenge.

It was no small task. At this point in the Internet game, e-commerce was already moving into new, creative areas with off-shoots of Amazon's basic storefront model. A site called Ebay became a quick hit with a business that let people create little auctions among themselves online. Consumers loved it. Priceline was the next big idea—and, really, the first breakthrough idea—to change e-commerce. Priceline's CEO, Jay Walker, saw that auctions could help airlines sell unused airline seats. Usually written off as losses, open seats could go to the highest bidder through the Internet. Things were happening fast. Van Horn's challenge wasn't just to "do something in e-commerce"—he had to catch up and leapfrog the rest, and fast.

The first idea for Everything.com was so ambitious it was nearly ridiculous. Allen wanted Everything.com to have information and services on everything—literally. It would start off with "everything" for men to draw the overwhelming majority of males who were online in 1998. Everything.com would lure them with articles on the things that men liked, then slip in subtle opportunities to buy related products. There were plans to create a site that had "everything" for women, along the same lines. Van Horn assembled a staff of about 20 versed in publishing. Their task was enormous: They were eventually going to put "everything" on the site. For now, they geared up for the challenge of "everything" for men. Their desks in Allen's drab Bellevue building piled high with reams of magazines and proprietary research about what men liked to read and buy. They began to write stories on things like hiking. Allen and Van Horn expected merchandisers who had no storefronts of their own to line up for a spot on Everything.com.

The plan for Everything.com was a really big idea. It was pie-in-the-sky, but that's the sort of stuff Allen likes. He's usually looking ahead around corners, and wants to be the one to create that view first. He says he doesn't mind waiting around for the rest of the world to catch up.

Allen's e-commerce plan for Everything.com was similar to an idea from the days of SkyPix. With the advent of interactive television, companies talked up big plans to let consumers interact with their televisions. One of those was to tie in content like television shows with commerce, where everything on the screen, or related products, was for sale.

Allen really wanted to push the envelope in the current e-commerce climate. Everything.com was too ambitious in many ways, but to Allen, it wasn't groundbreaking enough. He told Van Horn to find him some new ideas.

By now, Van Horn had a staff of about 35. He wouldn't have to do the thinking on his own; he could share the risk with the rest. The first thing he did was ditch the daunting "everything" name. Now that the company was definitely going be all-e-commerce-all-the-time, Van Horn came up with a name better suited to the company's new plan: Mercata. It's not a word, but is very similar to the Spanish *mercado* and the Italian *mercato*, which mean "market." With their new name for the site, Van Horn and the rest of the staff went to work on a new business concept.

This was a fun time at Mercata. The company's future was certain but unknown. It was wide open with possibilities. Mercata was cash-rich, with a guarantee of millions more from Allen behind it. Employees knew they were secure in their jobs, even if they didn't know what those jobs would be. Van Horn summoned everyone on staff and told them he'd shut down the company for a few days so they could all go away together to hash out the company's future.

Employees were heady with the prospects. "Anything was possible," recalls Wayne Wurzer, who was hired as copy chief in November 1998, when the company was still set on publishing articles. "Even though I had no business experience, after a month on the job, I was told, 'go and research an idea.' It was 'clean slate, think big.'"

Allen the "idea" man loved this. He was excited to hear back from Van Horn how it turned out.

The idea that became the business behind Mercata wasn't Allen's and it wasn't even Van Horn's—it came from a column in a business magazine that suggested the Web would be a great place for people to get together and find ways to save money on purchases by buying in bulk. Van Horn read this and ignored the dozens of other ideas presented at the company's retreat. He pulled out a white board and drew elaborate diagrams to show how such a thing could work over the Internet. He distributed materials to accompany his presentation. Van Horn, the pitchman with an MBA who had worked his way onto Allen's radar, was just warming up.

Mercata launched in May 1999. Over the next nearly two years, Van Horn would convince Allen, Oprah Winfrey, and investors that Mercata was just about the greatest thing ever to have happened.

The idea was simple. If consumers with a single purchase item in mind could find each other somehow, they could go to the retailer as a group and demand a lower price. Mercata would be the intermediary. It would start by suggesting items available for discount, usually overstocked goods. This was a good move for the other side of the transaction: Mercata gave merchandisers a way to make money on unsold products, instead of having to write them off as losses. Van Horn and his team even came up with a new name for it all: "we-commerce."

Allen stumped for Mercata. He talked about Mercata to the other companies in his portfolio. At one of his Synergy Summits in 1999, he singled out Mercata during his opening remarks. "He said it was special to him," recalls Brad Humphries, a former vice president who ran the company's merchandiser relationships.

Mercata drew customers, easily raised $75 million from eager venture capitalists (some who were just interested in establishing a connection with Allen), and landed the esteemed Goldman, Sachs investment bank to take it public. But to employees, Van Horn seemed to lose track of the big picture while he spent his time flogging the business. He loved talking about Mercata to journalists. He finagled a guest spot on "The Oprah Winfrey Show" and wowed Oprah with the "we-commerce" concept. Beyond that, he didn't seem to add much to the company. "He was exceptionally good at telling the story and could get just about anyone with a pulse excited about it," says Humphries, who calls his time there an incredible experience. "Now, running the company and managing the business—that was not his strong suit," he says. Van Horn hired friends and relatives, quickly bloating the management ranks with high-salaried executives. It seemed to employees and executives that Van Horn became a little heady with power and being part of Paul Allen's inner circle of confidants.

To some, it looked like Van Horn thought Mercata was his own personal company. He micromanaged staff down to their grammar. "He gave the company a lecture on the use of pronouns," recalls one former Mercata employee. Van Horn even issued a memo on the finer points of speech. "He was like a moldy old English teacher," says the ex-employee. Still, money kept pouring in—$89 million was raised. But there were no controls in place—Allen himself was off tending to his other investments and hobbies.

Since Mercata was not managed by Allen in the least, the few times he was around (even though his Vulcan office was upstairs, the Mercata crew rarely saw him), he wasn't any help to executives looking for direction. It was no secret that he had the final word on the company's business, though. Employees knew that, ultimately, Van Horn's job was to carry out whatever wishes Allen had for Mercata. When Allen saw something on the site he didn't like, he'd fire off an e-mail to Van Horn, who would follow Allen's direction.

Allen did come in for overview presentations, but the outcome was frustrating, more than anything else. "People tried to read his reactions," says Wurzer. Allen would maybe "perk up" one moment, or ask questions that staff tried to decode. They bemoaned his laissez-faire attachment to Mercata. "Part of being hands-off is good, because you get to do stuff. But the bad part is that you can become a fat and lazy company. We became a fat and lazy company," says Wurzer. With Allen as a source of capital behind it, Mercata never felt the impetus to push its business model toward profitability.

Mercata proved to be one of the Internet economy's most spectacular busts. It was pure dot-com era: It was a very intellectual concept that drew a lot of cash and attention, but didn't turn out to be a good business idea. Despite Allen and Van Horn's efforts and a splashy, award-winning ad campaign featuring the voice of the pitchman for Visa, Mercata didn't attract enough consumers to make the theory of group-buying work as a money-generator. The idea had sounded great in theory, but it required more consumers per product than were finding their way to Mercata. Mercata wasn't a practical stopping point, like Amazon, or entertainment, like Ebay's auction drama. Priceline was for the individual, so action of some sort was always guaranteed. Mercata's biggest problem was that it didn't always get a better price for consumers. It was Mercata's downfall. In 1999, Mercata rang up a net loss of $36 million and counted just $6 million in revenues. After $89 million in three rounds of venture capital financing and plans to raise $100 million in an initial public offering, Mercata was shut down by majority owner Allen who was tired of seeing his money wasted on an idea that wasn't working. In January 2000, days before Mercata planned to go public, Allen shut down the company and retained the intellectual property—the group-buying concept had been patented—so that someday, maybe, he could use it again.

Like so many CEOs of failed Allen companies, Van Horn was brought into Vulcan and put in a holding pattern. Allen wasn't certain what to do with Van Horn, but he knew he could trust him. That mattered.

There were many people who became stars for a period of time because of the Internet. Company founders like Jerry Yang at Yahoo!, Marc Andreessen at Netscape, and Steve Case at AOL found their pictures frequently splashed across national magazine covers. Even relatively obscure people in investment roles like John Doerr at venture capital firm Kleiner, Perkins, Caufield & Byers and Mary Meeker at Morgan Stanley were suddenly vaulted into national—and sometimes international— celebrity. Mercata made headlines and raised Tom Van Horn's profile for a while, but it only further tarnished Allen's image as the "accidental zillionaire."

Allen can't be blamed for all of it. The guy driving Allen's moves in the Internet economy was Bill Savoy, his trusted moneyman since 1990. At Vulcan Ventures, if Allen ruled the wired world, the guy who presided over the Internet was Savoy. The Internet economy's intense emphasis on venture capital and initial public offerings fell right into Savoy's purview.

Savoy was a short, wiry fellow with a shock of blonde hair that always fell into his face. He looked more like a teenager than an accomplished adult and some people derisively called him "David Spade" because of his resemblance to the diminutive comic actor. But Spade was funny. Savoy, on the other hand, struck many people as mean—and incredibly arrogant. "You could call me the guard at the door of the vault," he often said.

Savoy wasn't like the other guys who worked for Allen. He wasn't an old friend, like Bert Kolde or Vern Raburn, and he didn't appear to be as insecure about his position in the Allen clan, like Van Horn and the rest of Allen's rotation of top executives, who also insinuated themselves into Allen's personal life if they could. Savoy knew that he was a very powerful money manager. He didn't need to tag along with Allen to prove it. "My work persona is built around one person," he told *The Wall Street Journal*. "I don't want my social life to be that, too."

Savoy was cold and very unfriendly. Almost no one liked him. "He's arrogant. I don't enjoy working with him," says one financier. A woman who worked for Barry Diller when Allen first took a seat on the board of Diller's Home Shopping Network got to know Savoy on an eight-hour plane ride to a meeting overseas. The experience still makes her shudder. "He's the most arrogant human being," she says. Not everyone sees him like that. Says one executive from a former Allen company, "Very cocky—but not resentful."

Savoy's personal journey had taken him from New Braintree, Massachusetts, where he began life on his own at 16 and within 10 years he had come to preside over billions of dollars. That knowledge filled his head. "I totally groove on what I do," he told *Bloomberg* magazine.

David Geffen called Savoy "if not the center of the deal-making world, he's pretty close to it," while observing the 36-year-old huddled for hours with Nancy Peretsman, the star managing director at investment company Allen & Co. during one of Herb Allen's summer retreats. It was the summer of 1999 and Savoy had spent $2 billion on dot-com investments in less than two years. With all that dough and all the places it could go, Savoy was one hot property.

In 1991, Savoy guarded just $1.7 billion for Allen. By the time Internet mania swept the nation in 1997, Savoy was parsing out 10 times as much—Allen's fortune had amassed to $17 billion. It was Savoy's job to carry out the wired world vision through investments that fit that view. But with the Internet, Savoy found a way to shine in his own right.

As the dot-com deal-making whipped into a frenzy in the last few years of the decade, Savoy was the man on everyone's list, even if people didn't like to do deals with him. No fewer than 200 companies received investments from Vulcan thanks to Savoy's penchant for the Net. Thousands more lined up, hat in hand. Savoy funneled their business plans off to the now dozens of Vulcan employees who reviewed them and thought about how many millions to put into the lucky ones chosen. Vulcan backed companies with names like Zany Brainy, Siliscape, and iMotors. Through Savoy, the firm became seriously involved in dot-com investments, with a 6.2 percent stake in Priceline; 6.2 percent stake in chip maker Transmeta; 4.6 percent stake in Amazon spin-off Drugstore.com; 18.7 percent stake in electronics services company Value America; 10 percent stake in TheStreet.com; $20 million in online bookseller FatBrain; $30 million in music portal RioPort.com; $11 million in tech-information Web sites CNET; and others.

The pace of the investments alone did great things for Allen's image. *The Economist* called him "technology's archangel." A Dow Jones report called him a "market king." One fund manager from Stein Roe & Farnham in Chicago said, "He makes investors sit up, pay attention, and deliver 'buy' orders."

Most of the investments turned out to be duds. Even at the time, Allen's investing pattern left people scratching their heads. It was easy enough to say that they all fell into the wired world program. Of course they did: They were all based on the Web, a worldwide network like that Allen envisioned earlier in the decade. But Allen wasn't leading the way to the biggest hits of the Net. "Allen and his people have been creative and early, but since Microsoft, where are the Yahoos and the Amazons?" Keith Benjamin, one of the Internet's star investment analysts, wondered aloud to *The Wall Street Journal* in 1998.

Allen became technology's poster child. But as soon as the dot-com sector began going bust, it was all over, fast. Initial public offerings like Mercata's were canceled. Allen investments like ValueAmerica, an online shopping site, went down in over-heated flames. So did Allen and his brief moment as a "market king." But of course, Allen didn't really care how much money he lost. He had too much of it, anyway. "The advantage of having the re-sources I have is that you can be a more patient investor," he told *The Economist*. In Hollywood, one company would shortly test that patience.

By the fall of 1999, Allen's old pals at DreamWorks had come up with an idea for a Web site, a phenomenon that took a while to take hold among Hollywood brass. But once the Internet economy came to Hollywood, it left many people there feeling very uncomfortable. It used to be that movie breaks brought en-viable lottery-size cash-windfalls. Now, the dot-com people seemed to be the ones getting richer. They were flaunting their toys around the millionaires in Hollywood, who were suddenly not as rich as these multimillionaires (and the occasional billion-aire). They wanted in on it, too.

DreamWorks had a deal with Imagine Entertainment, a pro-duction studio owned by Ron Howard and Brian Grazer. After a brief huddle, the principals from each studio decided they should start an Internet venture together. It would be structured like the other dot-coms: It would start off in-house at DreamWorks, raise outside cash from venture investors and eventually be spun-off into a public company, and boom: lots of dough for the five guys with the big idea.

It wasn't a stretch to pull Paul Allen into the mix. He'd helped out the DreamWorks guys in the past, and this proposal fell squarely within his forte (as far as they were concerned). On a warm fall day at the end of October, a press release was issued announcing a new entertainment site, with backing from Allen's Vulcan Ventures. The site was called Pop.com.

Pop.com started the same way DreamWorks had: It was just a general idea that needed serious filling out. (It was also the way Everything.com had started.) There was no one running Pop.com and there was no business plan. That didn't stop the principals from thinking big. They approached every bold-faced name in the entertainment and media sectors to run the new venture. They asked talent agent Michael Ovitz (then dabbling in dot-coms, himself), *Vanity Fair* editor-in-chief Graydon Carter, and former Warner Bros. co-CEO Terry Semel (by this point a venture capitalist) to head up Pop.com. They asked every studio head in town to leave his or her position and become a dot-com CEO. You'll get rich, they promised them, Paul Allen's put up $50 million to back this thing.

Eventually, Kenneth Wong from Disney Imagineering took the job. Wong managed to come up with a business plan. Pop.com would buy and create programming for the Web. Like a studio, it would sign talent to a contract. Pop paid well and attracted top animation and comic talent, as well as some movie stars, including Drew Barrymore and Steve Martin, but it was too late. The initial plans called for launching the site—whatever it was to be—in spring 2000. But the market's crash in April 2000 dampened interest in the company from its Hollywood backers. The company's employees plugged away through the summer, while other entertainment dot-coms blew up around them, turning tens of millions of dollars into dust. But Pop.com kept going, first promising a summer and then a fall debut. That's when Allen sat up and noticed Pop.com wasn't happening.

Until now, Allen had been caught up in the enthusiasm from Howard, Katzenberg, and the rest. He had pretty much left Pop.com alone, but thanks to its celebrity backers, every major newspaper, business publication, and Hollywood trade magazine reported any new missteps or progress out of Pop.com. It was quickly viewed as a joke for its delays. Allen called up the principals for a chat. This Pop.com thing couldn't go on any longer like this, he told them. Meanwhile, Allen had also sunk $10 million into iFilm, a Web site that changed direction several times, but was generally focused on being a portal for short films and film industry information for insiders. He suggested the two merge and salvage what little there was to save of Pop.com. Executives on both sides of the table couldn't come to terms and Pop.com was simply folded.

Pop.com turned out to be a big, embarrassing failure for the principals at the two studios. For Allen, not as much. Instead of waiting for tens of millions to be sucked out of his many billions, he escaped with a mere $9 million loss. It was probably his smartest move as an investor in the Internet economy.

When it came down to it, the Net still didn't make much sense to Allen. All kinds of content and services offered for free? Not for him. But, he thought, the Internet made sense if he could use it as a way to test ideas he'd transfer over to the cable world he was building, while Savoy spent more of his time on the Net. Allen would view the Web as an environment in which to build new products and services. It was just like those days at Microsoft, when Allen used to haul out his simulator program that allowed programmers to develop languages for new machines before they were built. Cable wasn't ready yet, but ultimately, it offered a better environment for the real wired world he imagined. Some publications were calling cable the "heir apparent" to the Internet, which was running its course. Cable was high-speed and high-bandwidth. It could carry loads of content that could be sent back-and-forth, interactively, with consumers. And it was a connection that was going to both PCs and TVs. Allen saw how the Net could help him build up some of these things that he'd later put on his cable systems.

He thought his wired world would need a portal on any platform. The idea of a "portal" was a trendy one in Internet days, but Allen's idea was a holdover from Everything.com—a place that did "everything." Go2Net was a portal that seemed to be on its way toward "everything." In 1999, it was growing into a network of sites that offered all the essential services people wanted online: a financial site, a search engine and a shopping site. Consumers could go to Go2Net's home page and find all these things offered there. It was a portal Allen could understand. He wanted this sort of thing on his cable service, eventually. Even better: Go2Net was based in Seattle and it was run by a Lakeside alum. Russell Horowitz, Go2Net's CEO, graduated from Allen's alma mater in 1984. In 1996, he'd started Go2Net with another Lakeside chum, John Keister. It was all very familiar to Allen.

Allen didn't dillydally around with Go2Net. He had too many billions and was starting to make bigger investments, anyway, plunking down billions at a time for the various cable systems he was acquiring.

Allen plowed $750 million in *cash* into Go2Net on March 15, 1999. It was at the height of Allen's Internet-wisdom persona, when investors were following his lead. The move boosted Go2Net's stock by 30 percent. It continued to rise based on the news of Allen's interest alone, all the way from $90 on that day to $180 two months later. Savoy watched like a hawk over the events. Allen's money had been promised based on the deal day's stock price. He couldn't pay $180 for all the shares he wanted, but he still needed a 54 percent stake. The next month, the company agreed to give him a discount and he put up a total of $426 million for a 34 percent stake. Allen hardly held a majority of the company, but he acted as if he owned the whole thing.

"We consider Go2Net to be the glue to hold together our vision of the wired world," Savoy told *The Wall Street Journal*. For Allen, Go2Net didn't capture his fancy for being a cool, abstract intellectual concept like Mercata (which he had also hoped to port over to cable, only it became too expensive to wait for that). Go2Net was serious consumer candy. It was a portal that did many things. He wanted it to do more, though. He summoned some of the company's executives into his office. They showed him some of their plans for Go2Net's front page, including new content and services. Allen sat expressionless behind his desk while they filled him in on their plans. Suddenly, he cut them off. He didn't want to hear anymore. He wanted to know why the site's front page couldn't have a constantly running ticker, a video window, and other animated, moving objects that provided useful information or entertainment—all at once. He wanted a portal that did "everything."

The executives sat speechless. The Web couldn't handle all that. Well, it could, but most consumers' connections couldn't. What Allen was talking about required a fat broadband pipe— at least as wide as cable—that fewer than 5 percent of all households had. They went away upset and frustrated. Allen never relented.

Back at work, Go2Net management pushed on with their own plans. Flush with Allen's cash, Go2Net, like so many dot-coms of the day, went on a serious shopping spree. Over the next year, it gobbled up several companies, including Web hosting service Virtual Avenue, business directory United States Online, financial chart maker IQC, and search company Dogpile. It also made an investment in e-mail provider CommTouch. Go2Net, which had been public since April 1997, was well run. It exceeded expectations on Wall Street and had minimal losses. It survived the April 2000 stock market crash and in July 2000, Infospace, a Seattle-area listings site, agreed to acquire Go2Net for $4 billion—more than tripling Allen's investment. Allen and Savoy both came out clean.

For Allen, though, a sale wasn't necessary. He had really wanted Go2Net to be the portal for his cable plans. He didn't care about the money—Go2Net could lose all the money in the world, for all he cared. He needed a portal for his wired world.

Allen—or Vulcan, through Savoy—was surely one of the most active investors in the dot-com period. To observers who knew something about his wired world, it seemed like the Internet was right up Allen's alley. But ultimately, the Internet boom wasn't about ideas, it was about money. Lots of it, sunk hard and fast into hundreds of minicompanies with big dreams. Just one hit could turn a huge profit for its backers, so venture capitalists spread their bets around. It was like prospecting for gold.

For Allen, the dot-com boom did not turn out to be his shining moment, after all. Except for a brief moment, it didn't do much to validate his wired world theory, at least on Wall Street, where he'd gone back to being the "accidental zillionaire." A *Wall Street Journal* report at the end of 2000, eight months after Internet stocks fell crashing to earth, evaluated Allen as a stock picker and concluded that investors who follow Allen's lead, "won't become billionaires any time soon." The story reported that the average rate of return on investment for nine of Allen's stakes in public companies yielded not only a negative, but a whopping 43 percent loss in value. It said more about Savoy, though, since he was the one picking the stocks. Still, it didn't help Allen's Internet investment profile.

But Allen had moved on. His moneyman Savoy, told everyone who was listening that, since summer 2000, and in some cases, earlier, Allen's Internet holdings had been diminished. Allen had a new focus: he was a cable guy now.

11

# CABLE GUY

The dot-com bubble burst in 2000 and it was a disaster. Hundreds of companies in varying stages of development were stricken. Hopeful techies and MBAs alike, went home. Venture capitalists closed their wallets and consumers were left with fewer surfing and shopping choices than before. The Internet looked like it was over.

Paul Allen had long since moved on. His investment portfolio still held a few Internet stragglers, but his attention—and his wallet—was directed elsewhere, and had been, even while the world was still going nuts over dot-coms.

In 1998, Allen kicked off a spending spree bigger than any before. But now it went in an unlikely direction, cable. He looked quite serious, too. In a single instance, Allen plunked down $2.8 billion for a controlling stake in the country's ninth-largest system, Marcus Cable. Several months later, he paid $4.5 billion for St. Louis-based Charter Communications. He didn't stop. Through 1999, he scooped up several more cable companies for hundreds of millions of dollars apiece and merged them as he went along. When he was done, he'd spent $18 billion and was suddenly the owner of the fourth largest cable system in the country, Charter Communications. It gave him a direct connection into 6.2 million homes. "It was like you woke up one day and Paul Allen owned half of cable," says one interactive TV executive.

It did seem like a rather sudden change in course, even to the closest Allen watchers. Allen had always been the tech guy, not the cable guy. Technology was fast moving, new, and geeky. Cable was very old-school. It had its roots in mom-and-pop ownership of systems delivering cable connections to just a few thousand subscribers each. The business had evolved through the 1980s and early 1990s as government restrictions on cable ownership gradually eased and restrictions on the rates they could charge were similarly loosened. It made cable a credible business. Big companies eyed cable as a growth target as more and more households signed up each year. By the 1990s, cable began to resemble big business, with companies like AT&T and Time Warner scooping up systems to become major cable operators covering large geographical areas around the country. But still, cable wasn't all that sexy. It felt very clunky in a world increasingly going wireless.

Consumers, too, thought cable was very low-tech. Many people were unhappy with their cable companies. There were no instant connections. They had to wait for service and repair technicians to come to their homes, lay down cable lines and drill holes in walls so the cable could go through. A box had to be carried into the house. When there was a problem with the service, another trip had to be made to the home to determine the problem. The whole process was slow and riddled with headaches. Why would a high-tech guy want to get into a business so heavy on maintenance and installation and have to deal with customers, on top of it?

The truth was, a smart strategy was unfolding. Allen first started thinking about cable in 1992, after his vision for SkyPix failed to materialize. He thought for the first time then about not just providing services to consumers in a wired world, but controlling the connection to their PCs or TVs—or whatever it was that gave them access to the wired world. Now, Allen tweaked his plan to get to a wired world. The four ingredients—software, hardware, infrastructure, and content—were still essential, and still four areas he targeted with his investment activities. But when it came to cable, he got very specific. Now, there were three areas that, if managed accurately, could converge to create a cable-connected wired world. He looked at it like three circles that overlapped: connections to consumers; the content to give them; and communications systems that managed the interactive experience. Where these came together, a wired world would be born.

After SkyPix failed, Allen didn't give much more thought to the satellite business. It was too difficult to get into, anyway. In 1992, there weren't mature, ready-to-buy satellite operators like DirecTV. It was an extremely nascent business with no proven track record. There was no guarantee that owning a satellite broadcast system would get the signal into the home without a special device. But cable, on the other hand, had already proved itself. People were allowing boxes into their homes because they were eager to get cable content like MTV and CNN. Millions were signing up. Allen wanted in.

At the time, Savoy said no. As Allen's main financial man, he said with authority that cable was not a good investment. In 1992, the government had just imposed a rate cap on cable operators and growth in that business looked limited. Savoy later said to *Bloomberg*, "I was right timingwise about cable, but anything else that I haven't done that he told me to do I've ended up regretting." For the time being, Allen accepted Savoy's answer and turned his attention elsewhere.

Over the years, cable continued to nag at Allen. He wanted some way in to people's homes. That was why he had wanted control of AOL.

Throughout the decade, Allen turned his attention elsewhere. He built a music museum, bought a football team, played with his celebrity friends, and tried never to miss a Trail Blazers' game.

The dot-com boom happened. He kept busy enough. But he was still the "accidental zillionaire" with just one success—Microsoft—behind him. Executives close to him thought he still wanted a success all his own. Cable became his big hope.

Meanwhile, cable itself went through many changes in an effort to keep up with changes in media toward the trendy concept of interactivity. More practically speaking, cable owners also had to prove to Wall Street that they weren't, in fact, aging dinosaurs, as some people had come to believe. In the early 1990s, when everyone was talking about a new idea called "interactive TV," cable operators and cable channel owners began buzzing about video-on-demand and giving consumers access to the Internet through cable connections. Most of it was just talk. Cable was an old-boys' network run by tough-talking men like Tele-Communications Inc. chief John Malone, a plain-speaking New Englander who had been in the cable business since 1972. As a business, cable resembled the real-estate industry—cable companies needed to dominate a market to get the most out of their expensive infrastructure. The men who ran cable systems walked around like swash-buckling prospectors eyeing each other's properties and sitting down often for a land-swap. Their properties grew and gained in value.

Meanwhile, thanks to some Silicon Valley developments, cable and television also became credible components of the hot Internet industry. AtHome was a Redwood City, California, company that delivered Internet access through a cable modem. WebTV, based in Mountain View, California, built a set-top box that let people surf the Web with a remote mouse and keyboard pointed at their television sets. Cable owners were buying in to these companies, but none of them were very serious about it.

Paul Allen was among the most prescient about the potential of cable and, in 1998, he decided that if he didn't get going on his cable idea, it would be too late. Cable companies were getting expensive, and some of them were getting smarter—but none had delivered the ultimate interactive experience, yet. If he got in now, he could lead the way toward the wired world future.

This time, Savoy ran the numbers and told Allen he would likely get some return on his investment. That hardly mattered to Allen, who once said he could be patient with his investments. It was more important that he find a way to enable the wired world. Cable seemed to be the answer.

In fact, Allen was already late to the cable game. In 1997, a year before Allen started investing, his old pal and partner Bill Gates had become a cable guy first. Gates had met Brian Roberts, the frank, wiry CEO of Comcast Cable, in 1995. Roberts had been in Seattle with other cable industry leaders who were exploring technologies for cable systems. The talk then was upgrading cable networks to handle digital technologies. Gates thought digital cable connections could open up a new market for Microsoft, so at a dinner of cable executives, he asked Roberts how he could help him get it done faster. "I just blurted out as a joke, 'Well if you are really interested, why don't you buy 10 percent of everyone in the room here. And then that would make a real statement,'" Roberts told the *Washington Post*. Two years later, Gates put $1 billion into Comcast for an 11.5 percent stake.

Charter Communications was a private company that financial folks were watching. Based in St. Louis, Charter was run by Jerry Kent, a plain-speaking, hard-working, 15-year cable veteran. Kent and his two partners, Barry Babcock and Howard Wood, had started Charter from scratch in St. Louis in 1992 after their previous employer, Cencom Cable, was acquired and moved its headquarters out of the area. Now on their own, the trio raised $300 million and started shopping for cable properties. They called the company Charter Communications. By 1998, they'd grown Charter to 1.1 million subscribers in various markets in the south and southwest. In 1998, Kent and his partners decided that if they were going to grow any further, they would need to bring in another partner. Otherwise, they'd have to sell out to another cable operator. Through a banker, they found Allen.

Bankers liked Kent. Most people did. He was a really personable, hard-working guy. He was easy to get along with. Maybe that's why Allen picked him to run the cable empire he was building. Charter was only the second of what he knew would be many more cable acquisitions, necessary to create a sizable system for deploying the broadband services in a wired world. Allen had already promised the guys at his first cable acquisition, Marcus Cable, that they would get to run his cable holdings. But then he met Kent and seemed to forget what he'd told the Marcus executives. Allen handed Kent and his team the business he was amassing. Marcus executives were stunned. A few years later, one former executive still bitter over the incident told *Cable World*, "They did the deal with us, told us we were king of the world, then did the deal with" Charter, he said.

Kent would not be remembered as an Allen disciple in the fashion of Bert Kolde or even Tom Van Horn. To Kent, the relationship with Allen was demanding and one-sided. After it was all over, he told *The Wall Street Journal* their relationship "wasn't healthy." Kent wanted merely to run a successful cable business. Allen had a slightly different plan—he had a wired world that mattered more than one cable company. His concern was a grand network of operations. While Allen had been bulking up Charter, he'd also been getting involved with other kinds of companies. Some of these businesses ran right up against what Kent was trying to do at Charter. But Allen owned 94 percent of all voting shares, so it didn't really matter what Kent thought.

At any rate, Kent carried out the wired world vision well enough. In many ways, it lined up with his view of cable's future in interactive, digital television. He agreed that Charter's systems should speed up the upgrade to digital and focus on moving more of its subscribers to digital cable services. With Allen's impetus and Kent's acumen, very quickly, Charter boasted the greatest percentage of digital cable subscribers in the industry. Its digital services, like basic Web surfing, weren't incredibly sexy, but they outstripped the competition.

Kent's real talents lay in business building. He knew how to create a strong financial profile for cable systems. For Allen, Kent managed the intense pace of acquisitions to build Charter into the fourth largest system. It was Kent who became the face of Charter to Wall Street. Charter planned to go public to raise money to cover the debts from all the acquisitions. It was a good move. In November 1999, Charter pulled off a record-breaking IPO, raising $3 billion and making Wall Street history as the fourth largest IPO ever. The IPO was great news for Charter, but it was the beginning of the end for Allen and Kent.

More than anything else, owning Charter and pushing it aggressively to become a digital platform was extremely good for Allen's image. He gained some true respect as a businessman from people in a wide array of industries for the first time. Wall Street thought he had finally become a shrewd investor. Charter had losses from all the acquisitions and system upgrades, but the pitch from Kent about untold riches in a digital cable future sold investors on the company. Cable operators welcomed Allen, especially if he could bring additional cash and credibility to their industry. Even techies dug Allen's new big plan. They drooled over his wide-bandwidth pipes to consumers and his control over the cable "headend." The headend was where the magic happened. It was the piece of technology, *interactive* technology, between consumers and the system operator. While many people were developing set-top boxes that could do neat things with television, Allen's control over the headend meant he could control exactly what went into each home.

Allen continued to spend his money on cable systems. But he also assembled a cadre of companies that looked like they all centered around a wired world delivered over Charter's increasingly high-speed, high-bandwidth connections. He sunk money into new cable networks TechTV and Oxygen Media. Through these channels, he could control the programming to consumers. This was the content piece of the wired world puzzle. He bought a controlling stake in High-Speed Access, a company that could deliver Internet access over cable modems—a communications component. And then, in a move that doomed his relationship with Kent—he put a whopping $1.65 billion into a New Jersey-based company called Residential Communications Network (RCN).

RCN was an "overbuilder." It was a new kind of cable and telecommunications company that was laying down fiber-optic networks in major cities around the country, in the hopes of luring customers away from cable and phone companies. For the first time, thanks to companies like RCN, consumers would actually have a choice of cable providers. Better yet, these were brand-new lines, which meant they had state-of-the-art technologies. Allen loved it. Cable companies occasionally frustrated him, since they were mired in ancient technologies. Allen thought there was no harm in getting behind both cable and these overbuilders to see who got the job done first, or better.

Kent and other Charter executives were furious when they heard about Allen's plan to invest in RCN. They weren't given much warning. When they learned the news, the deal was practically done and it was too late to change Allen's mind. They were in shock. Didn't he realize that RCN was a direct inhibitor to the very progress Charter was trying to make? RCN only needed to take 30 percent of the subscribers in a local market to do well;

cable became more efficient the more people who subscribed. Losing that 30 percent could affect their bottom line dramatically. But Allen had been won over by RCN. RCN CEO David McCourt made no apologies and didn't cow to his nemeses, cable industry executives who were voicing their complaints to the media. "Paul wants to get something done," McCourt told the *Wall Street Journal.* "And he knew he wasn't going to be able to do that hanging around with the [cable] monopolists." It was an arrogant statement from an executive whose future was about to hit a multitude of road-bumps.

RCN turned out to be one of those pie-in-the-sky ideas along the lines of dot-com dreams of changing the world. It wasn't a bad premise—why not offer consumers an alternative to their cable systems? It was one area where consumers were pretty much forced to go with whatever cable company operated in their area, unless they opted for satellite, which was also becoming a thorn in the side of the cable industry. But RCN wasn't like the satellite business, which could simply launch a transmitter and wait for people with receivers to pull down the signal. RCN was, like the cable business, deeply involved in real estate and construction— capital-intensive real estate and construction. RCN's business required sending out tractors, electricians, men in hard hats with shovels, and others to dig up roads and lay down miles of fiber- optic lines. RCN was blowing through cash—hundreds of millions of dollars every quarter—but what was worse was that it wasn't even a reliable system. After loads of consumers reported outage problems, regulatory officials began an investigation into the company. Its stock, which hit $72 per share in February 2000, fell to just a few dollars by the end of 2001.

Still, Allen didn't back down from RCN. He believed in the concept. Why not control all the options into the household? But obviously, RCN was in such serious trouble it needed a way out. Allen thought about merging it with Charter.

Every step of the way, Kent fought some of Allen's views that he believed would cripple the cable system he had first begun piecing together from nothing almost 10 years earlier. RCN was the last straw. In September 2001, Kent abruptly resigned from Charter. The straight-talking Kent did little to cover up his troubled relationship with Allen. He told *Cable World* that differences with Allen ran "across all aspects. It's strategic; it's operational; it's personnel; it's all across the board. No one [thing] stands out. There have been some events that occurred over the last couple of weeks that certainly had an impact, but, really, this has been building upon for 18 to 24 months, and it just wasn't going to work going forward."

As it turned out, while Charter was a Wall Street favorite, holding strong while other cable stocks dipped, it wasn't the company or even Allen that investors loved as much as it was Kent himself. Charter's stock dropped 20 percent when Kent left.

If you subscribed to Charter Communications in 2001, you got a sense firsthand of Allen's aggressiveness. He practically forced the wired world down his customers' throats. While its connections were being upgraded to digital, Charter still had too many people buying only analog (in other words, cheaper) services from the company. Allen moved many of the premium channels to the digital service, so that if subscribers wanted channels like HBO and Showtime, they would have to upgrade their plans and costs to digital. He sent them elaborate remote controls with confusing buttons on them, many of which were simply placeholders for digital services still in the works.

Charter made no apologies for its abandonment of the average cable consumer. "The low-end customers that we were working hard to recruit with discounting were not paying off in terms of generating revenue. Continued aggressive growth for the sake of leading the industry didn't make sense to us," a spokesman told *Business Week* in 2001. It worked—by then, 28 percent of all Charter customers were digital subscribers, more than any other cable system.

Allen was barreling through the industry, paying heed to no one. He even shunned regulatory concerns. "Paul Allen's 'wired world' is like a Digital Concentration Camp," says Jeffrey Chester, executive director of the Center for Digital Democracy.

Chester had his eye on Allen. Allen was a culprit in an industry he believed was going to eliminate the open-access nature of the Internet and turn it into a toll-road only. He showed government agencies, such as the Federal Trade Commission (FTC), how closely tied the cable companies were and objected to certain deals on the table. Chester stepped up when Allen's cable-modem Internet access company, High-Speed Access (HSA), was picked as an alternative Internet access service to be offered to customers of AOL Time Warner's cable system. In Chester's view, it was a good thing that AOL wasn't going to make its customers choose only AOL to sign on to the Internet, but Chester didn't think that HSA was the right alternative. Its financial lineage to Charter Communications meant there were still conflicts of interest, he told the FTC: Charter and AOL jointly backed other services, and Charter was a significant buyer of AOL programming like the cable networks HBO, CNN, and TBS. If AOL Time Warner wanted a disinterested third-party alternative to AOL, one it couldn't possibly influence in the least, it should look elsewhere.

This was a relatively small issue, but Chester believed Allen's plans were far more sinister. He pointed out to the FTC that all of Allen's properties were contractually bound to work with one another, to the detriment of an open and free-market environment. HSA's financial filings revealed that "Under our programming content agreement with Vulcan, Vulcan has the right to require us to carry, on an exclusive basis in all cable systems we serve, content it designates . . . may include start-up and related Web pages, electronic programming guides." That wasn't all. Vulcan could also call the shots on which companies would not be carried by HSA: "Vulcan has the right to prohibit us from providing content or telephony services that compete with Vulcan content at Vulcan's discretion and can require us to remove competing content."

It was Chester's job to paint the most extreme picture, but Allen's motivations weren't that far off. He was, in fact, pulling together what seemed to be the final pieces of an evolving wired world vision that he had updated since getting into the cable business. And it was one that was eerily under his complete control.

In Allen's new and improved wired world view, the cable connection into the home wasn't simply a means to bring consumers entertainment, shopping services, news, financial information and instant-messaging through TVs, PCs, or other devices. He realized that, with that connection to the home, he could control not just those communication devices, but also pretty much anything in the house that ran on a computer chip or had the potential to be controlled by a computer chip.

The new wired world view looks something like this: Imagine an eight-year-old boy comes home from school and the house "knows" it. It lets him in, warms up a snack for him in the oven, sets the television to the programs his mother has approved, keeps the house locked, and sends a message to the parents that he's there. The wired world is a world that surrounds us completely with technology that is practically alive—brought to you by one Paul Allen.

For Allen, it was like 1992 all over again. SkyPix was the big dream back then for getting into consumers' homes. Now, it was Charter. Charter was panning out nicely, even with the occasional

pushback from people like Jerry Kent. RCN was another bet wagered, and he had invested in all entertainment and services for
consumers living in a wired world. But he wasn't done. He needed
a big plan to make it all happen. Allen wasn't the "big plan" guy.
He had the ideas, but others carried them out. He was just the
guy who saw where the world was headed. It had always been like
that. With Everything.com and Mercata, Tom Van Horn had figured out how to make it happen (sort of). Even as far back as Altair days, Allen hadn't been the one to carry things out as much as
identify the need for the version of BASIC he and Gates created.
Allen had seen that the microcomputer Altair needed was a language like BASIC and, from that, a universe of personal computers could spawn. He didn't figure out how to make it happen, he
just told Gates to get to work with him on creating BASIC. Even
earlier, he saw that the world would ultimately be connected
through its personal computers. He tried various ways to help
bring that about, only to be stymied by the Greenbergs at SkyPix
and Steve Case at AOL. Now, he needed someone to help him
carry out an idea that was ready to go. He needed a sidekick—a
CEO or other executive to implement his idea. As one former employee observed, "Paul Allen is the uber-strategist and the CEO
becomes the master tactician."

It was an exciting new era. Allen's wired world was coming together: He was in charge of the connection to consumers. He
could charge a toll; he could dictate what they received. He was
the ruler of this wired world. He asked his top lieutenants at
Charter, RCN, Vulcan, and Go2Net (before it was acquired by
InfoSpace) to huddle on a regular basis and figure out how it was
all going to work. The group was called Broadband Partners.
    Paul Budak became involved with Broadband Partners in 2000.
At the time, he was directing software development on set-top

boxes at Vulcan-backed BSquare, an interactive TV company. He had become something of a technical expert in interactive TV software. He met with the group a few times to discuss what was available in the market and what they might consider using. Microsoft had an interactive TV platform it was working on. But there were many others, including a company called Liberate Technologies, which was later chosen by Charter to handle some of its interactive TV needs.

Budak watched as Broadband Partners transformed quickly from a loose cabal of interactive cable people into a real company. It had to. It had become clear rather early on that if there was going to be a strategy to roll out the wired world, one dedicated company should handle it. Allen agreed. He picked longtime loyalist, former Asymetrix CEO Jim Billmaier to head up the new company, called Digeo—combining "digital" and "video."

If Charter had been the late 1990s' equivalent of SkyPix, then Digeo was what Starwave was meant to be in the very beginning, a multimedia company that provided all of the content and services sent through the interactive channel to the consumer. Budak, who'd been hired on to the original Starwave when it was just 10 people strong, saw the similarities to Digeo. "It was just like SkyPix and Starwave, just different people and a different place, 10 years later," he says.

Digeo started off in stealth mode. Billmaier went on a hiring spree that, naturally, included other Allen-company regulars, as well as some of his own friends and relatives. Their job was to figure out what the set-top box would do for consumers. Before Go2Net was acquired by InfoSpace, it was supposed to provide a kind of interactive-cable portal with shopping, news, and entertainment for Charter customers. When that company left the Vulcan fold, Microsoft's MSN was chosen. Digeo and Charter executives used MSN as the front page in presentations to investors on Charter's digital future.

This was a twist. For the first time, Microsoft became a vendor to Allen. In addition to its MSN portal, Microsoft executives hoped Allen would choose their interactive TV software platform, too. It was an odd shift in dynamics between Allen and Gates, but Gates had fallen significantly behind in cable. His $1 billion investment in Comcast really hadn't gotten him very far. A few deals with Comcast and AT&T were inked for Microsoft's interactive TV platform, but nothing had been rolled out yet. Allen had been the smart one to realize the only way to make a difference in cable was to take the giant step into becoming an owner of the pipes. Only by owning the connection could anyone make a difference in cable. It put Charter and Allen in a position of power with Microsoft. In late 2000, when Digeo was firming up its plans, Microsoft needed to be in on them, badly.

Getting it wrong in cable wasn't the first time Gates had miscalculated the road ahead. He had completely underestimated the impact of the Internet and the Web in the early 1990s and by mid-decade had had to play significant catch-up. With millions of dough in its coffers, Microsoft scooped up enough companies in the dot-com evolution and handily became a mega-force on the Internet.

Cable wasn't like the Internet, though. Microsoft was learning that. The cable industry wasn't too well-versed in technology, and though Microsoft had a big name, it still couldn't call the shots. Executives at its interactive TV group in Mountain View, California, office had been hitting their heads up against a wall for years now, trying to break into the cable business. Charter and Allen seemed among their last hopes.

Allen did eventually choose Microsoft's interactive TV platform. In the fall of 2001, a press release was sent out announcing the selection. But after several months of talks and planning between Microsoft and Digeo and Charter, the deal fell apart. Microsoft was just not ready.

If anyone was watching a race between Bill Gates and Paul Allen, in the spring of 2002, Allen was in the lead. Gates's interactive TV plans were having a hard time of it. Microsoft's interactive TV group, split between Redmond and Silicon Valley, had gone through a major change at the top and two deep rounds of layoffs. By May, the interactive TV group in Silicon Valley was all but gone, as were Microsoft's original plans to develop software and an interface that dominated the interactive TV sector. New plans were being drawn up. But it wasn't really Gates's fault; he was embroiled in a federal justice department probe of Microsoft's business practices. It had been going on for years. Gates had begun to lose his focus.

Even before Microsoft staggered in interactive TV, Allen was on top of the world. In 2001, Charter's stock soared; Jerry Kent, before he left, was a solid if occasionally difficult-to-manage leader for the company; and cable was giving Allen back some of his credibility. When the Microsoft deal fell apart in November 2001, it wasn't Allen who got a bad rap; it was Microsoft. *The Wall Street Journal* said Charter's commitment to Microsoft's interactive TV offerings had been viewed "as a big vote of confidence." People were watching Allen to see what he'd do next with his money and his cable empire.

What he did next was scoop up one of the hottest new companies out of Silicon Valley. Moxi Digital was a company started by Steve Perlman, an entrepreneur built in Allen's image with a steadfast belief in his own vision of the future. (*Business Week* noted that Perlman "gets frustrated when his ideas aren't lauded by others.") His last company was WebTV, which Allen had backed in its earliest days. Now, with Moxi, Allen was back again. He took part in the company's $67 million round of fundraising before the product was unveiled. In January 2002, at the Consumer Electronics

Show in Las Vegas, Moxi wowed the crowd. This box was amazing. It could receive cable or satellite signals, record programs and play them back almost as they were happening, like the digital video recorder TiVo. It could also play DVDs. Even better, it served as a hub that could send the same content wirelessly to other TVs around the house. The Moxi box would eliminate the need for many VCRs or DVD players in a single home, or having several cable hook-ups. All those needs would be taken care of by this single, brilliant box.

But behind the excitement, Moxi was in trouble. The technology was so expensive that the company was blowing through cash. Within several months, it would be gone, if no one came to the rescue.

Paul Allen came to the rescue. Moxi was seen as a good fit with Digeo, which was also focused on making TV watching and Web surfing more compatible and less awkward experiences. Digeo had done some neat things, like creating interactive channels—called "i-channels"—for Charter subscribers, but more interactivity was still needed. Moxi could bring a combination of software and hardware to the table. In March 2002, Allen bought Moxi and merged it with Digeo. Perlman had been pushed out in February, so Moxi's future was all Allen's; he had no headstrong founder to fight with. Moxi quickly became a component of the Digeo plans. Soon enough, the Moxi name was eclipsed by Allen's Digeo brand.

It really seemed like cable was going to be Allen's place to finally prove himself. It was far less groundbreaking than what he had hoped for when he first left Microsoft in 1983, but at least his wired world was coming to fruition. At this point, he was just waiting for the rest of the world to catch up. He had built his business in a way that could be mimicked by other cable companies. If they all followed his lead, consumers would get the wired world experience.

Allen fashioned his lifestyle to reflect some of his hopes and dreams for that future. His interactive movie house, recording studio, and automated areas throughout his Mercer Island home were meant to be a case study in wired world living. "I've built myself the equivalent of what will be available to everyone in the near future," he told the *Seattle Times*. "Not everyone will have all this stuff on their own, of course, but it will be available through cable service or satellite."

Cable was offering Allen his first credible second chance. He was being forgiven for mistakes in the dot-com era—heck, many people had overspent during all the hoopla. His role in Microsoft still gave him a lot of tech credibility, and many people admired him for taking his money and living well. In contrast, Gates started to look like an overachieving workaholic who had lost touch with reality; Allen was still living in the real world—enjoying life as well as working on new ideas for the future.

But, unfortunately, Allen still couldn't shake the "accidental zillionaire" moniker, even after so many people from the Internet economy had become instant, lucky millionaires—and hadn't put nearly the eight years into their companies that Allen had put into Microsoft. Allen was considered lucky because he lived off riches that accumulated once he was gone.

He was also the "accidental zillionaire" because he just couldn't make the kind of money he got from Microsoft, even in cable.

His Charter holdings were doing all right, but the stock price was starting to slip. A general recession, the end of the dot-com boom, and a leveling off of growth in the cable industry pushed prices back down to earth. In May 2002, Charter had sunk so low that Allen was forced to sell off shares he'd bought on margins he never expected the company would dip below. It was a blow to his investment profile.

It was time to consider again how well Allen had done not as a visionary, but as an investor. The Web site News.com posted an update story on the "accidental zillionaire," detailing his losses throughout the 1990s, from AOL to Mercata to Metricom.  The story noted his Charter stake had declined in value by 55.2 percent and RCN by 97 percent; and that he'd sunk at least $187.4 million into Mercata, Metricom, and Interval Research, all of which had become disasters he ultimately shut down. He wasn't going to get off the hook for those companies, no matter how much time passed.

Allen drags his past around with him. It's okay when he's being sentimental; when he's building things in honor of childhood memories, like his museum for his rock idol Jimi Hendrix. In business, however, Allen wanted more than anything to shake the past. Yet he was always being reminded that he was, to many people, just an "accidental zillionaire."

# EPILOGUE

In the summer of 2002, business wasn't a fun place to be. A recession had pushed stock prices to record lows. Worse, since the previous fall, corporate America had found itself in the midst of one of the most intense series of business scandals in its history. It began with energy company Enron in Houston and cut through some of the biggest corporations, bringing established firms like Arthur Andersen and WorldCom to their knees. Heads of these firms were being called before Congress, and some of them were even sentenced to jail.

Paul Allen had never had much luck making a success out of the companies he owned, but so far, they had all escaped this kind of scrutiny. To some degree, it seemed unlikely Allen's business methods would ever be called into question. These other companies came under investigation for unethical and illegal accounting practices, often motivated by the fact that they had no real revenues to report. Allen's companies had occasionally had trouble logging revenues, too, but they always knew they could go back to Allen for more cash, which presumably lessened the temptation to mess with the books.

Meanwhile, Charter was not entirely without its troubles, even of the legal sort. Allen's cable investment may have established him in a single field, once and for all, but Charter itself was a financial mess. Among other things, its stock price had been dragged down in the undercurrent of the recession. Once a history-making IPO target, Charter shares began the summer trading for $7 and falling. On top of that, Charter's $17 billion debt was becoming a distraction too enormous to ignore. Wall Street analyst Karim Zia at Deutsche Banc Alex.Brown kicked off an increasingly circumspect approach to Charter by downgrading his recommendation of Charter's stock from a "strong buy" to just a "buy," on April 2. Zia said he was concerned about Charter's subscriber base dwindling. The downgrades continued. On May 1, Williams Capital adjusted its view of Charter stock from "buy" to "hold." June 11 saw AG Edwards drop its "strong buy" recommendation to "hold"; two days later, another, less serious downgrade from RCB Capital Markets from "top pick" to "outperform." Charter executives painted a rosier financial picture: First-quarter losses were lower than the previous year and cash flow had increased more than 10 percent. The company had been spending money upgrading its systems, but those expenditures were nearing an end. Charter's officials assured analysts that things could only get better.

But it wasn't enough. Scandal had come home to the cable industry. It began with the sixth-largest cable operator, Adelphia Communications. Adelphia filed for bankruptcy protection in March, after failing to pay off huge amounts of debts. Adelphia's systems were valuable to some other cable operators, including Allen, who tried to acquire them. He wanted the Adelphia customers in the Los Angeles market, where Charter still needed to up its subscriber base. But before Allen did a deal, a federal investigation broke wide open. According to the feds, Adelphia founder John Rigas and his two sons, Timothy and Michael, had been taking billions of dollars out of the company for personal use and failing to record it on the company's books. In July, they were charged with securities fraud, wire fraud, and bank fraud. They were indicted in September and faced up to 30 years in prison.

Well before the Rigases were even charged, news of the scandal reverberated throughout the entire cable industry. Charter was quickly assumed to be guilty by association, and so were Comcast, Cox, and AOL Time Warner. Everyone in the business was eyed suspiciously by analysts, shareholders, and federal authorities, but especially corporations like Charter and Adelphia. "Investors are

no longer willing to take the risk that a cable company will generate free cash flow in the next three to five years," said SoundView
Technology Group's Jordan Rohan. "And when the company is
owned by one person, other shareholders may or may not be
treated fairly. That's not a great position to be in."

Stocks dropped lower. By the start of July, Charter's shares
had sunk to $5, but that wasn't the least of it. Soon enough, sev-
eral shareholder lawsuits and the SEC would allege that Charter
was up to some suspicious business, too.

While Charter's debt climbed and Adelphia looked like it was
for sale, Allen mulled over his cable universe. He could
have been inspired by the splash made by Digeo at the National
Cable Television Association conference in New Orleans in May.
Not only was Allen's yacht-board party the buzz of the four-day
affair, but Digeo itself was front-and-center on the conference
hall, difficult to miss and always packed with industry folks intrigued by Allen's latest endeavor. As Allen strolled the floor of
the convention hall, he couldn't have missed the excitement
around his wired world.

But just as his spirits were lifting, one of the cable industry's
leading financial analysts, Jessica Reif Cohen at Merrill Lynch,
came out with a shocking report on July 18: Charter's executives
had "a more aggressive capitalization policy," she said, that resulted in higher earnings results than were appropriate. She said
the company was lumping data-only subscribers with basic-cable
subscribers to boost the numbers of cable customers, and count-
ing new-channel fees as advertising revenues. Interestingly, although Cohen cast doubt on Charter's accounting practices, she
also made a point of saying in the same report that she still saw
great things for Charter's future, and maintained a "strong buy"
recommendation for longer-term investors.

Charter defended its methods by saying that its financial data were "properly reported in accordance with generally accepted accounting principles and have previously been disclosed in various SEC filings," according to a Charter spokesman at the time.

CEO Carl Vogel also piped up, explaining in more detail why things looked the way they did. The new-channel fees were logged as ad revenues because the ads supported the new channels. "It's based on our market rate," he told USA Today on August 14. "If we run the ads, we have to recognize it as ad revenues." The grouping of data-only subscribers with basic-cable subscribers was also on the up-and-up, he said: "We're selling multiple products off our broadband pipes." In any event, he said, all such practices had been reviewed and approved by the company's auditor, KPMG.

It wasn't enough of an explanation for shareholders, who began filing suits, left and right, beginning at the end of July and continuing into the fall. They claimed the company's executives had overstated Charter's revenue, inappropriately accounted for new-channel costs and artificially inflated the number of subscribers for the company's basic cable services. On August 16, the federal government fell in line with the skeptics, launching an investigation into the company's accounting practices.

All the while, Allen was nowhere to be seen. He made no statement about his company's predicament and was even somewhat removed from the top management there. But he was clearly thinking about Charter. He was quietly considering playing the white knight, at least when it came to Charter's staggering debt. He'd already purchased an additional 929,000 shares in the company in May, giving him 55.4 percent of the company. Charter's stock was so low, he could buy up the rest of it for a mere $857 million, just a smidgen of the $18 billion he'd paid to assemble his cable empire, and take it private. Or, he could eliminate the controversial $17 billion debt by exchanging it for equity. He did not discuss this with Charter executives; Allen revealed his consideration of these possibilities in a filing with the Securities and Exchange Commission in early August.

This time, when one of Allen's companies started spending far more than what it was bringing in, he didn't bat an eye. Most other cases, Allen called a halt to his companies' excesses. But here was Allen, about to pour cash into this money pit. Cable, after all, was the key to bringing about the wired world.

It would be nice to say that, in conclusion, Allen has undergone some sort of change over the years, that he's learned some lessons along the way or improved his skills as a businessman, or even as a technologist. But there's little proof of that. Mistakes were repeated and unique business models never established in a way that made Allen a paragon of business. Allen hasn't become a better entrepreneur or a better investor, or even better at reading the future. Charter's situation (aside from the shareholder suits and the federal investigation) is only more of the same in the history of Allen companies: They are merely run, not inventively so. Don't expect to find *Paul Allen's Guide to Business* hitting the bookshelves any time soon.

If there's one area where Allen has evolved, it is in his social life. Over the years, he has improved his ability to enter celebrity circles; his parties have grown in popularity and notoriety. The rest seems to be a lot of continuity. Many of the people I interviewed liked to say that Allen's story was whatever it was: "It's his journey" was a phrase I heard over and over. He obviously remained undefined to them, too.

Still, if there's one thing he's got, it's his wired world. It won't be surprising to see him continue to push the concept in his spare time away from Hollywood parties and his billionaire toys. When *Forbes* released its list of the country's richest people in September 2002, Allen remained third on the list, with a fortune of $21 billion, behind Warren Buffett's $36 billion and Bill Gates's $43 billion. Allen has so much more money yet to spend and he moves it around in larger and larger chunks at a time, into farther corners of the earth. His money is what makes headlines—usually after the fact. He moves stealthily. He moved undetected into cable; into Seattle's civic scene; into sports, entertainment, and technology. Most of these moves came quietly, but in huge bounds, involving billions of dollars at a time, catching people off-guard. He surprised some Allen watchers when he dumped his $568 million stake in USA Networks in May 2002. Allen may be a name to some, but because his identity has been so hard to pin down, he's been able to enter certain worlds undetected.

Allen still has something to prove—that he's more than Microsoft. The wired world is his chance, finally, to do something "groundbreaking," as he once said was his goal after leaving Bill Gates. You can be sure he'll keep trying. One day, you may wake up to find that Paul Allen owns a piece of your world, and you can be sure the part that he owns will fit, in his view, into his own, "wired" world.

# SOURCE NOTES

A ccidental *Zillionaire* is the result of dozens of interviews with friends, family, colleagues, underlings and acquaintances of Paul Allen, as well as from official sources such as government institutions. A great deal of the information on Allen comes from previously published articles and books. Much of Allen's history with Bill Gates comes from two excellent books, *Hard Drive*, by James Wallace and Jim Erickson; and *Gates: How Microsoft's Mogul Reinvented an Industry—and Made Himself the Richest Man in America*, by Stephen Manes and Paul Andrews. Both teams of top-notch journalists meticulously researched and reported the details and dynamics of those early years. The rest of the source material is indicated here in reference to specific facts and quotes in the book.

## Chapter 1

Page 3      "Edna Faye enrolled . . ." University of California at Los Angeles alumni records.

Page 3      "In 1950, when . . ." James Wallace reported in the *Seattle Post-Intelligencer* that Kenneth Allen graduated from the University of Washington in 1951. The university's alumni association says Allen attended, but did not graduate, and would not release the years of his attendance. What's known is that Edna Faye Gardner Allen graduated from UCLA in 1948 and that she received her first teaching certificate from the Washington State Board of Education in January, 1952. Sometime between those years, the

Allens would have moved to Seattle. According to the same story and others in the *Post-Intelligencer*, the family moved to Wedgwood.

**Page 4**    "On January 21, 1953 . . ." State of Washington Department of Health birth certificate records.

**Page 4**    "Faye, as she now . . ." By 1948, when she graduated from UCLA, she had dropped Edna in favor of Faye. As a public figure, she goes by Faye G. Allen, as evidenced by the Seattle buildings and programs in her name.

**Page 4**    "When Paul was just . . ." *Seattle Post-Intelligencer*, April 22, 1996.

**Page 4**    "He grew into . . ." Interviews with former classmates and friends of Paul and Jody.

**Page 4**    "He read a lot . . ." *Rolling Stone*, June 22, 2000.

**Page 4**    "In high school, Kenneth . . ." Allen has told reporters over the years about his father's knee injury, including the *Seattle Post-Intelligencer*, April 22, 1996.

**Page 5**    "If anything . . ." *Rolling Stone*, June 22, 2000.

**Page 5**    "In 1968, they . . ." *Seattle Times*, June 23, 2000.

**Page 5**    "Jody learned to . . ." Ibid.

**Page 6**    "Amost every year . . ." Ibid.

**Page 6**    "In 1966, Paul . . ." Allen's initial exposure to Hendrix's music has been retold in several accounts in connection with his building of the Hendrix-related Experience Music Project in 2000, including *Rolling Stone*, June 22, 2000.

## Chapter 2

**Page 18**    "In the fall . . ." *Fortune*, October 2, 1995.

**Page 18**    "This microprocessor's only . . ." This account of events around the 4004 was reported in *Gates*, Doubleday, 1993.

**Page 18**    "Years later, Gates . . ." *Fortune*, October 2, 1995.

**Page 20**    "Bill Gates had entered . . ." Information on Gates's final years at Lakeside; Allen's involvement in the remaining

Lakeside projects; their plans to start their first company, Traf-O-Data; and their work for TRW comes in large part from *Gates*, Doubleday, 1993, and *Hard Drive*, John Wiley & Sons, 1992.

Page 23    "One day over . . ." *Fortune*, October 2, 1995.

Page 24    "When he wasn't . . ." Gates's college days are delved into much deeper in books focused on him, specifically: *Gates*, Doubleday, 1993, and *Hard Drive*, John Wiley & Sons, 1992.

Page 25    "Paul saw that . . ." *Seattle Post-Intelligencer*, May 13, 1991.

Page 25    "I bought a . . ." *Seattle Post-Intelligencer*, May 13, 1991.

Page 26    "Well, here's our . . ." *Seattle Post-Intelligencer*, May 13, 1991.

Page 26    "I told them . . ." Interview with Ed Roberts, Spring, 2002.

Page 27    "We were increasing . . ." Interview with Ed Roberts, Spring, 2002.

Page 28    "He was a . . ." Interview with Monte Davidoff, Spring, 2002.

Page 28    "Of my friends . . ." Interview with Monte Davidoff, Spring, 2002.

Page 29    "Paul's part was . . ." Interview with Monte Davidoff, Spring, 2002.

Page 30    "It was clear . . ." Interview with Monte Davidoff, Spring, 2002.

Page 30    "No one had . . ." Interview with Monte Davidoff, Spring, 2002.

Page 30    "Sometime in March . . ." The story of how Paul Allen and Bill Gates created Microsoft has been covered so many times it has become folklore. Some of the sources for this section include *Gates*, Doubleday, 1993, and *Hard Drive*, John Wiley & Sons, 1992, as well as the PBS series "The Triumph of the Nerds," June 12, 1996. Some of the events were reconfirmed by Davidoff, Roberts, and David Bunnell in interviews, Spring, 2002.

Page 31    "He didn't have . . ." Interview with Roberts, Spring, 2002.

Page 32    "Next time we . . ." Interview with former MITS employee, Spring, 2002.

Page 33    "Paul was, as . . ." Interview, Roberts, Spring, 2002.

Page 33    "He was one . . ." Interview with David Bunnell, Spring, 2002.

Page 35    "He was much . . ." Interview with Davidoff, Spring, 2002.

Page 36    "He viewed it . . ." *Personal Computing*, January, 1977.

Page 37    "It was not . . ." Interview with Davidoff, Spring, 2002.


## Chapter 3

Page 39    "Sometimes they grew . . ." Accounts in *Hard Drive*, John Wiley & Sons, 1992, and in *Gates; How Microsoft's Mogul Reinvented an Industry—and Made Himself the Richest Man in America*, Doubleday, 1993.

Page 40    "Allen argued that . . ." *Gates*, Doubleday, 1993.

Page 41    "Gates later told . . ." *Gates*, Doubleday, 1993.

Page 41    "Newly returned to . . ." *Puget Sound Business Journal*, March 3, 2000.

Page 42    "It made him a . . ." *Hard Drive*, John Wiley & Sons, 1992.

Page 42    "One of the earliest . . ." *Hard Drive*, John Wiley & Sons, 1992.

Page 45    "Zilog threatened to . . ." *Gates*, Doubleday, 1993.

Page 46    "On December 12 . . ." *Dow Jones News Service*, December 12, 1980.

Page 47    "It encouraged strict . . ." "Triumph of the Nerds," PBS, June 12, 1996.

Page 50    "Another Microsoft executive . . ." *Fortune*, October 2, 1995.

Page 51    "Microsoft did not tell . . ." *Gates*, Doubleday, 1993.

Page 51    "Then, with an agreement . . ." *Gates*, Doubleday, 1993.

Page 52    "While Gates was . . ." *Seattle Post-Intelligencer*, April 22, 1996.

Page 53    "Gates was still . . ." *Fortune*, October 2, 1995.

## Chapter 4

Page 57     "Allen never made it . . ." Fact-checking interview, former Microsoft executive Scott Oki, Spring, 2002, based on accounts in *Gates* and *Hard Drive.*

Page 57     "I'd had little bumps . . ." *Fortune,* October 2, 1995.

Page 57     "Then one day . . ." *Fortune,* October 2, 1995.

Page 59     "It's a huge shock . . ." *Rolling Stone,* June 22, 2000.

Page 60     "Radiation treatment can . . ." American Cancer Society.

Page 60     "His absence did . . ." Interview, Mark Ursino, Spring, 2002.

Page 60     "He was getting . . ." Interview, Mark Ursino, Spring, 2002.

Page 60     "In 1982, he . . ." *Fortune,* October 2, 1995.

Page 61     "It was hard . . ." *Fortune,* October 2, 1995.

Page 61     "To be 30 . . ." *Fortune,* October 2, 1995.

Page 61     "While once they . . ." *Hard Drive,* John Wiley & Sons, 1992.

Page 61     "According to an . . ." *Gates,* Doubleday, 1993.

Page 62     "It was a real change . . ." *Fortune,* October 2, 1995.

Page 63     "He loved it . . ." *Rolling Stone,* June 22, 2000.

Page 64     "He'd once told . . ." Paul Allen Web site, *www.paulallen.com.*

Page 64     "Also in his father's . . ." *The Oregonian,* September 22, 1991.

Page 65     "She even made up . . ." Paul Allen Web site, *www .paulallen.com.*

Page 65     "They had been . . ." *Seattle Times,* June 23, 2000.

Page 66     "I took that . . ." *Fortune,* October 2, 1995.

Page 67     "You realize how . . ." *Business Week,* May 21, 1990.

Page 69     "Ideas, he believed . . ." Interview, Mark Ursino, Spring, 2002.

Page 70     "In a single day . . ." *Seattle Times,* March 31, 1986.

Page 71     "I'm pretty happy . . ." *Hard Drive,* John Wiley & Sons, 1992.

Page 71     "As time passed . . ." Refers to comments he made to anonymous sources and journalists about the excessive amount of his money, including the *New York Times*, November 5, 1995, when he said, "There's just so much money."

## Chapter 5

Page 75    "People were just . . ." Interview, Pam Miller, Spring 2002.

Page 76    "There was this . . ." Interview, Jeff Day, Spring 2002.

Page 76    "When Microsoft was . . ." *San Francisco Examiner*, May 21, 1990.

Page 77    "But Allen's attitude . . ." Interview, Day, Spring, 2002.

Page 77    "The manager says they . . ." Interview, Day, Spring, 2002.

Page 77    "Other people weren't . . ." Interview, Mark Ursino, Spring, 2002.

Page 77    "Many reports have . . ." Allen's reputation as "shy" is a notion created in part by Allen's preference for privacy, but also by various press reports over the years, both those with whom he spoke and those he declined, including *Seattle Post-Intelligencer*, April 22, 1996, *Associated Press*, May 17, 1997, *Fortune*, May 15, 2000, and others.

Page 77    "He was extremely . . ." Interview, Miller, Spring, 2002.

Page 78    "These guys are . . ." Interview, Ursino, Spring, 2002.

Page 82    "It wasn't my idea . . ." *Seattle Times*, February 9, 1993.

Page 83    "At Paul Allen . . ." Interview, Paul Budak, Spring, 2002.

Page 84    "But then, many . . ." The examples of Allen-backed ventures allowed to keep spending without a balanced return on investment are numerous, from Asymetrix's development of Crucible and ToolBook to Allen's Interval Research to a dot-com effort called Mercata (Chapter 10). Allen has spoken publicly about this, citing his patience with his investments, as in *Fortune*, July 11, 1994.

Page 84    "We're *gonna* go . . ." The quotes from an anonymous senior executive at Starwave in this section all come from a Spring, 2002, interview with the same former member of the executive management team, who was privy to many strategic decisions at the company. His comments and characterizations of Starwave, Mike Slade, and Allen's interactions with the company were affirmed by other managers at the company at that time.

Page 86    "Starwave chief technology officer . . ." Federal court filing, U.S. District Court, Los Angeles.

Page 88    "Allen got wind . . ." Interviews with former senior Disney executives, Spring, 2002.

Page 88    "Allen made a profit . . ." Based on Allen's investment by 1996 of $96 million and the reported $350 million Disney paid for Starwave (confirmed by Disney executives involved in the transaction), Allen's take would have been at least $200 million, accounting for additional spending in the company by the time of Disney's acquisition in the Spring of 1997.

Page 89    "Liddle said that . . ." *The New Yorker*, February, 1998.

Page 90    *"Harper's* magazine showcased . . ." *Harper's*, December 1, 1994.

Page 90    "Allen tended to have . . ." Interview, Michael Naimark, Winter, 2002.

Page 91    "When Interval began . . ." *Wired*, December, 1999.

Page 91    "Vanderbilt professor Donna . . ." Interview, Donna Hoffman, Winter, 2002.

Page 91    "In a single day . . ." Company press release, November 13, 1996.

Page 92    "In late 1997 . . ." *The New Yorker*, February, 1998.

Page 92    "He also gave . . ." Interval's shift to more of a broadband-cable focus was well-covered in the media. The most involved piece was probably *Wired*, December, 1999.

Page 92    "For the first time . . ." *Wired*, December, 1999.

Page 93    "In April 2000 . . ." *Fortune*, May 15, 2000.

## Chapter 6

**Page 101**    "As Allen has . . ." *Wired,* August, 1994.

**Page 103**    "This guy says . . ." Interview, Stephen Burakoff, Spring, 2002.

**Page 104**    "There were other . . ." Interview, Stephen Burakoff, Spring, 2002.

**Page 105**    "By the end of . . ." Interview, Stephen Burakoff, Spring, 2002.

**Page 106**    "He's a straight-shooter . . ." Interview, Thomas Youngman, Spring, 2002.

**Page 106**    "Once Layered was . . ." *Bloomberg Markets,* November, 2000.

**Page 107**    "It's not like . . ." *Bloomberg Markets,* November, 2000.

**Page 108**    "Cable titan John . . ." *Multichannel News,* May 6, 1991.

**Page 109**    "We all worked . . ." Interview, anonymous former SkyPix employee, Spring, 2002. Sentiment echoed by other former SkyPix employees in interviews, Spring, 2002.

**Page 111**    "TV will basically . . ." *Seattle Times,* September 27, 2002.

**Page 111**    "He told *Business Week* . . ." *Business Week,* November 18, 1996.

**Page 111**    "Once everybody's wired . . ." *Fortune,* July 11, 1994.

**Page 112**    "Periodically, you have . . ." *Fortune,* July 11, 1994.

**Page 113**    "I can afford to . . ." *Fortune,* July 11, 1994.

**Page 113**    "For Allen, Vulcan was . . ." *Fortune,* July 11, 1994.

**Page 114**    "The unique thing . . ." *Fortune,* July 11, 1994.

**Page 115**    "The CEO of one . . ." Interview with anonymous former CEO of Silicon Valley-based Internet company that counted funding from Allen's Vulcan Ventures, Winter, 2002.

**Page 115**    "Ticketing just naturally . . ." *Fortune,* July 11, 1994.

**Page 117**    "He was dumpy . . ." Interview with anonymous former senior executive, Winter, 2002.

**Page 117**   "He wanted to . . ." Interview with anonymous former senior executive, Winter, 2002.

**Page 117**   "He seemed to . . ." Interview with anonymous former senior executive, Winter, 2002.

**Page 118**   "A story, in . . ." *Wired*, August, 1994.

**Page 118**   "He became mortal enemies . . ." Interview with former senior officer at *Wired* magazine, Winter, 2002.

**Page 119**   "As soon as . . ." Interview with Charlie Jackson, Summer, 2002.

**Page 119**   "Ten years from now . . ." *Bloomberg Markets*, November, 2000.

## Chapter 7

While Allen's dalliances with America Online were for the most part well played out in the press at the time, especially when relations became contentious, one reporter had more of an inside scoop than the rest: Kara Swisher, author of *AOL.com*, who spent a year inside AOL headquarters. Much of the characterization of the relationship between Allen and AOL comes from *AOL.com*.

**Page 123**   "Steve Case had . . ." *AOL.com*, Times Business, 1998.

**Page 127**   "When it came to . . ." *Bloomberg Business News*, June 17, 1992.

**Page 127**   "Paul validated . . ." Interview with former investment analyst covering AOL stock in 1992, Spring, 2002.

**Page 128**   "Steve Case and Paul Allen . . ." *AOL.com*, Times Business, 1998.

**Page 130**   "He did originally want . . ." July 30, 1994.

**Page 130**   "This is America . . ." *AOL.com*, Times Business, 1998.

**Page 130**   "AOL wasn't totally . . ." Interview with former investment analyst covering AOL stock in 1992, Spring, 2002.

**Page 130**   "Besides, Case didn't . . ." *AOL.com*, Times Business, 1998.

**Page 131**   "I got calls . . ." Interview with former investment analyst covering AOL stock in 1992, Spring, 2002.

Page 132   "A key criterion . . ." *Wall Street Journal*, September 20, 1994.


## Chapter 8

Page 135   "People commented on . . ." "Nice" is one of the most common adjectives used by people who have had some dealings with Allen.

Page 136   "Geffen had worked . . ." *The Operator: David Geffen Builds, Buys and Sells the New Hollywood*, Random House, 2000.

Page 138   "We initially talked . . ." *Rolling Stone*, June 22, 2000.

Page 138   "Allen had stars . . ." *Rolling Stone*, June 22, 2000.

Page 138   "We were talking . . ." Interview with powerful Hollywood investor, Spring, 2002.

Page 138   "He's so hard . . ." Interview with powerful Hollywood investor, Spring, 2002.

Page 139   "The new venture was . . ." *Keys to the Kingdome*, Morrow, 2000.

Page 139   "He said 'Hey . . .'" *USA Today*, March 21, 1995.

Page 139   "Since 1990, I've . . ." *Red Herring*, July, 1998.

Page 141   "By the measure of . . ." Reporters were piling onto Dream-Works' story early on, including *Los Angeles Times*, June 26, 1996.

Page 141   "What if the hero . . ." *Los Angeles Times*, May 7, 1995.

Page 142   "Paul would come down . . ." Former senior executive at DreamWorks, Spring, 2002.

Page 142   "Paul looks at Steven . . ." Former senior executive at DreamWorks, Spring, 2002.

Page 142   "I did mention . . ." *Rolling Stone*, June 22, 2000.

Page 142   "It was just like . . ." *Rolling Stone*, June 22, 2000.

Page 143   "Allen failed to . . ." *Empire*, Spring, 2000.

Page 144   "Said Storyopolis's spokeswoman . . ." *The Oregonian*, February 6, 1995.

**Page 145**    "Soon enough, that . . ." *Seattle Weekly,* June 17–23, 1999, as well as deposition transcripts, Los Angeles County Superior Court.

**Page 145**    "Someday, he has . . ." *Los Angeles Times,* May 7, 1995.

**Page 146**    "Allen had had . . ." E-mail interview with anonymous classmate; other interview subjects, including Monte Davidoff from Harvard days, recalled meeting or speaking with serious girlfriends of Allen.

**Page 146**    "He was really . . ." Interview with freelance journalist who covered Allen and his hobbies for a mainstream publication, Winter, 2002.

**Page 147**    "He was very . . ." Interview with freelance journalist who covered Allen and his hobbies for a mainstream publication, Winter, 2002.

**Page 147**    "According to Wertheim . . ." *Venus Envy: A Sensational Season from Inside the Women's Tour,* HarperCollins, 2001.

**Page 148**    "The information hit . . ." The reports of Jerry Hall's appearance on Allen's yacht are numerous, including *New York Daily News, The Independent, The Guardian, The Observer, The Times-Picayune,* all between August 10 and August 15, 1999.

**Page 148**    "The movie producer . . ." A report in *W* magazine, March, 2002, confirmed reports from friends interviewed Spring, 2002.

**Page 149**    "He no longer . . ." Interview with anonymous source, Spring, 2002.

**Page 149**    "That's happened several . . ." Interview with anonymous source, Spring, 2002.

**Page 149**    "The depositions were . . ." All information and direct quotes in this section are taken directly from transcripts of depositions held in Seattle for a sexual harassment suit filed by Abbie Phillips in Los Angeles Superior Court.

**Page 152**    "Being sued for . . ." Nondisclosure agreements are a staple with Allen and Vulcan. All of his employees are required to sign, as was told to me by many former employees who were fearful of breaking them. Some of them spoke anyway (anonymously, though), others declined. For his parties, he required them, as reported in *National Post*, August 15, 2001 and *Seattle Times*, August 31, 1998.

**Page 152**   "It's the best . . ." *Rolling Stone*, June 22, 2000.

**Page 152**   "Added Howard Rosenmann . . ." *Rolling Stone*, June 22, 2000.

**Page 153**   "As soon as . . ." Interview with Hollywood screenwriter, Spring, 2002.

**Page 154**   "It was incredible . . ." A long-time friend of the host, Douglas Adams, recounted the events of this night and his relationship with Adams. All tales were confirmed by another close friend of Adams who was also present at the events recounted, Spring, 2002.

**Page 155**   "He's completely hopeless . . ." Despite the negative or biased tone of this interview subject, there was no reason to believe that this person held a grudge against Allen. Allen had invested in his business and had him over as a guest. Interview conducted Spring, 2002.

## Chapter 9

**Page 158**   "Gates, who spent . . ." *Rip City*, 2001.

**Page 159**   "I said, 'I can't . . .'" *Seattle Times*, June 1, 1988.

**Page 159**   "The decision to . . ." *Seattle Times*, June 1, 1988.

**Page 159**   "We had a deal . . ." *Atlanta Journal and Constitution*, October 30, 1988.

**Page 160**   "Owning the Blazers . . ." *Rip City*, 2001.

**Page 160**   "In Portland, some . . ." Interviews with season ticketholders in the 1980s, Winter, 2002.

**Page 161**   "The team's former physician . . ." *Seattle Post-Intelligencer*, April 22, 1996.

Page 161    "We are a performance-oriented . . ." *Seattle Post-Intelligencer,* April 22, 1996.

Page 161    "This was unheard of . . ." Interview with John Lashway, Spring, 2002.

Page 161    "We were always . . ." Interview with John Lashway, Spring, 2002.

Page 162    "But back in Seattle . . ." Several reports referred to Seattle as "Allentown," including *The Oregonian,* June 17, 2001, and *Seattle Times,* August 23, 1997.

Page 163    "Paul Allen's a guitar . . ." Interview with longtime music executive now working in the tech field, Spring, 2002.

Page 163    ". . . one eye on . . ." *Rip City,* 2001.

Page 163    "I really like . . ." *Seattle Weekly,* February 19–25, 1998.

Page 164    "In the process . . ." *Seattle Times,* November 27, 1994.

Page 164    "Hendrix later claimed . . ." *Los Angeles Times,* April 20, 1993.

Page 164    "Jimi's music sold . . ." *The Independent,* August 8, 1995.

Page 165    "One newspaper report at . . ." *The Oregonian,* August 7, 1995.

Page 165    "Mr. Allen's motives . . ." *The Oregonian,* August 7, 1995.

Page 166    "Jody had to . . ." *Seattle Times,* June 23, 2000.

Page 166    "One local Seattle paper . . ." *Seattle Weekly,* February 19–25, 1998.

Page 166    "Anything that's at . . ." *Seattle Times,* June 23, 2000.

Page 167    "This didn't work so well . . ." *Seattle Weekly,* February 19–25, 1998.

Page 167    "He wasn't really . . ." *Seattle Weekly,* February 19–25, 1998.

Page 168    "There are threads . . ." *The Oregonian,* May 21, 2000.

Page 168    "Seattle's 'Allentown' is . . ." *The Oregonian,* May 21, 2000.

Page 168    "People need to . . ." *Seattle Times,* April 24, 1996.

Page 170    "They coached the . . ." *Forbes,* October 14, 1996.

**Page 171**    "I had them . . ." Interview, Richard Carter, Spring, 2002. The events relayed by Carter were reitered by several articles, including *Forbes*, October 14, 1996, and other members of the Friends of Sperry Peninsula group.

**Page 171**    "I'm lobbying for . . ." This account was told to Richard Carter, who headed up the campaign to win back Camp Nor'wester. Carter relayed it to me in an interview, Spring, 2002.

**Page 172**    "In summer, the . . ." Interview, Richard Carter, Spring, 2002.

**Page 172**    "Don't mention Richard's . . ." Ibid.

**Page 173**    "Then all of a . . ." Ibid.

**Page 174**    "There was absolutely . . ." *Seattle Times*, August 20, 1996.

**Page 174**    "Really, he's being . . ." *The Oregonian*, August 18, 1996.

**Page 174**    "Please, we get . . ." According to a letter received by Richard Carter.

**Page 175**    "In a ranking . . ." *Worth*, April, 2000.

**Page 175**    "He had a . . ." *Chronicle of Philanthropy*, database of donors.

**Page 176**    "To say it . . ." *Seattle Times*, April 24, 1996.

## Chapter 10

**Page 177**    "Eventually, everyone is . . ." *Fortune*, October 2, 1995.

**Page 178**    "Paul Allen's primary . . ." *Bloomberg Markets*, November, 2000.

**Page 178**    "Say you've got . . ." *Seattle Times*, September 27, 1992.

**Page 179**    "I'm an idea . . ." *Seattle Times*, June 14, 1998.

**Page 180**    "Do something in . . ." Interviews with former employees of Mercata, the successor to Everything.com, Spring, 2002.

**Page 182**    "He says he doesn't mind . . ." Allen has spoken publicly about this, citing his patience with his investments, as in *Fortune*, July 11, 1994.

Page 183    "Employees were heady . . ." Interview, Wayne Wurzer, Spring, 2002.

Page 184    "He said it was . . ." Interview, Brad Humphries, Spring, 2002.

Page 184    "He was exceptionally . . ." Interview, Brad Humphries, Spring, 2002.

Page 184    "He gave the company . . ." Interview with anonymous former employee, Spring, 2002.

Page 185    "Part of being . . ." Interview, Wayne Wurzer, Spring, 2002.

Page 187    "You could call me . . ." *Wall Street Journal*, April 9, 1998.

Page 187    "My work persona . . ." *Wall Street Journal*, April 9, 1998.

Page 187    "He's arrogant . . ." Interview with powerful Hollywood investor, Spring, 2002.

Page 187    "He's the most arrogant . . ." Interview with said executive, Winter, 2002.

Page 187    "Very cocky, but . . ." Interview with former executive at one of Allen's Hollywood holdings, Winter, 2002.

Page 187    "I totally groove . . ." *Bloomberg Markets*, November, 2000.

Page 187    "David Geffen called . . ." *Bloomberg Markets*, November, 2000.

Page 188    "*The Economist* called . . ." *The Economist*, November 15, 1997.

Page 188    "A Dow Jones report . . ." *Dow Jones Newswires*, March 6, 2000.

Page 188    "One fund manager . . ." *Wall Street Journal*, November 15, 1999.

Page 189    "Allen and his people . . ." *Wall Street Journal*, April 9, 1998.

Page 189    "The advantage of . . ." *The Economist*, November 15, 1997.

Page 193    "We consider Go2Net . . ." *Wall Street Journal*, March 16, 1999.

Page 193    "The executives sat . . ." Interview with former senior executive at Go2Net, Winter, 2002.

Page 194   "A *Wall Street Journal* . . ." *Wall Street Journal*, December 5, 2000.


## Chapter 11

Page 197   "It was like . . ." Interview with anonymous interactive TV executive who has known Allen through various connections over the years, Spring, 2002.

Page 199   "I was right . . ." *Bloomberg Markets*, November, 2000.

Page 200   "Executives close to . . ." Interviews with former executives at his companies, Winter and Spring, 2002.

Page 201   "I just blurted . . ." *Washington Post*, August 28, 2000.

Page 202   "Allen had already promised . . ." *Cable World*, October 8, 2001.

Page 202   "They did the deal . . ." *Cable World*, October 8, 2001.

Page 202   "After it was all . . ." *Dow Jones News Service*, September 24, 2001.

Page 205   "Paul wants to . . ." *Wall Street Journal*, November 11, 1999.

Page 206   "He told *Cable World* . . ." *Cable World*, October 8, 2001.

Page 206   "Charter's stock dropped . . ." *Associated Press*, September 24, 2001.

Page 206   "The low-end customers . . ." *Business Week Online*, November 13, 2001.

Page 207   "Paul Allen's wired . . ." Interview with Jeffrey Chester, Center for Digital Democracy, Spring, 2002.

Page 209   "Paul Allen is . . ." Interview with executive who had worked with two of Allen's startups, Spring, 2002.

Page 210   "It was just . . ." Interview with Paul Budak, Spring, 2002.

Page 212   "The *Wall Street* . . ." *Wall Street Journal*, March 20, 2002.

Page 212   "*Business Week* noted . . ." *Business Week*, March 4, 2002.

Page 214   "I've built myself . . ." *Seattle Times*, June 4, 1998.

Page 215   "The Web site . . ." *News.com*, May 13, 2002.

## Epilogue

**Page 218**   "Zia said . . ." *Cable World,* May 6, 2002.

**Page 218**   "Investors are no . . ." *USA Today,* August 14, 2002.

**Page 219**   "Charter's executives had . . ." *St. Louis Post-Dispatcl,* July 19, 2002.

**Page 220**   "Charter defended its . . ." *St. Louis Post-Dispatcl,* July 19, 2002.

**Page 221**   "When *Forbes* released . . ." *Forbes,* September 13, 2002.

# INDEX

Printed in the United States
55590LVS00002B/118

9 780471 234913